I0795785

IMAGES
of America

SYLVA

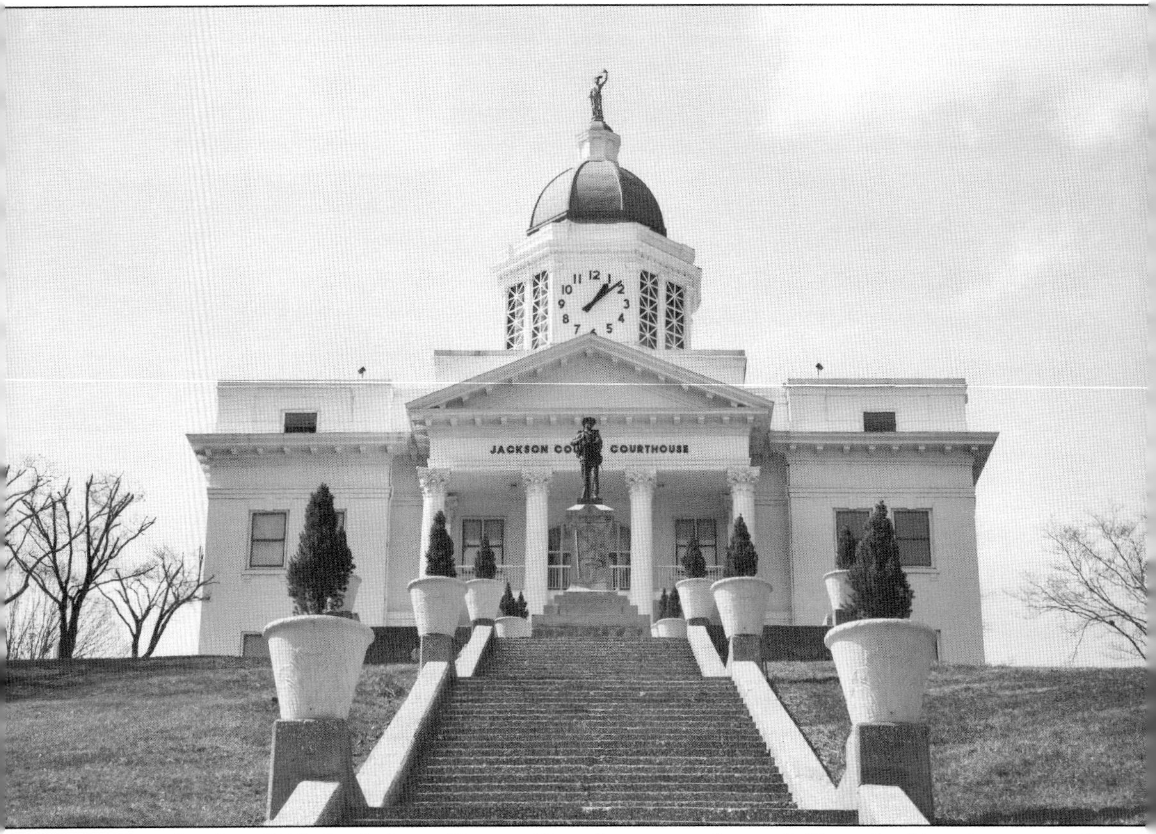

Completed in 1914, the Jackson County Courthouse stands on a hill overlooking downtown. It is believed to be the most photographed building in western North Carolina. (Photograph by Nick Breedlove.)

On the Cover: Employees line up in front of Sylva Laundry around 1950. Floyd Patterson, whose head is between the words "Sylva" and "Laundry," was manager of the business at the time. His son J. D., who worked there during the summers of 1956 and 1957, remembers that the laundry's telephone number was 25J. Bookkeeper J. T. Gribble stands second from the right, and owner Harry Ferguson on the far right. LifeWay Community Church (formerly the Sylva Coal and Lumber Company) now extends into the space once occupied by the laundry, which stood mostly on the Railroad Avenue lot now owned by retired *Sylva Herald* publisher Jim Gray. In 1950, the buildings on Railroad Avenue included Sylva Coal, the Sylva Hotel (Potts House), Sylva Laundry, and the Farmers' Federation warehouse. (Courtesy of J. D. Patterson.)

IMAGES
of America

SYLVA

Lynn Hotaling

ARCADIA
PUBLISHING

ISBN 978-0-7385-5411-2

Published by Arcadia Publishing
Charleston, South Carolina

Printed in the United States of America

Library of Congress Catalog Card Number: 2008921293

For all general information contact Arcadia Publishing at:
Telephone 843-853-2070
Fax 843-853-0044
E-mail sales@arcadiapublishing.com
For customer service and orders:
Toll-Free 1-888-313-2665

Visit us on the Internet at www.arcadiapublishing.com

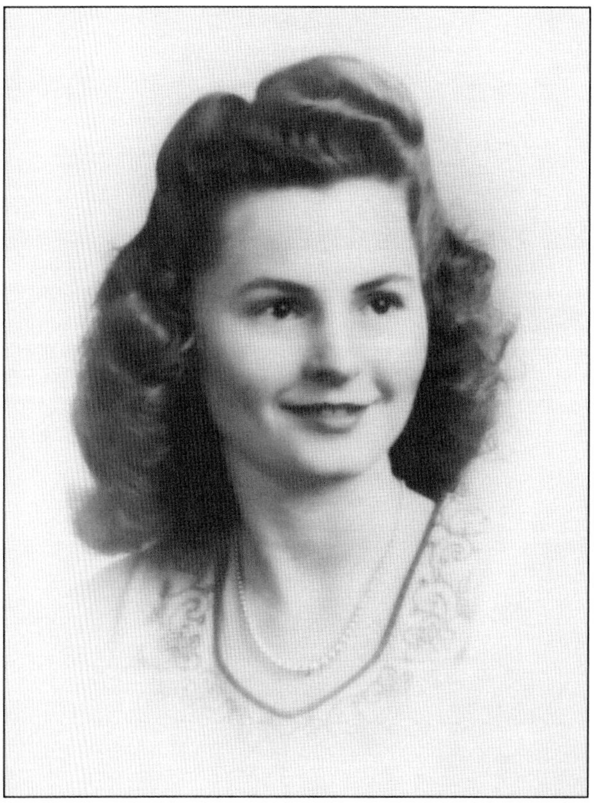

This glimpse of Sylva's past is dedicated to local historian Rachel Brown Phillips in recognition of her commitment to the book and her untiring effort to see it to completion. In addition to rounding up many of the photographs, she read every page and tracked down dates and names among her wide circle of friends and acquaintances. Without her promise of help, I am not sure I would have attempted to write a book about my adopted hometown.

Contents

Acknowledgments		6
Introduction		7
1.	Downtown	9
2.	Community Life	59
3.	Trade and Commerce	105
4.	Postcards from Sylva	121

ACKNOWLEDGMENTS

This book would not have been possible without the cooperation and assistance of a great many people, and I wish they could all be listed here. The names of those who shared their treasured photographs are listed on the pages where those images appear, and I thank them all. Certain individuals made extraordinary contributions, and I am honored to have had their support. Thanks to *Sylva Herald* photographer and editor Nick Breedlove for scanning and cataloging hundreds of images as well as sharing his postcards; to newspaper publisher Steve Gray for his generosity in allowing the publication of *Herald* file photographs and his personal postcard collection; to George Frizzell, director of special collections at Western Carolina University's Hunter Library, for sharing his considerable knowledge and allowing us to include images and documents from the archives; to sports editor Carey Phillips, whose grandfather started *Sylva Herald* forerunner the *Ruralite*, for his research assistance and proofreading; to Rachel Phillips, Hattie Hilda Allison, and Dorris Beck, who brought their photographs and memories one afternoon to get the book off to a good start; to my husband, Richard, for his research assistance and proofreading; and to my daughter Elizabeth, who gave up a weekend to read the final manuscript for consistency and style.

Introduction

Looking at early photographs of a town nestled between the Plott Balsam and Great Smoky Mountains, a visitor might conclude that Sylva takes its name from its location in the tree-covered (sylvan) hills of western North Carolina, but the tale of the town's naming is more dramatic. Sylva's name comes from a man who was a "total stranger to this county—a wandering wayfarer whose life is a mystery to everyone concerned," according to the *Sylva Herald*'s 1951 Centennial Edition.

William D. Sylva appeared at the Webster home of Judge Riley Cannon at dusk on the evening of January 6, 1879. Though he looked like a tramp, the Cannons allowed him to spend the night. After they got to know him, the family took a liking to the young man and persuaded him to stay with them for a month. Sylva then took a job with E. R. Hampton, who owned much of the property where the town now stands. Hampton's sawmill, which "hummed over the present site of Sylva," was located near the east intersection of Main and Mill Streets.

When Hampton's petition for a post office was granted by the federal government, he asked his daughter what its name should be. Young Mae, who had also taken a liking to William, immediately replied, "Sylva." (William Sylva later died in Cleburne, Texas, on May 3, 1927.) Hampton opened the post office in 1879, and the North Carolina General Assembly chartered the location as an incorporated town on March 9, 1889. Sylva was incorporated again on February 16, 1899.

While it is not clear exactly why the town was chartered twice, the 1899 charter is the one under which Sylva continues to operate. That document describes the town's corporate limits. Sylva's center was said to be at the southeast corner of the depot, with the town's boundaries extending from that point three-quarters of a mile in each compass direction, as well as three-quarters of a mile at the four points in between, to form a perfect octagon. Looking at a map of current city limits, portions of that original octagon remain; however, annexations through the years have added several "arms" reaching out N.C. 107, Skyland Drive, and the Asheville Highway (Business 23).

The town of Sylva developed as a center of local commerce after the coming of the railroad in the 1880s. Some 30 years later, early industrialist C. J. Harris led a successful campaign to have Sylva replace Webster as the county seat.

In addition to the railroad, Sylva's early growth was spurred by the 1903 establishment of Harris's tannery. Churches and schools had already formed, including the Sylva Collegiate Institute, a Baptist boarding school that opened in 1900. The Jackson County Bank followed in 1905, and during those years, the county's newspaper, the *Tuckaseigee Democrat*, was published in Sylva rather than in Webster. Sylva also became the site of the county fair, which drew large crowds each year.

Harris's effort to make Sylva the county seat was contentious. The main reasons given by the removalists were that Sylva had a railroad and its economy was beginning to boom after Harris moved his tannery there from Dillsboro to get away from frequent flooding along the Tuckaseigee River. A bill setting a May election that would allow the voters to settle the county seat question was approved by the general assembly in February 1913. County residents, by almost a two-to-one margin (1,413 to 733), voted for removal, and construction of a new courthouse and jail overlooking downtown Sylva began in August of that year. Harris, who had promised voters he would build a courthouse in Sylva for a sum not to exceed $30,000 if the removal measure succeeded, was awarded the contract and completed the structure in 1914.

Sylva's story since that time is one of steady progress. The Jackson County Courthouse still watches over Main Street, though court functions and county administrative offices were moved to the Justice Center in 1994. Extensive repairs were begun in 1995 to shore up the historic structure; county commissioners voted in 2007 to make Courthouse Hill the site of a new county library by renovating the Jackson County Courthouse and constructing an addition to house the facility.

While space limitations preclude a more in-depth history of the town, much information is available in both *The History of Jackson County* and the two-volume *Jackson County Heritage Book*. This volume is intended more to provide glimpses of Sylva's past through photographs and accompanying captions than to deliver the town's complete history; it attempts to tell Sylva's story and that of those who have shaped it. It includes views of Main Street from various eras and multiple angles and features photographs of many Sylva notables, though some, like the town's most famous journalists—John Parris and Bob Terrell—appear as children. When available, images of individuals who made their marks outside of Jackson County—like Dr. John R. Brinkley and musicians Harry Cagle and Samantha Bumgarner—became part of the book, as did photographs of those who made political history.

Most of Sylva's downtown buildings date from the 20th century's first three decades, though the stores and enterprises inside them have rotated through the years. It is my hope that the images collected will lead readers to take a closer look at their hometown through the prism of its past.

One

Downtown

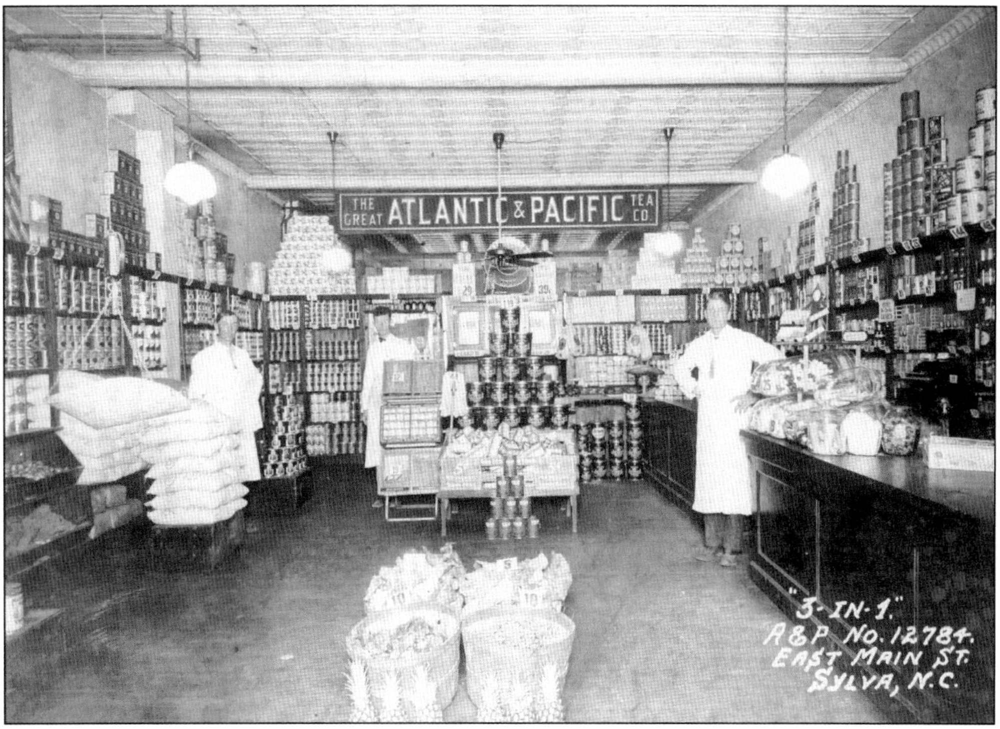

Grocery stores were once a fixture on Main Street. The Great Atlantic and Pacific Tea Company (A&P) opened across from the *Sylva Herald* around 1926 and remained in that location (now Jake's Mountain House) for some 30 years. The man in the center is T. Walter Ashe, who worked at the store for a year around 1930. The A&P moved to the east end of town, to the current site of Family Dollar, in 1956 and then to a much larger building at Sylva Plaza in 1978. The store closed in January 1998 after more than seven decades in Sylva. Other Main Street shops have included Winn-Dixie, which operated from about 1940 until 1963, and Sylva Supply Company, which sold groceries for the first half of the 20th century. (Courtesy of Ray Ashe.)

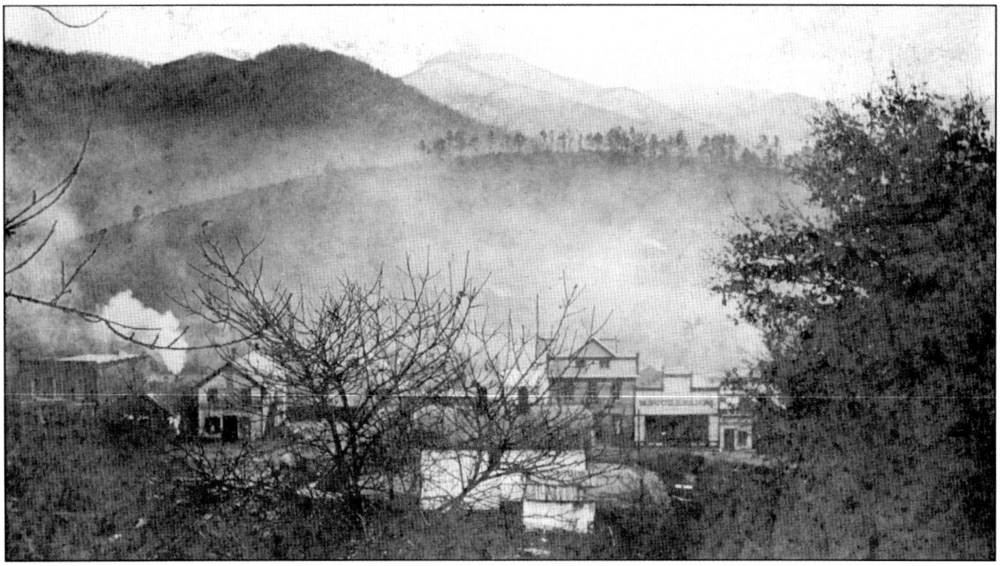

These images date back to 1895, when Sylva was not yet Jackson's county seat. In the above view, looking down from the Jackson Street area, the prominent structure with the peaked roof was located next to the site of present-day Jackson's General Store, which was built by early industrialist C. J. Harris in 1902 to house Sylva Supply Company. The building seen here once housed the Wilson brothers' Sylva Cash Store and later the Hanley-Morris dry goods store. M. Buchanan's store was located to the right of the taller structure. The photograph below shows the same buildings in reverse, with Mill Street in the foreground. It was taken near the site of the old depot, which was demolished in the late 1970s. (Courtesy of Lynn Hotaling.)

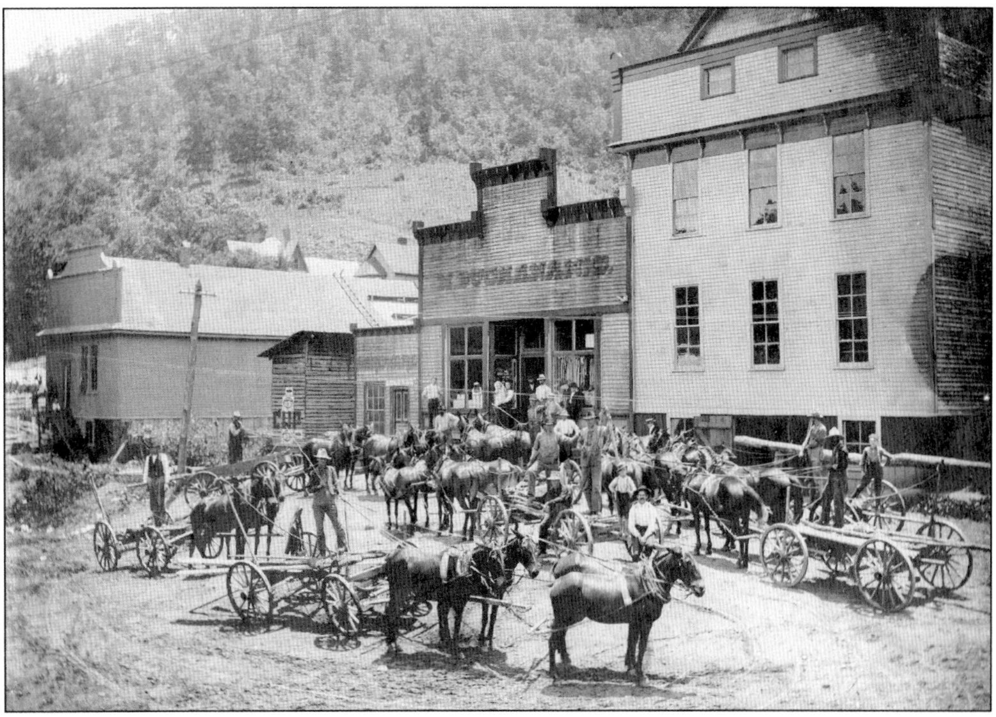

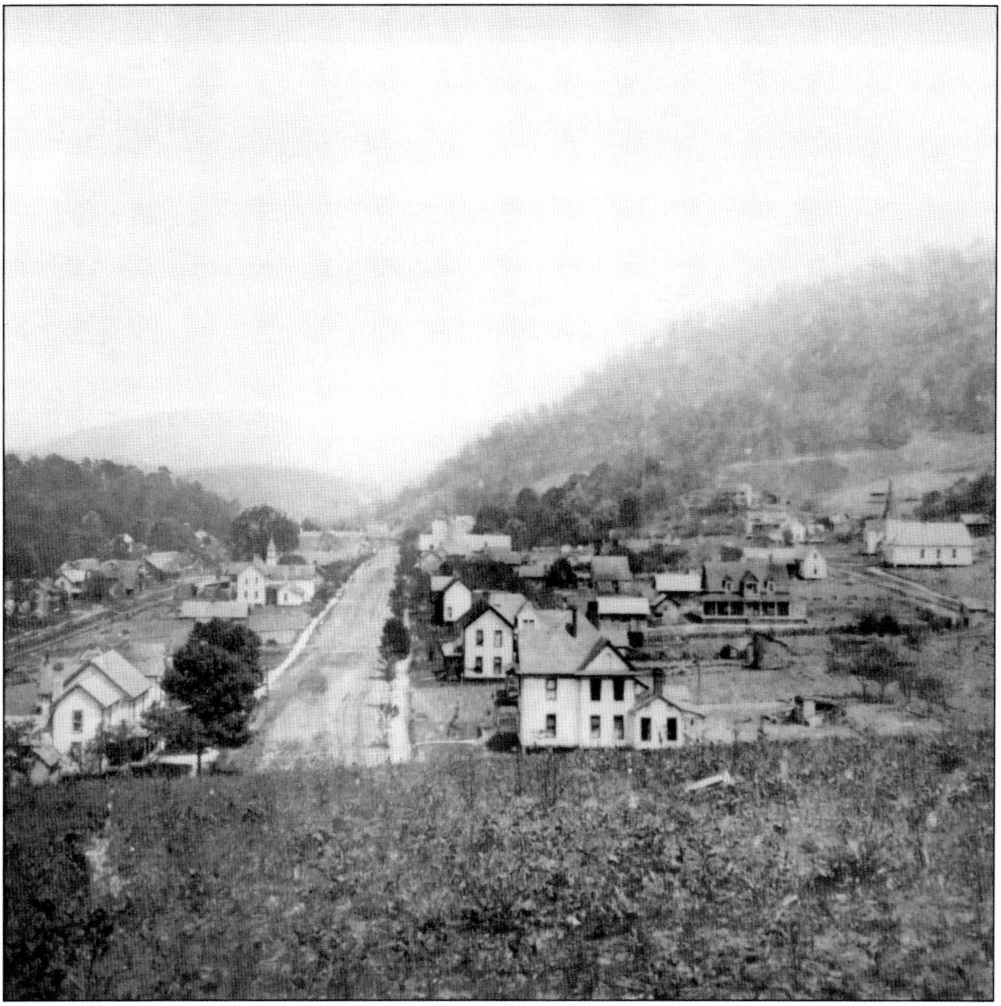

This view of downtown was taken between 1906, when the Hooper House (right foreground) was constructed, and the 1914 completion of the Jackson County Courthouse. The Hooper House, which is now home to the Jackson County Chamber of Commerce and Travel and Tourism Authority and the Downtown Sylva Association, is the only structure visible that is still standing today. Sylva First United Methodist (right background) remains in the same location, though church facilities have expanded over the years and the church is using a completely different building now. Other prominent buildings, generally from left to right, include the Osborne Buchanan home (left foreground), at the west end of Main Street opposite the Hooper House; the Dillard and Mollie Love house, which was an Episcopal church and school; the Judson Allen (later W. W. Watt) home; the Billy Davis house, later known as the Pangle house; and the Henry Curtis house. (Courtesy of Bill Shuler.)

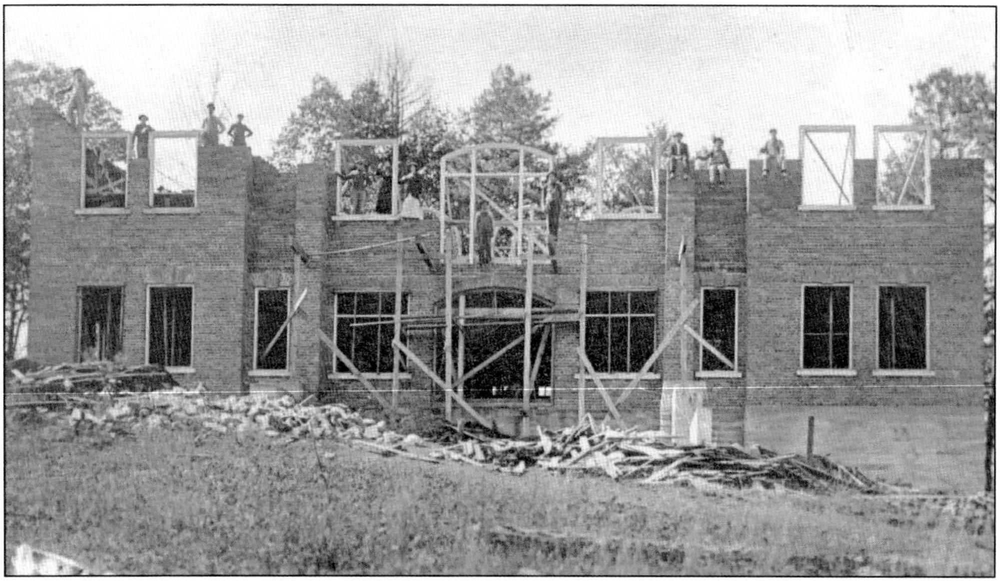

Jackson County's famous courthouse was built quickly once the voters made the decision in May 1913 to relocate the county seat to Sylva from Webster. Some 10 months after the election, most county offices had been moved to the new building. The contractor for the project was industrialist and entrepreneur C. J. Harris, who had also orchestrated the effort. The main reason given at the time for removal was Sylva's location along the railroad tracks, which proved a boon to economic development. The Jackson County Courthouse was patterned after Madison County's, designed by English architect Richard Sharp Smith and erected in 1907–1908. (Courtesy of Rachel Phillips.)

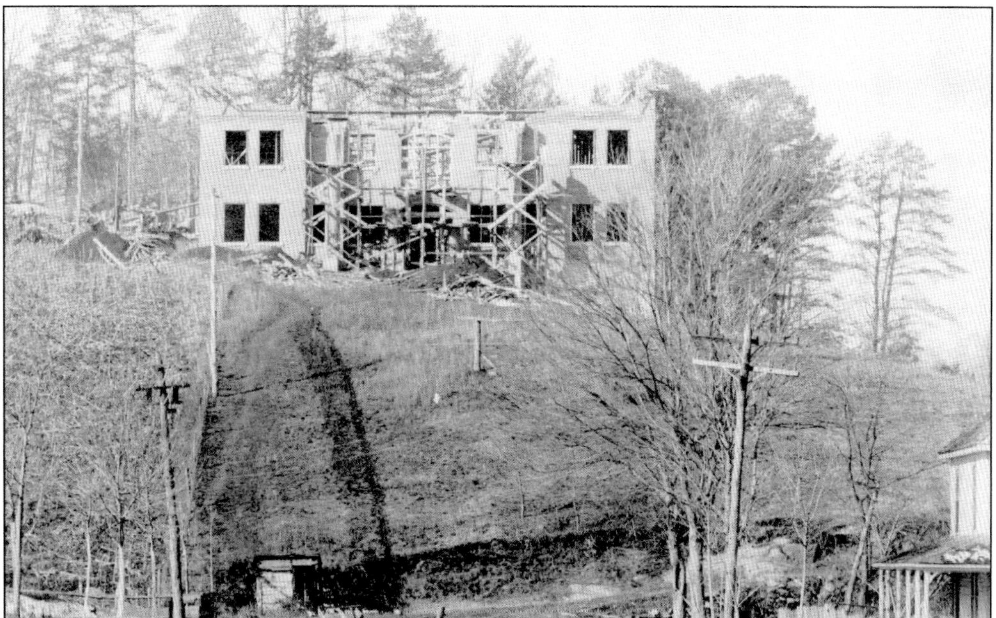

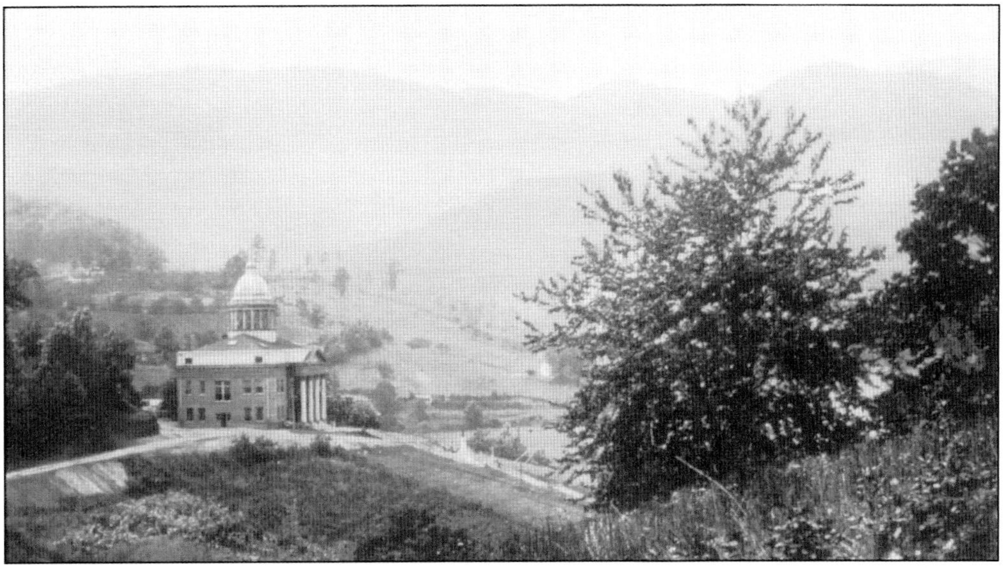

Reportedly the most photographed building in western North Carolina, the Jackson County Courthouse is viewed from Kings Mountain (above) and from Main Street (below) shortly after its completion in 1914. The structure was created in the Neoclassical Revival style, fronted with a Corinthian portico, and topped with a 16-ton cupola. Completed in 10 months, the stately courthouse still presides over Sylva's Main Street. The building, unoccupied since the sheriff's office moved out in 2003, is slated to become part of a new Jackson County library. (Above courtesy of Hattie Hilda Allison; below courtesy of Betty Foxx.)

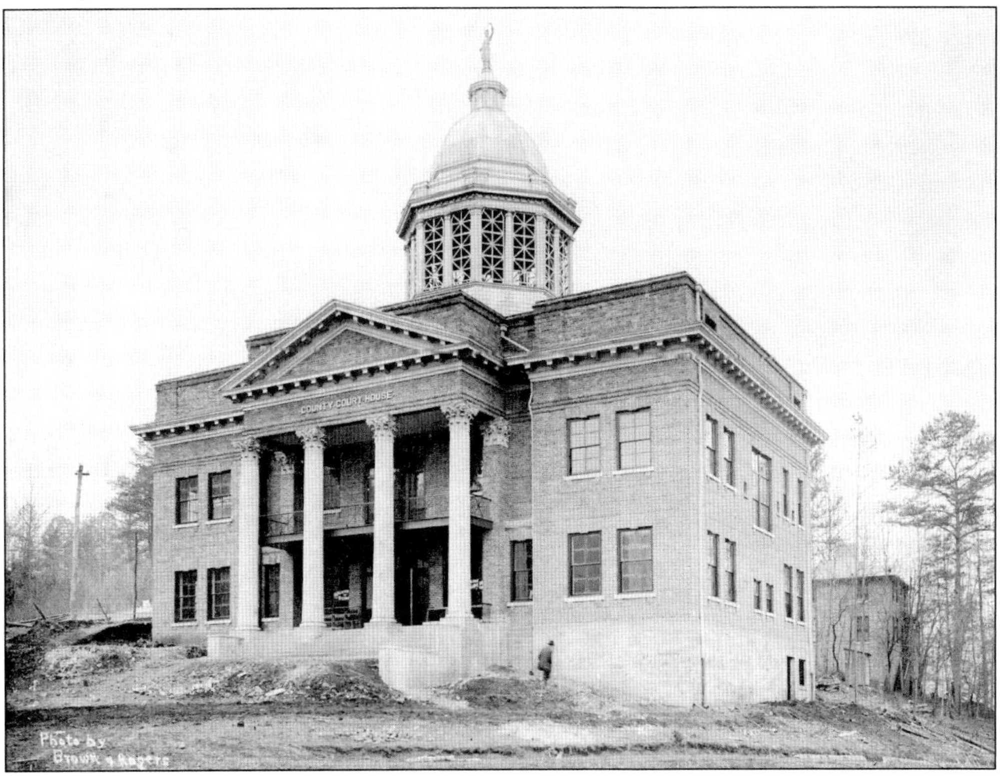

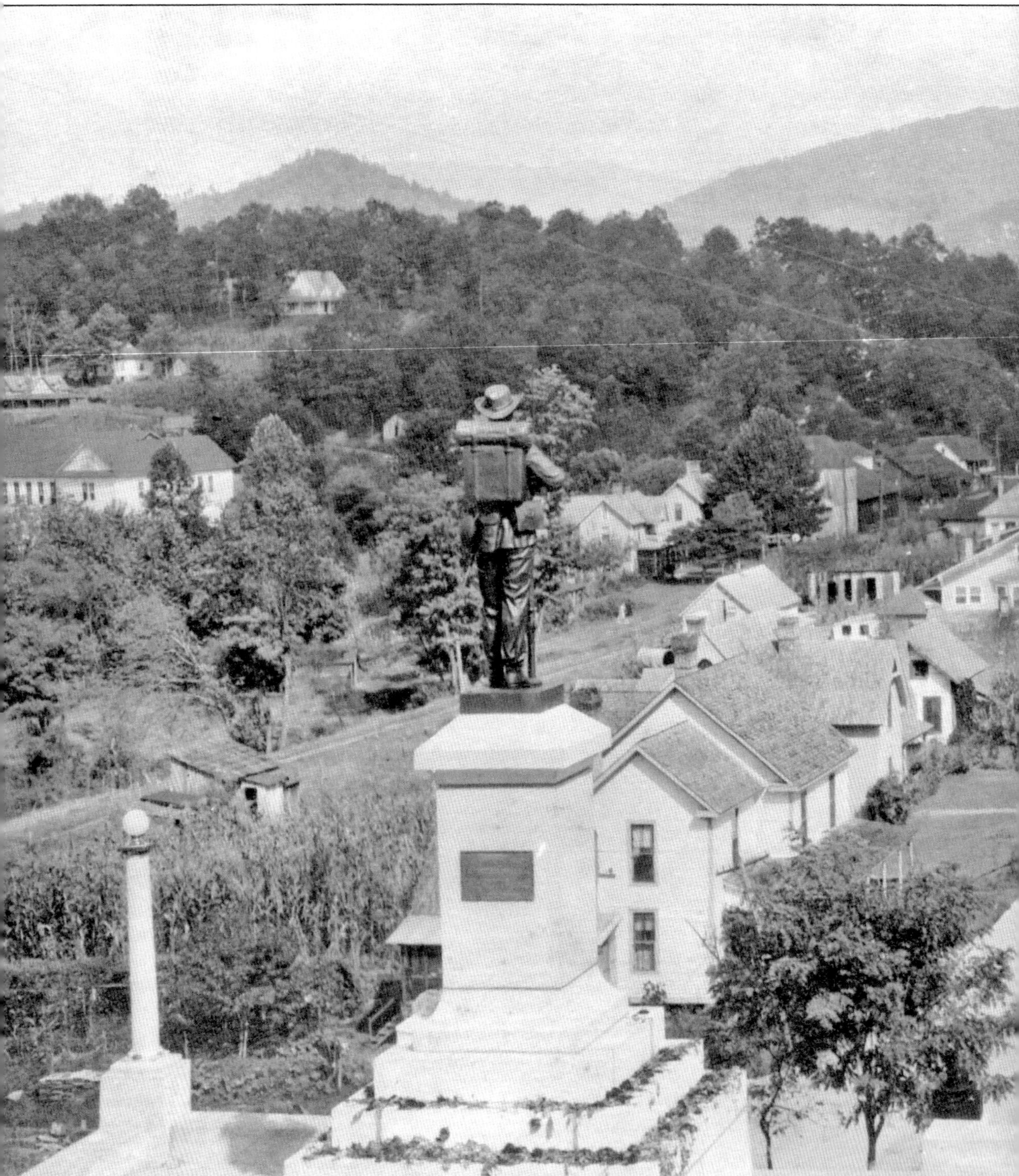

Looking down from the Jackson County Courthouse, this September 1915 view shows Sylva's west end covered in houses. From front to back, houses lining the still-unpaved street on the left are those of Osborne Buchanan (later Ernest Wilson), Ellen Picklesimer, Bess Barrett, James Cathey, and Dr. Alvin "Little Doc" Nichols (later Denning and Charles Miller); the Coward House (a boardinghouse); and Mollie Love's house (the site of first Belk's and then Peebles). The large building at left center is the Sylva Graded School, and behind it are the A. O. Allison and Logan Buchanan houses. The John R. Jones (later Mrs. Tom Wilson) house is above and slightly right

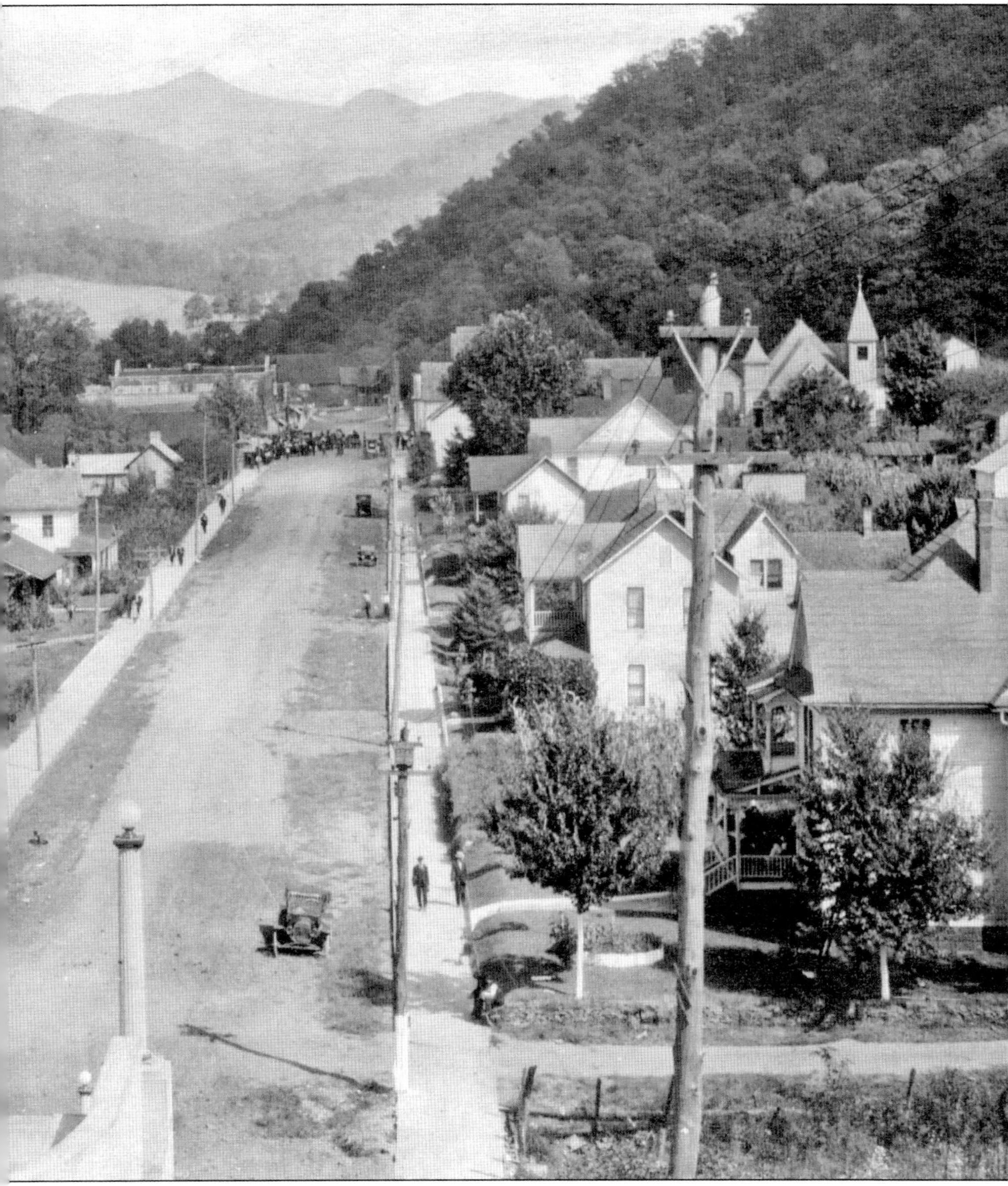

of the school. On the right, from front to back, are the D. D. Hooper house (restored in 2002 to become the Chamber of Commerce), the J. W. Keener (later Sam Allison) house, the W. W. Watt house (later Bess and then Kent Coward house), and the Charles Wells (later Leonard Holden) house. The prominent building behind and slightly right of the homes is the old Baptist church, which was located in the parking lot adjacent to the Sylva Post Office and torn down after the new sanctuary was completed in 1965. (Photograph by George Sherrill, courtesy of Ann Melton.)

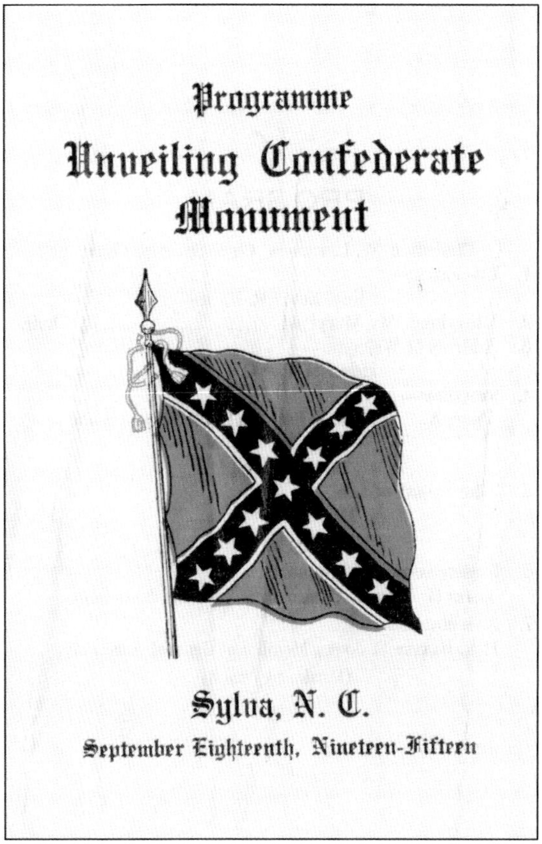

A Confederate monument was erected on the courthouse steps to honor the county's Civil War veterans on September 18, 1915. Jackson County's remaining Confederate veterans (below) gathered near the statue that day to hear music and speeches. According to the program for the event (left), a choir sang "Maryland, My Maryland," "Dixie," and "The Old North State;" Beulah Dills, daughter of Dillsboro founder William Allen Dills, performed "The Sword of Lee" accompanied by the band; Lucye Grindstaff sang "The Flag of Dixie;" the statue was presented by James H. Cathey; and the unveiling was by "eight little boys and girls, dressed in white and gray, assisted by twelve young ladies dressed in red, white and blue, bearing 12 state flags." The eight children in gray and white represented the eight companies of Confederate soldiers who volunteered from Jackson County. Dinner followed. (Left courtesy of Western Carolina University Special Collections; below photograph by George Sherrill, courtesy of Ann Melton.)

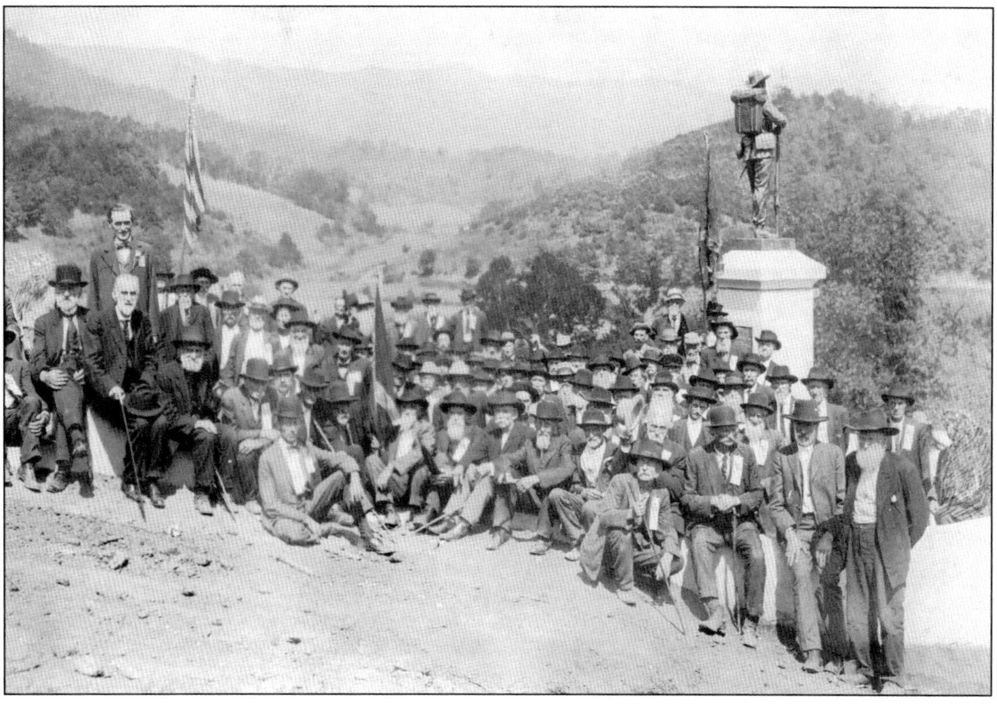

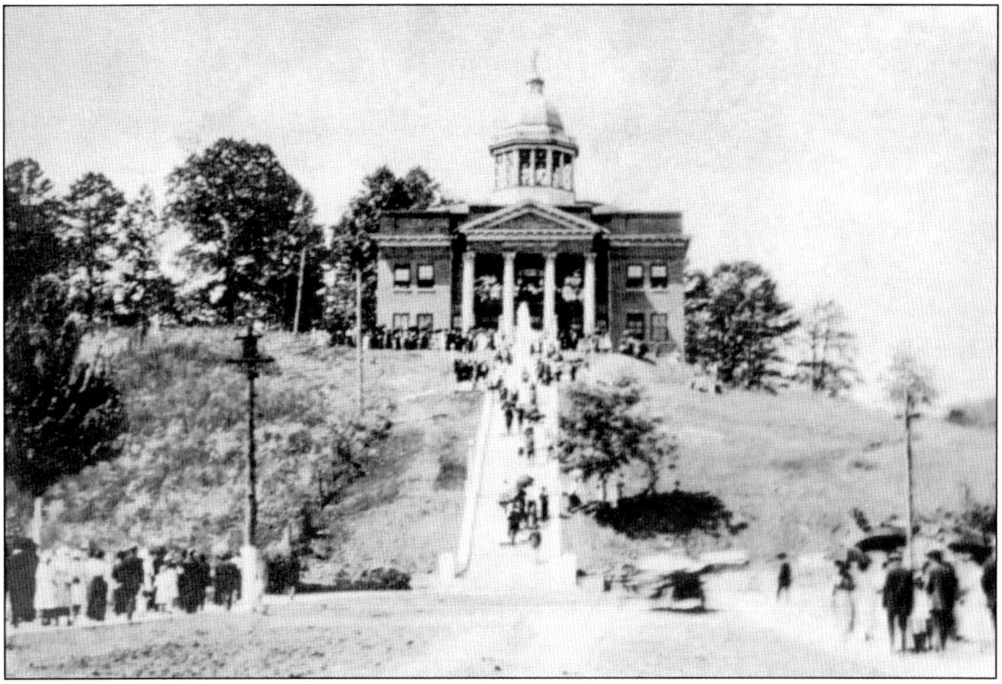

Jackson County's famous courthouse (above) was only one year old in September 1915 when more than 3,000 people crowded into downtown Sylva to witness the dedication ceremony for the Confederate monument. According to the *Sylva Herald* Centennial Edition, the people came in "crowded train coaches and long processions of wagons, buggies, carriages and automobiles flanked by riders on horseback" for the biggest occasion in Jackson County's then-63-year history. (Above courtesy of Patsy McGuire; below courtesy of Western Carolina University Special Collections.)

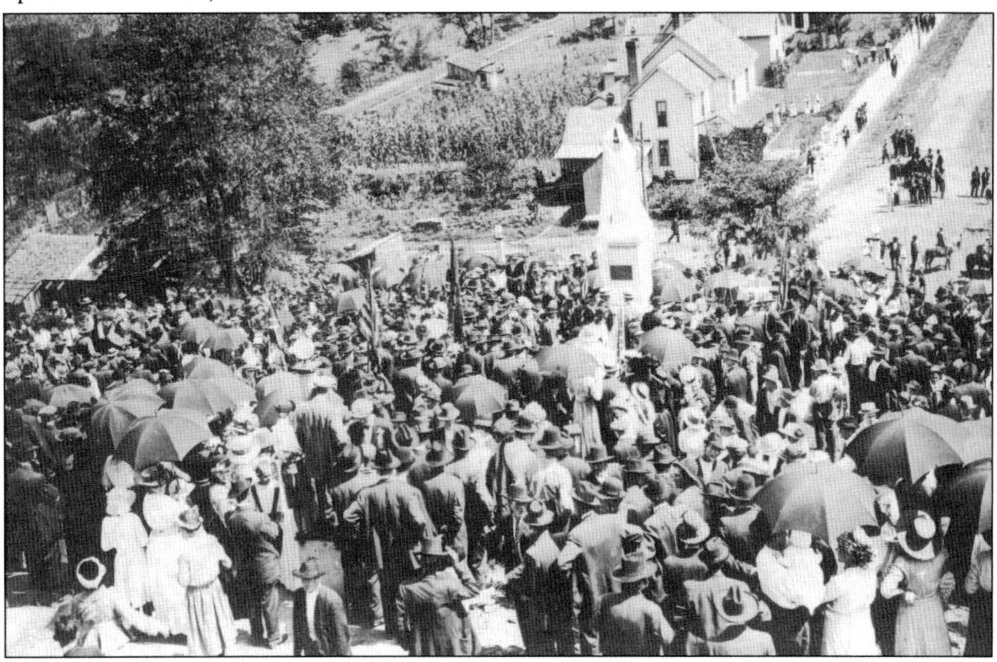

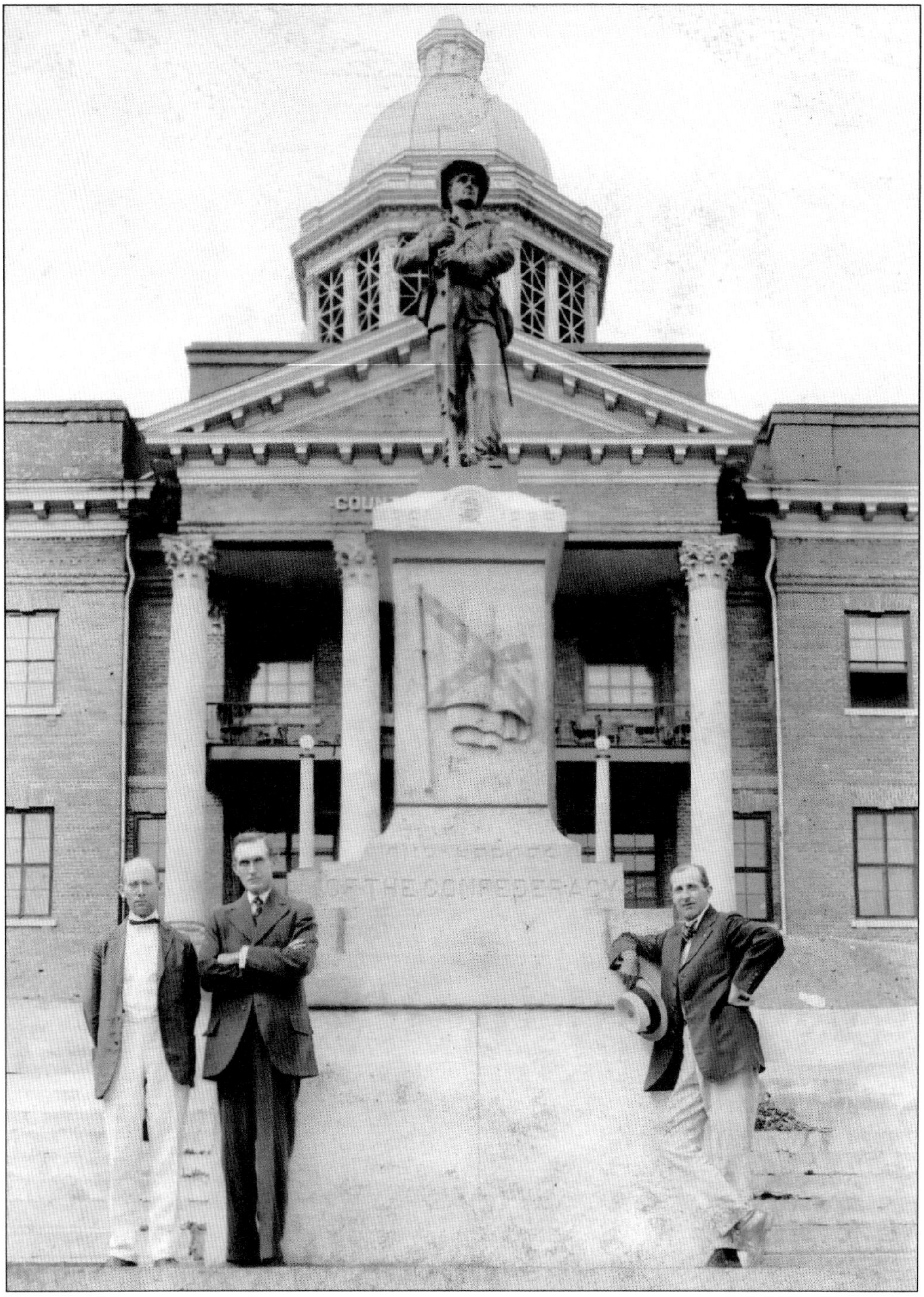

Three men, believed to be the members of the Monument Association (chairman James Cathey, Coleman Cowan, and Corsey Buchanan), pose with the statue on Dedication Day. Commemorating the deeds of the Confederate soldiers and their wives, this statue still stands on the steps of the Jackson County Courthouse. During the Civil War, 164 county men served in the Confederate army; only 84 returned home. (Photograph by George Sherrill, courtesy of Ann Melton.)

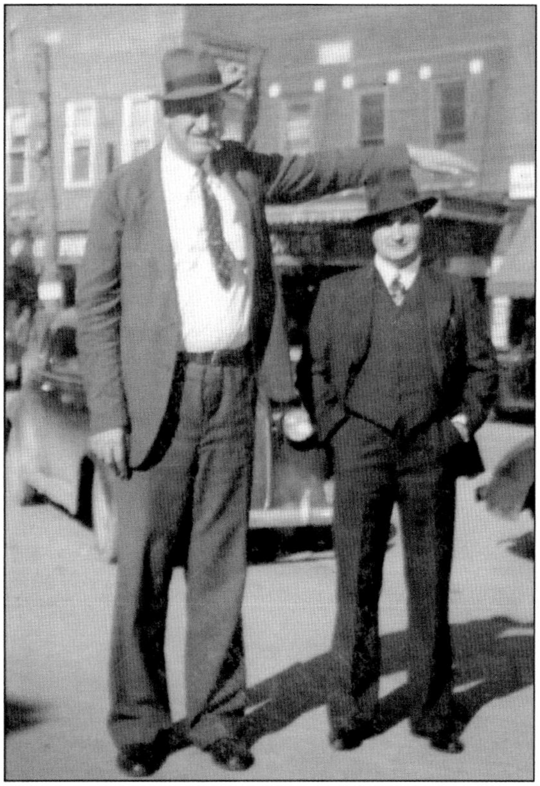

Chunk Cowan (left), on Main Street with Charlie Campbell, was the tallest soldier in the U.S. Army during World War I. He was 7 feet tall. (Courtesy of the *Sylva Herald*.)

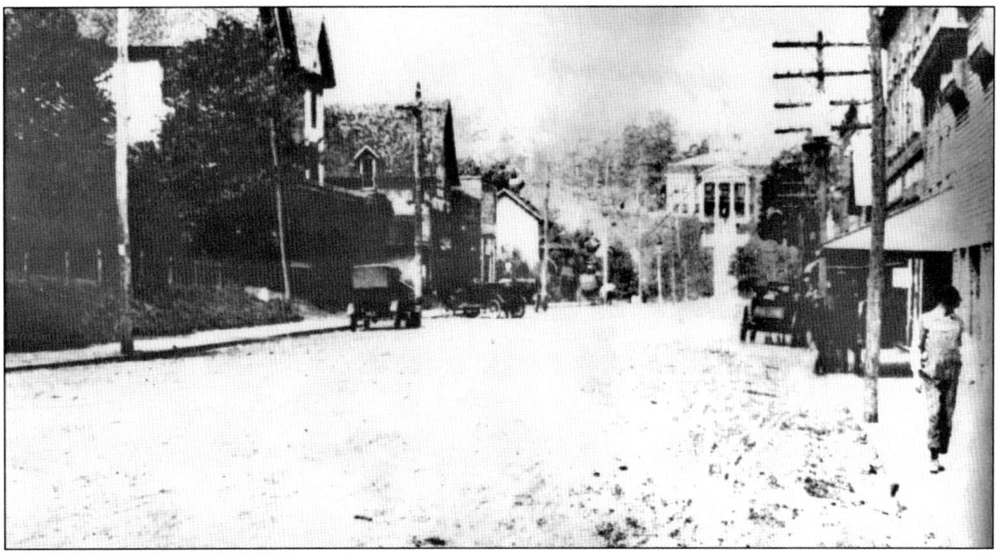

Lister Hooper took this photograph of Main Street from the back seat of a car in 1918. Former *Sylva Herald* graphics technician Mike Lyons reproduced the rare image of downtown Sylva. The first building on the left is the Commercial Hotel, which was located on the corner of Main and Spring Streets and burned in 1923. The fire was believed to have started in Zachary's Barber Shop, which extended out toward the street from the hotel. After the fire, the current First Citizens building was constructed on the site to house the Tuckaseegee Bank. (Courtesy of the *Sylva Herald*.)

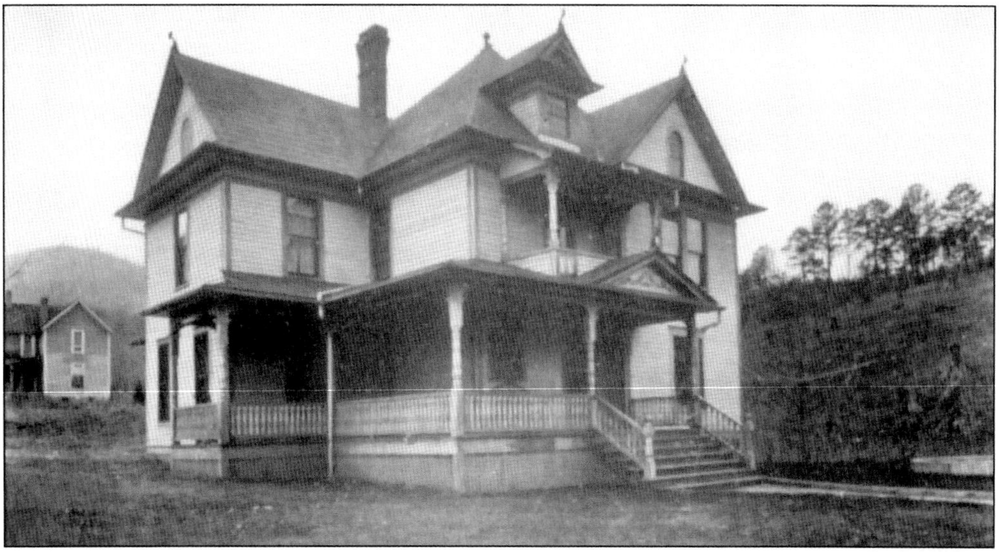

Main Street's Hooper House, home of the Jackson County Chamber of Commerce since 2002, was constructed in 1906 by Dr. D. D. Hooper to serve as both his office and residence. Hooper, who began his medical practice in Sylva, lived in the house until his 1973 death. Jackson County bought it in 1986 with an eye toward tearing it down and expanding the public library, but preservationists were able to convince commissioners in 1999 to turn the property over to the Hooper House Foundation to be remodeled for the chamber. (Courtesy of the *Sylva Herald*.)

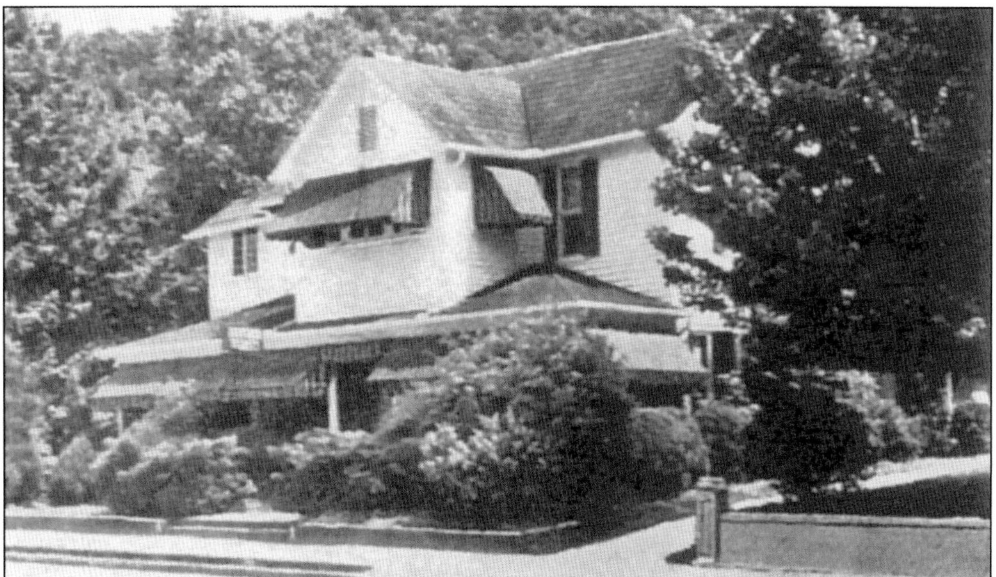

Just down Main Street from the Hooper House, this residence was constructed in 1886 by Jasper Allen and razed around 1970 to make way for the Jackson County Library. It served as the town's first school but was remodeled into a 10-room boardinghouse in 1895 after the 1894 construction of the Sylva Graded School. For a number of years, it was used as a union church building for Baptists, Methodists, and Episcopalians. The property was later purchased by W. W. Watts, who used it as a summer home, and then by Verona Bess Howard, who sold it to Kent Coward. Coward sold the house to Jackson County for the library. (Courtesy of Barbara Bess Carson.)

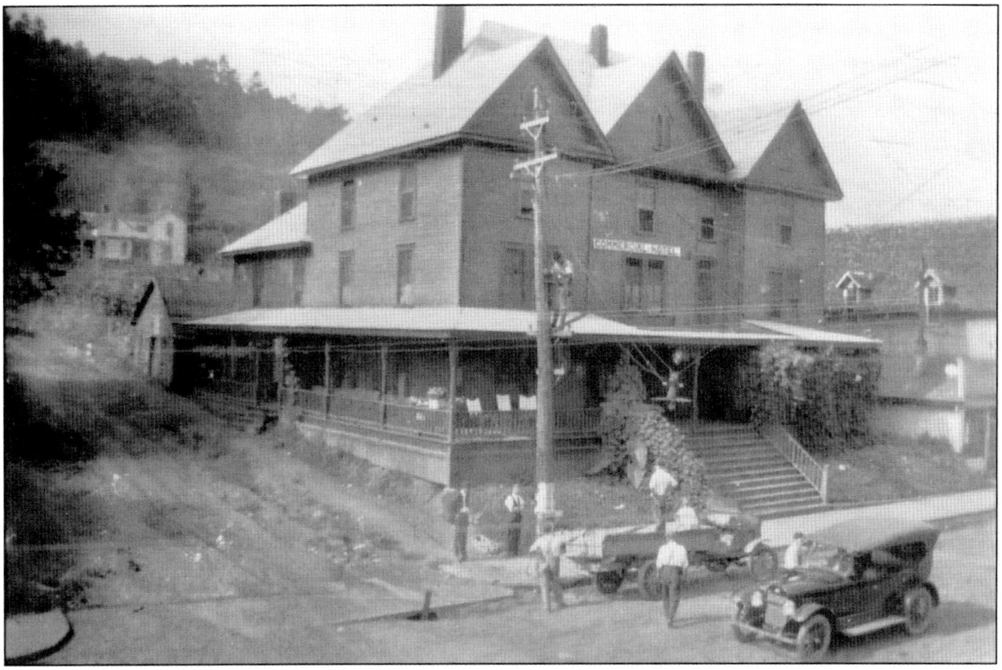

The Commercial Hotel, described in *The History of Jackson County* as a "new, two-story, up-to-date building," burned to the ground on April 6, 1923. Owned by the Hastings family, it was located on the corner of Main and Spring Streets on the site of the present First Citizens Bank parking lot. The fire, which was visible as far away as the Maple Springs community, also destroyed Medford Furniture, Zachary's Barber Shop, and a nearby home. The fire's intense heat broke out plate-glass windows on the opposite side of Main Street. (Courtesy of June Bess Anderson.)

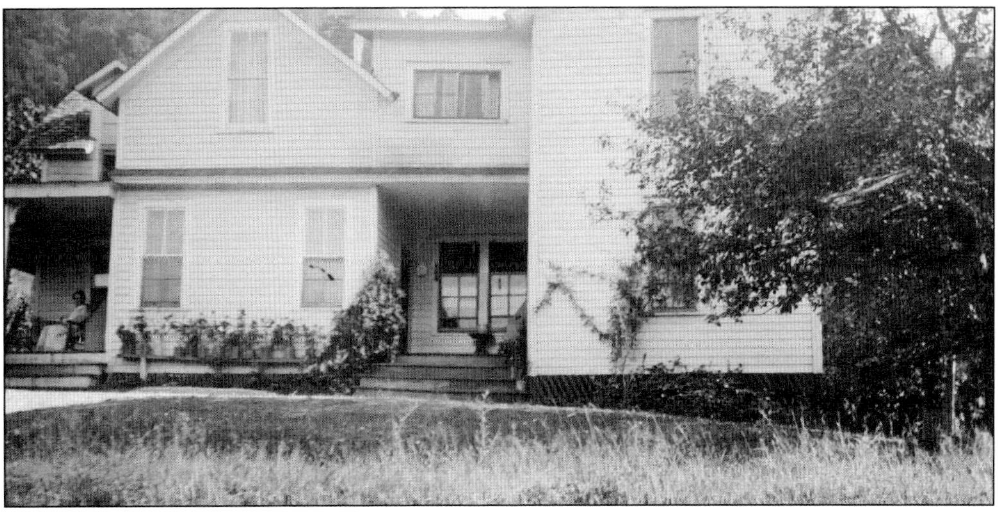

The old Manus Hanley and Mary Jane Long Morris house stood on the corner of Jackson and King Streets in a portion of the current Sylva First Methodist Church parking lot. The Morrises initially owned and operated the Commercial Hotel; their home is also visible in the upper left corner of the previous image. Manus Morris sold the house to Dr. Ralph Morgan around 1970, and it was subsequently demolished to create parking for Morgan's medical office, located at the corner of Spring and Jackson Streets where City Lights is today. (Courtesy of Jack Morris.)

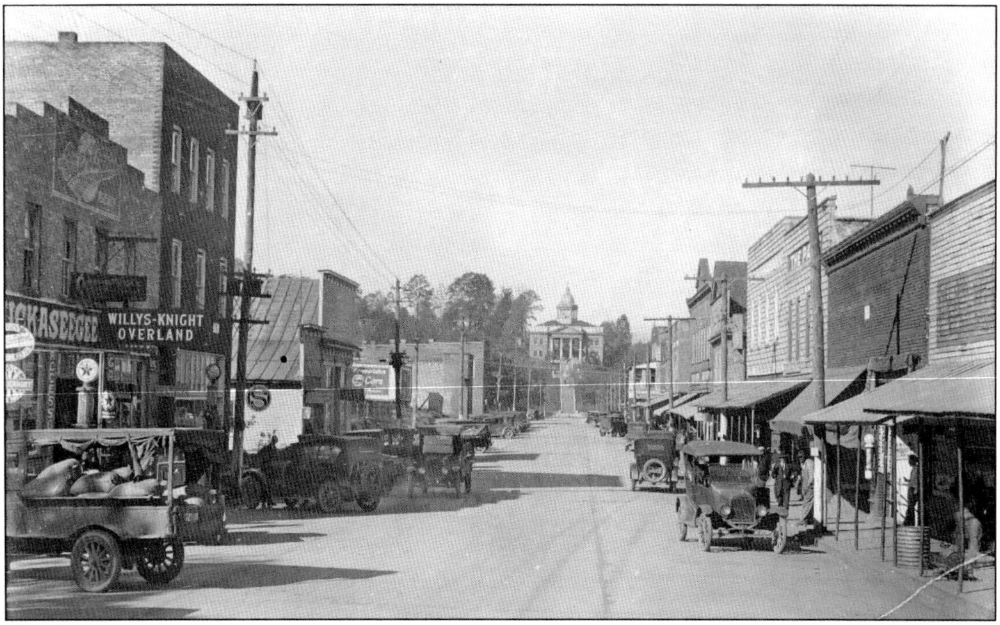

These Main Street views date from the 1920s. The buildings that now house the *Sylva Herald* are the first two on the left in both photographs. At that time, the first building housed Tuckaseegee Motors, a Willys-Knight/Overland dealership, and the second served as the McGuire dental offices. Buildings on the right side of the street in the above photograph include, from left to right, Sylva Supply Company (now Jackson's General), Jackson Hardware (now Nick and Nate's), and the Paris (now Motion Makers). Of interest on the right in the below image is the old Higdon House (past the New Jackson Hotel), built by E. R. Hampton, who once owned most of the land where Sylva developed. A third floor was later added to the hotel building. (Above courtesy of the *Sylva Herald*; below photograph by George Sherrill, courtesy of Ann Melton.)

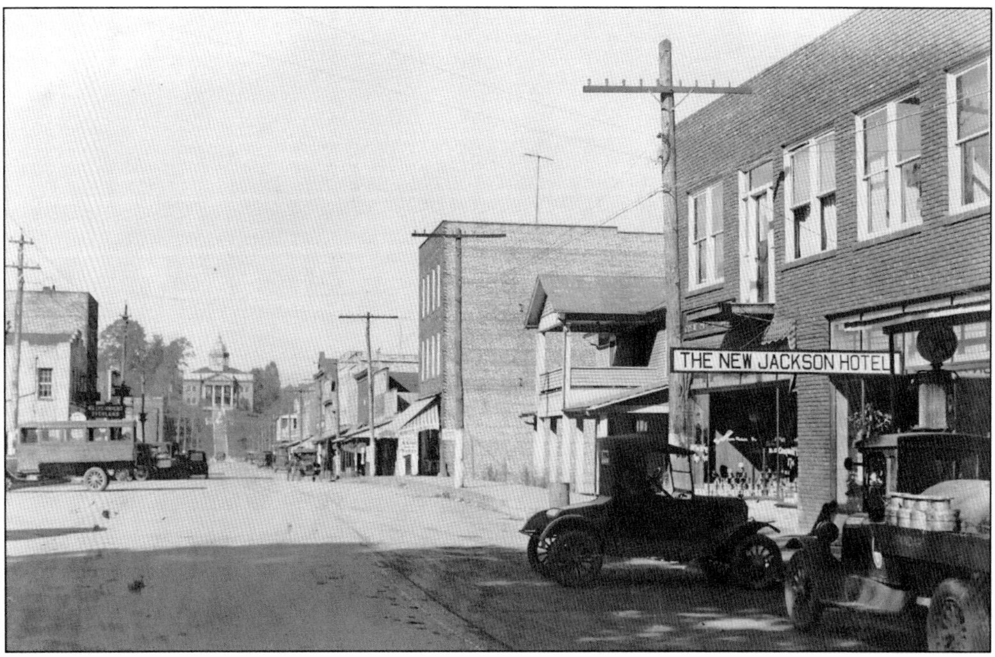

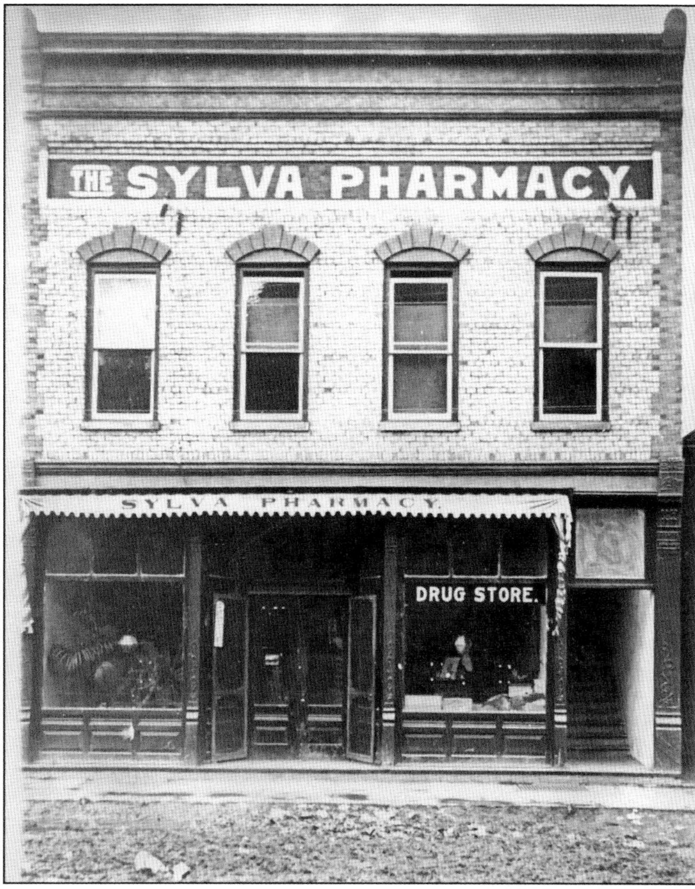

Sylva Pharmacy (above), operated by Gilbert Bess, was once located on Main Street in the building that now houses Hollifield Jewelers. The stairway to the right went upstairs to the law offices of E. P. Stillwell Sr. and David Stillwell. Main Street was still unpaved when this photograph was taken in the early 1920s. The store's interior is shown below, with the soda fountain at the back and the pharmacy area on the right. Those pictured include, from left to right, Bess, Odell Richardson, and Tom Wilson. (Courtesy of June Bess Anderson.)

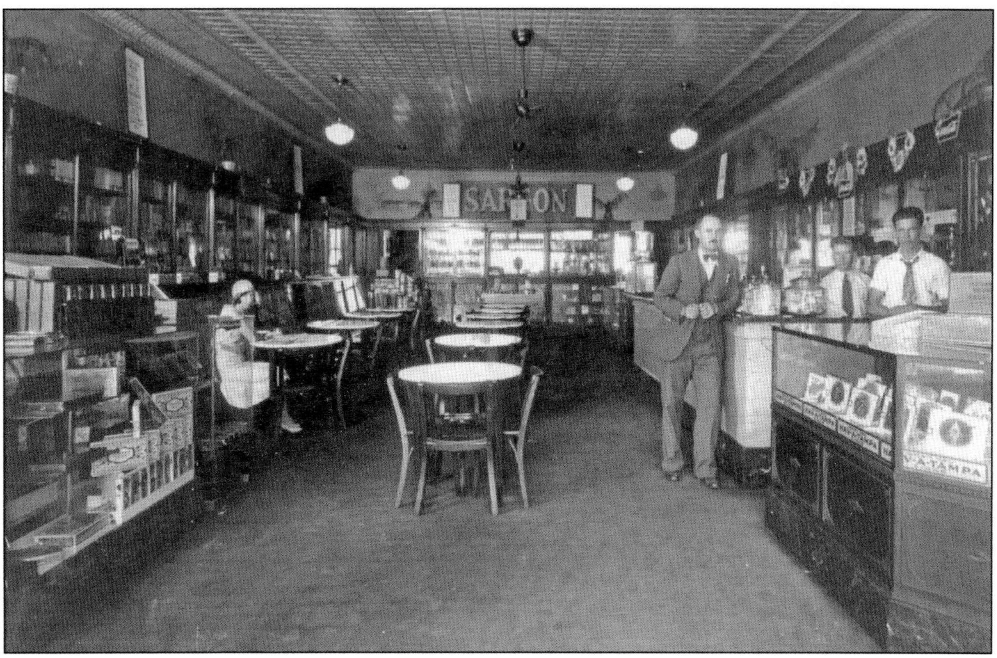

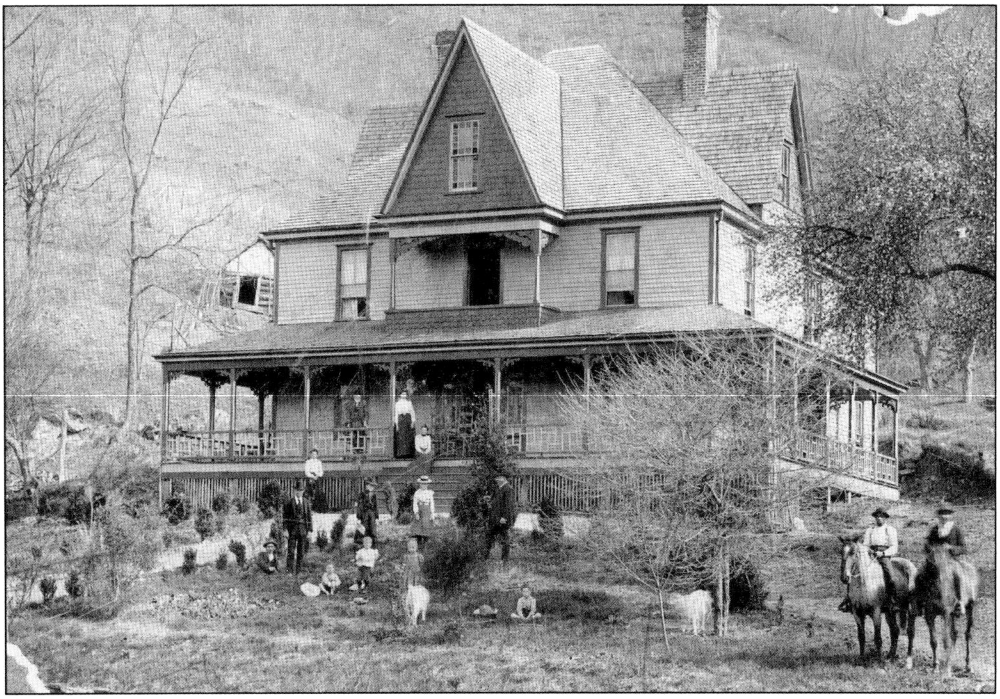

This house once stood on Main Street across from Livingston's Photo, where the Frank Massie home is today. The photograph dates from the 1890s, when the house belonged to Marcellus Sr. and Belle Buchanan, who operated it as a boardinghouse. There was a hill on Main Street in those days that was eventually leveled when the street was paved during the 1920s. (Courtesy of Elsie Massie.)

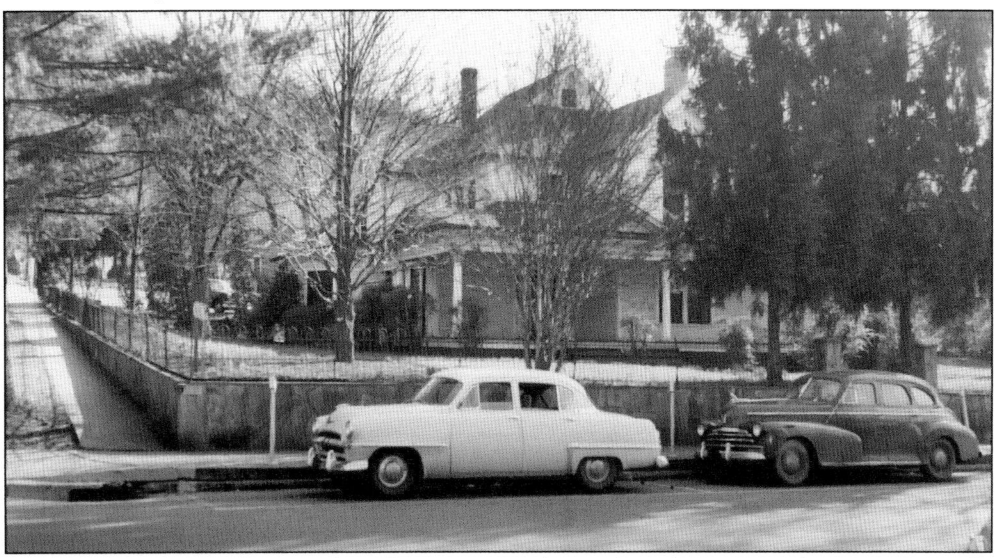

The home of E. L. and Gertrude Dills McKee was located on the corner of Main and Landis Streets where First Baptist Church stands today. The photograph was likely taken in 1952, when First Baptist bought the property from the McKee family. In 1958, the Baptists constructed an education building behind the McKee home before the house was demolished to make way for the sanctuary, completed in 1965. (Courtesy of the *Sylva Herald*.)

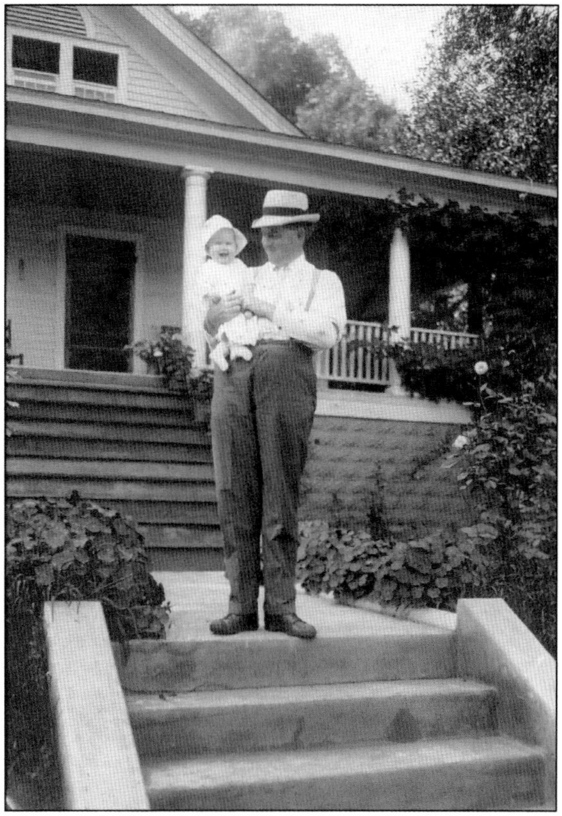

Longtime Sylva dentist Dr. Wayne McGuire (right) stands on the steps of his home holding his oldest daughter, Noracella, in 1915. Drs. Wayne and Daisy McGuire's dental office (now the *Sylva Herald*) was in front and to the right of the house, which was extensively remodeled around 2002 for use as Alan's Restaurant. Since then, various eateries have operated there, including the McGuire House, Karen's, and most recently, 553 Restaurant. The Thad Bryson home (below), one of the first built in Sylva, stood on the corner of King and Jackson Streets. From left to right are Loy "Curly" Bryson, Thad Bryson and his wife, Gerson and T. C. Bryson Jr., and Josephine Dills. The home of Wayne and Daisy's daughter and son-in-law, Drs. Patsy and Harold McGuire, now stands on the site of the Bryson residence. (Right courtesy of Patsy McGuire; below courtesy of Jeannette Bryson.)

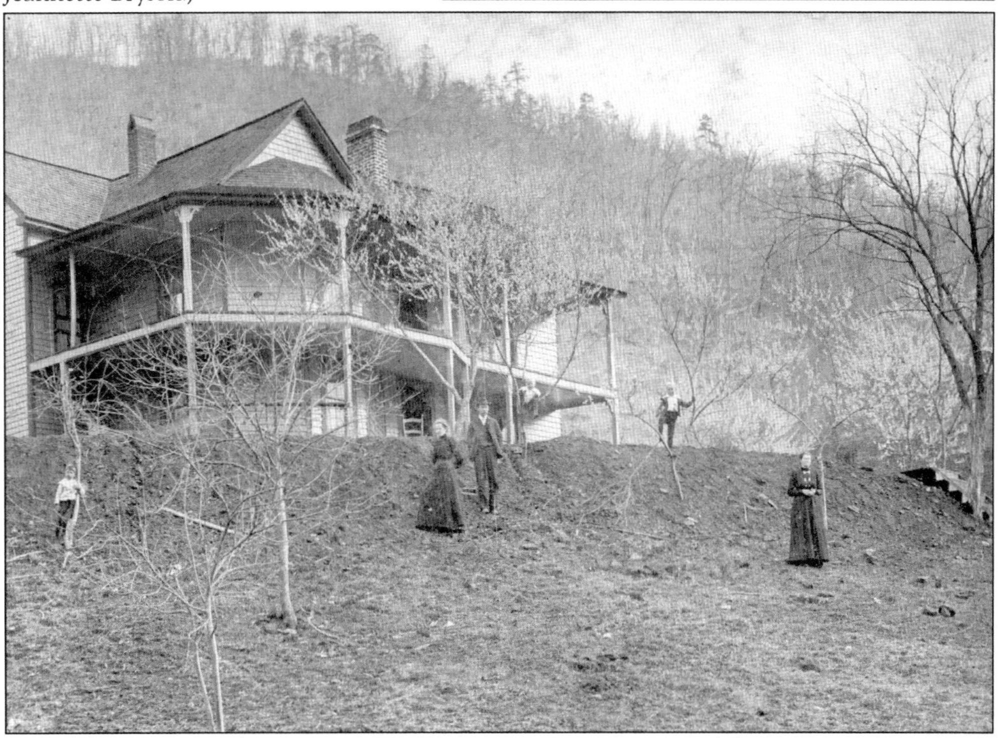

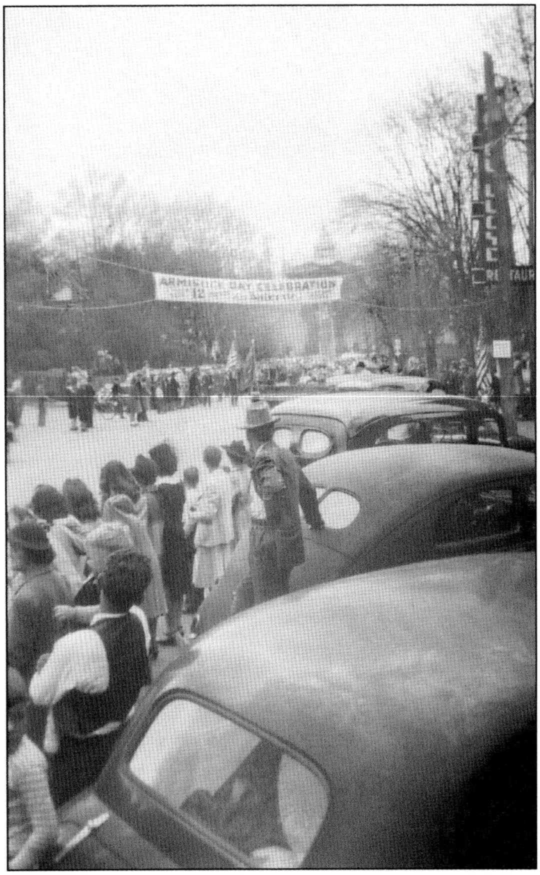

Armistice Day parades, like the one at left in the late 1930s or early 1940s, once lured large crowds to Sylva. Also visible is the sign for the Hotel Lloyd, which now houses the Jewelry Outlet. The below photograph shows a 1920 or 1921 Armistice Day parade as it rounds the curve at the courthouse end of town. The precursor of Veterans Day, Armistice Day (November 11) marked the 1918 end of World War I, when world leaders signed a peace agreement on the 11th day of the 11th month. When the armistice was signed, the whistles of the Sylva Tanning Company reportedly sounded and church and school bells all over the county rang out. The two buildings behind the floats are Early's Service Station (left), thought to be run by Sion Early, and Osborne Buchanan's barn. Buchanan was the grandfather of lifetime Sylva resident Allie Huff. Armistice Day was changed to Veterans Day around 1953. This end of Main Street was reconfigured in 1998 during downtown construction and renovation. (Left courtesy of Western Carolina University Special Collections; below courtesy of the *Sylva Herald*.)

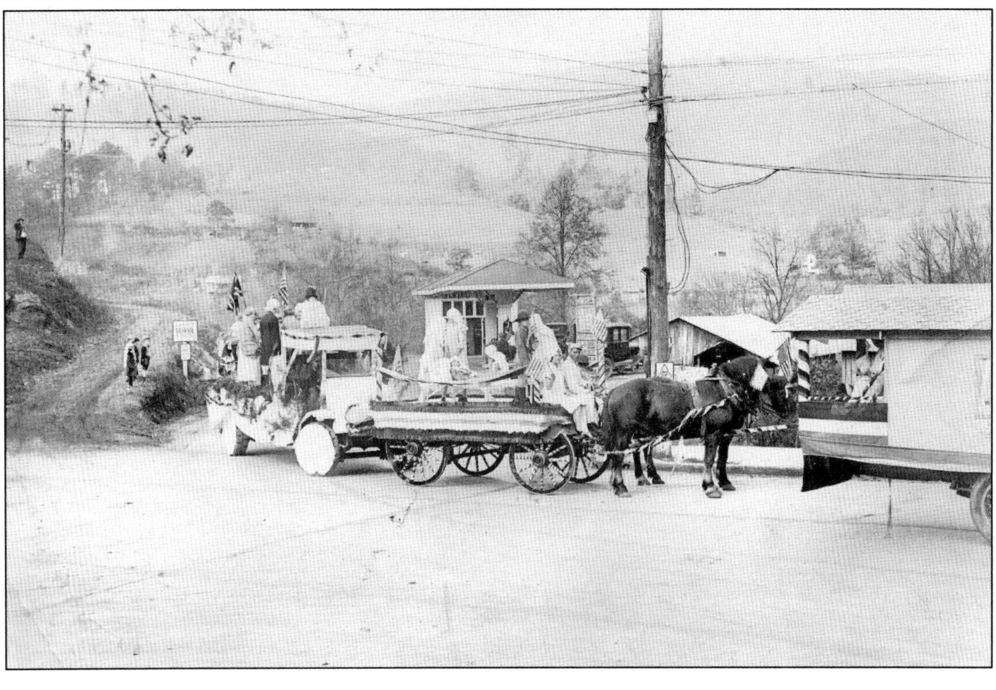

Tuckaseegee Bank's original Sylva location (right) was adjacent to the white marble building constructed in 1928 that now houses First Citizens Bank. Tuckaseegee became insolvent in 1930 and was forced to close; First Citizens still uses the original building, now painted white, for office space. Jackson Savings and Loan (below) once operated out of the Hotel Lloyd building. Here area residents pose in front of the bank when it opened in 1958 or 1959. Pictured from left to right in the first row are Lloyd Cowan, W. C. Hennessee, Tom Clayton, Dick Sellers, Joe Sellers, Bob Jackson, and Bob Parker. The rest include Eddie Queen, Mary Cowan, Bjorn "Johnny" Ahlin, Lou Bryson, Martie Franklin, Jean Franklin, Linda Barnes, Burt Wilkey, Peggy Parker, Pete Davis, Dick Green, Wayne Wilson, Andy Wilson, Clyde Franklin, Bert Lloyd, Bob Barefoot, and Bea Wall. The boy at right is thought to be a Messer. Jay Ball opened his Jewelry Outlet in the former bank building in 1987. (Courtesy of the *Sylva Herald*.)

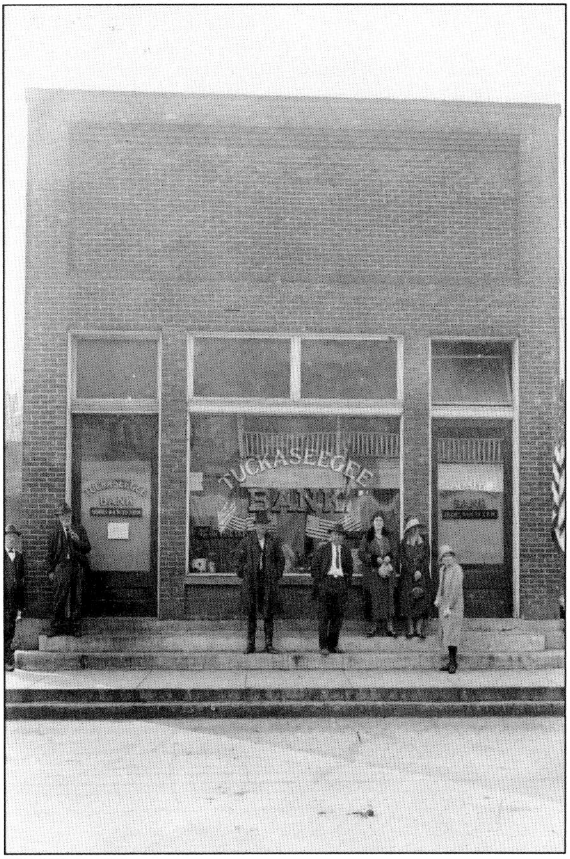

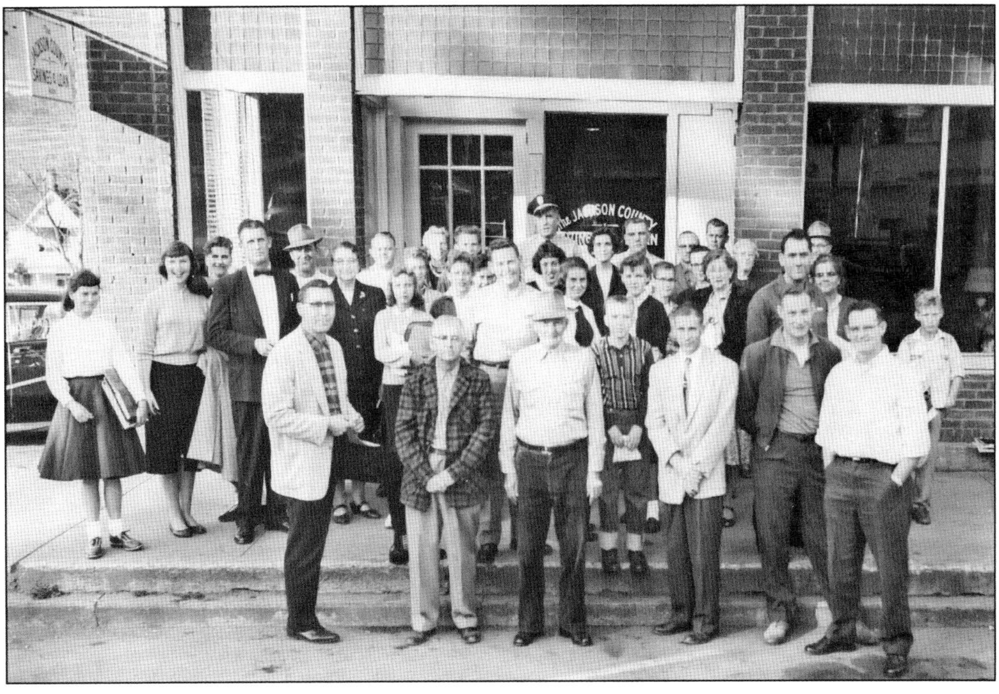

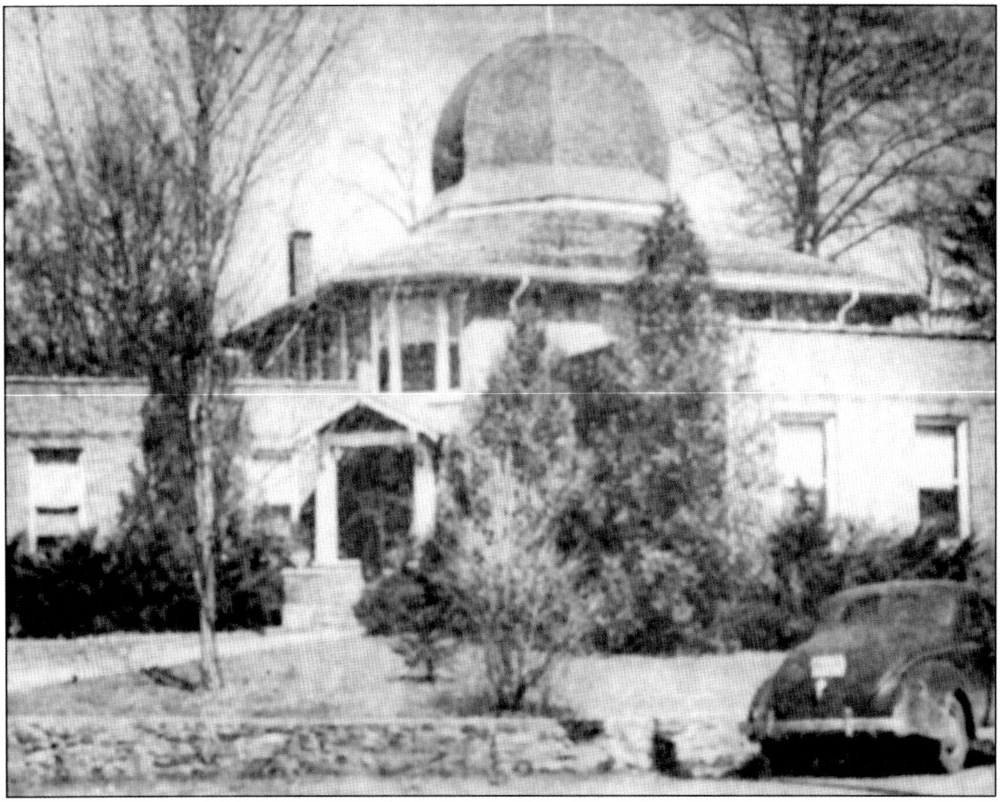

Sylva's first hospital (above), originally known as Candler-Tidmarsh, stood on Courthouse Hill overlooking the Jackson County Courthouse and downtown Sylva. It was organized in 1925 by Drs. C. Z. Candler and Harold Tidmarsh. Dr. Alvin Nichols purchased Tidmarsh's interest in 1928, and the name was changed to Candler-Nichols Hospital. By 1930, the burden of caring for the facility's large number of charity patients proved too great, so the two doctors accepted help from the Duke Foundation and C. J. Harris. In the below photograph, a nurse stands outside the original hospital. (Above courtesy of the *Sylva Herald*; below courtesy of Western Carolina University Special Collections.)

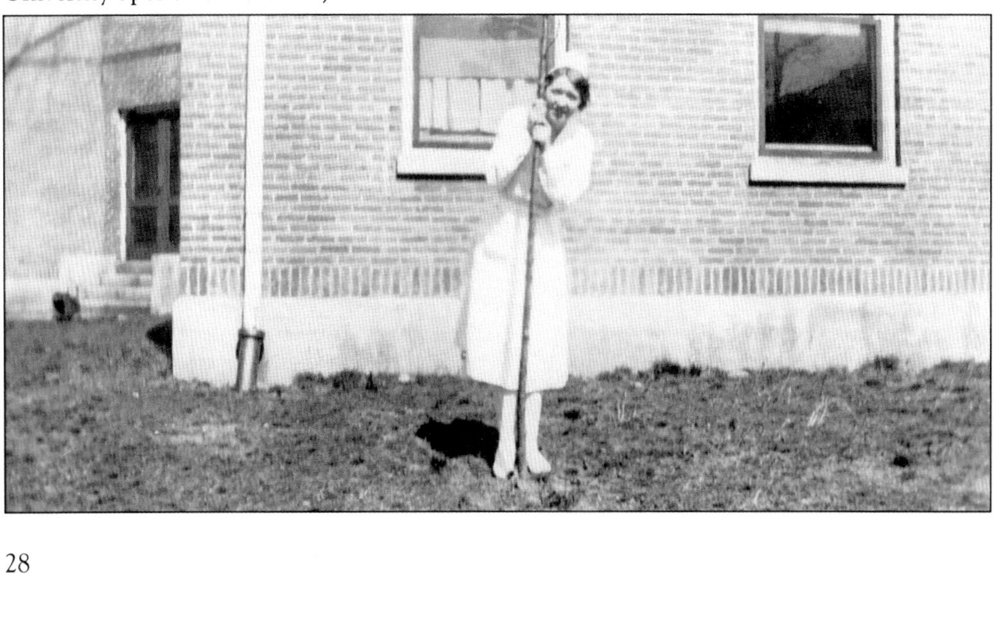

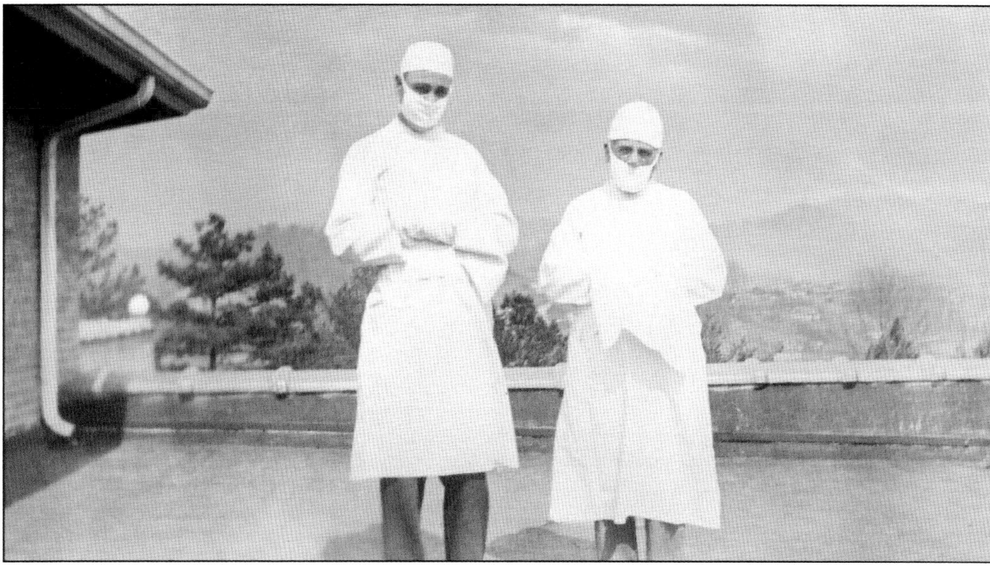

These photographs were taken outside Sylva's original hospital. The identities of those pictured are unknown. In 1930, the facility was renamed C. J. Harris Community Hospital in honor of the entrepreneur Harris, who had been a generous contributor. The hospital expanded with the 1948 opening of the T. N. Massie Wing, constructed at a cost of $37,000, with some $20,000 raised through public contributions. Hospital trustees were facing another critical shortage of space by the mid-1950s. Local medical and civic leaders, supported by the growing community, launched a fund-raising campaign for a new hospital. Before construction could begin, fire damaged one of the existing hospital's main wings in April 1958; the county was without a hospital for 35 days until it reopened in May. The new hospital opened at Harris Regional Hospital's present location in November 1959. (Courtesy of Western Carolina University Special Collections.)

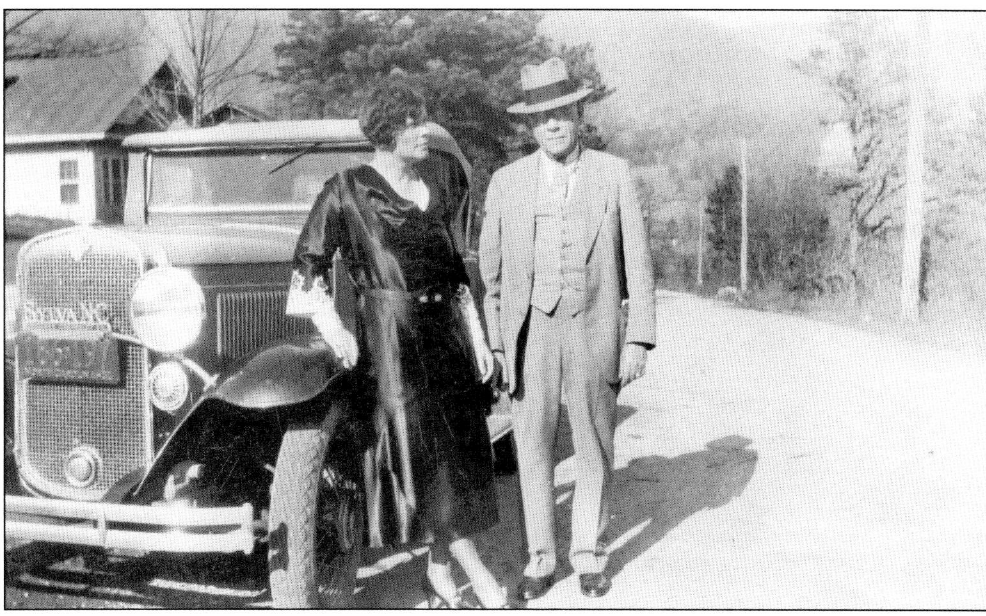

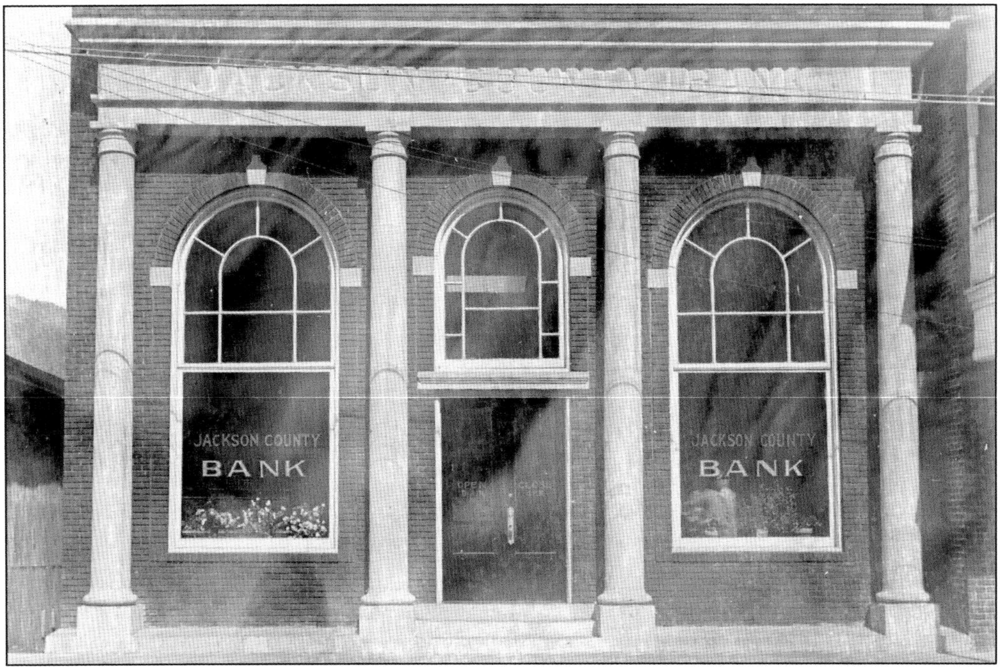

The Jackson County Bank opened in Webster in October 1905. By the mid-1920s, the bank had moved to Sylva's Main Street, where it was first located in the C. J. Harris building (now Jackson's General), until the above building was constructed. The institution merged with the statewide First Union National Bank in 1962, but the First Union name vanished 40 years later when that bank bought out Wachovia and kept the Wachovia name. The local First Union branch was sold to Central Carolina Bank (CCB). SunTrust, which currently occupies the building, purchased CCB in 2004. (Courtesy of the *Sylva Herald*.)

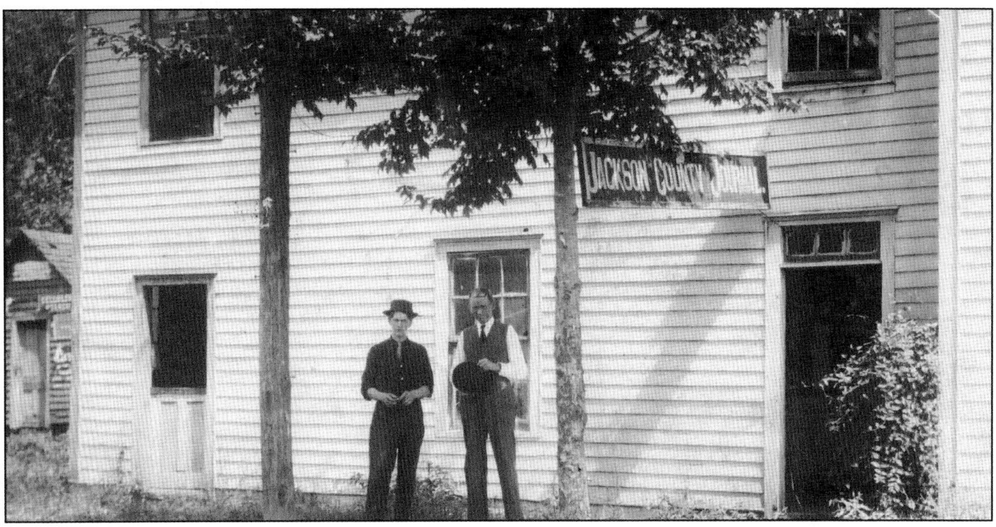

In 1910, the *Jackson County Journal* was published from a house on Allen Street located near where Hooper Builders Supply operated for years. Everette E. Brown (left) served as editor and N. B. Moore as business manager. Dan Tompkins took over as editor two years later and held that post for some 31 years. The *Journal*, termed a "casualty of World War II" in *The History of Jackson County*, ceased publication in October 1943. (Courtesy of Rachel Phillips.)

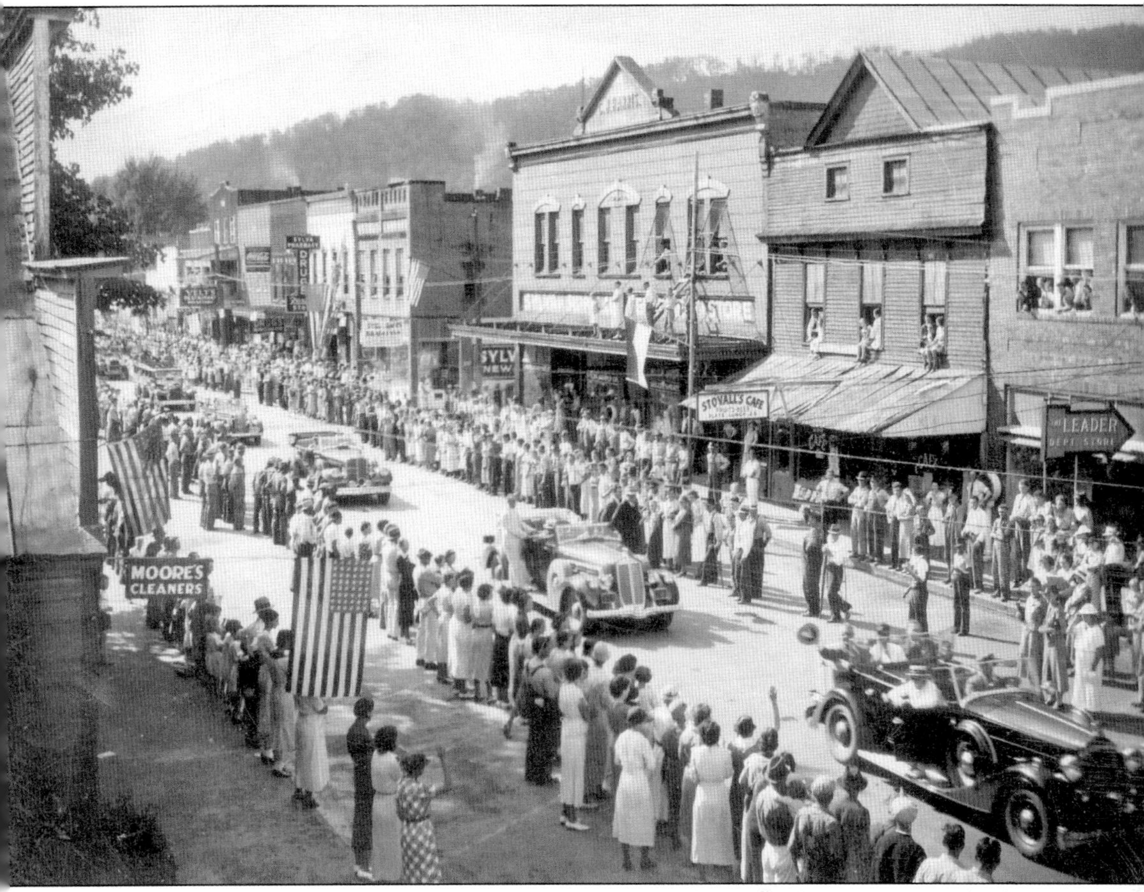

Thousands turned out to welcome Pres. Franklin D. Roosevelt, in the first car waving his hat to the crowd, to Sylva on September 9, 1936. All of these buildings are still standing except for the one housing Stovall's Café, which was then located to the right of the C. J. Harris Building (center, operating as Sylva Supply Company). The Stovall building was torn down around 1938 and replaced by a new café; that structure is now part of the Blackrock Outdoor Company. Roosevelt is the only president to have ever visited Sylva. (Courtesy of Western Carolina University Special Collections.)

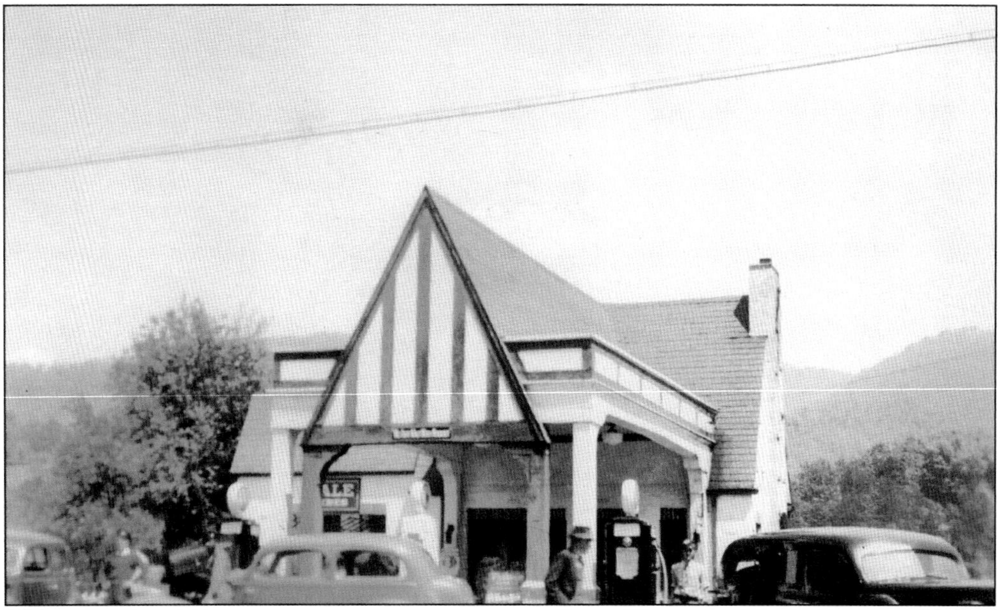

The West End Service Station, one of two Pure Oil service stations on Main Street owned by David Hall Sr. and his brother-in-law James H. Councill, was located on the present Moody Funeral Home parking lot. Before being razed, it was enlarged to accommodate the bus station and later other businesses. The East End Service Station was situated at the corner of Main and Broad Streets where Performance Motors is now. (Courtesy of Bob Hall.)

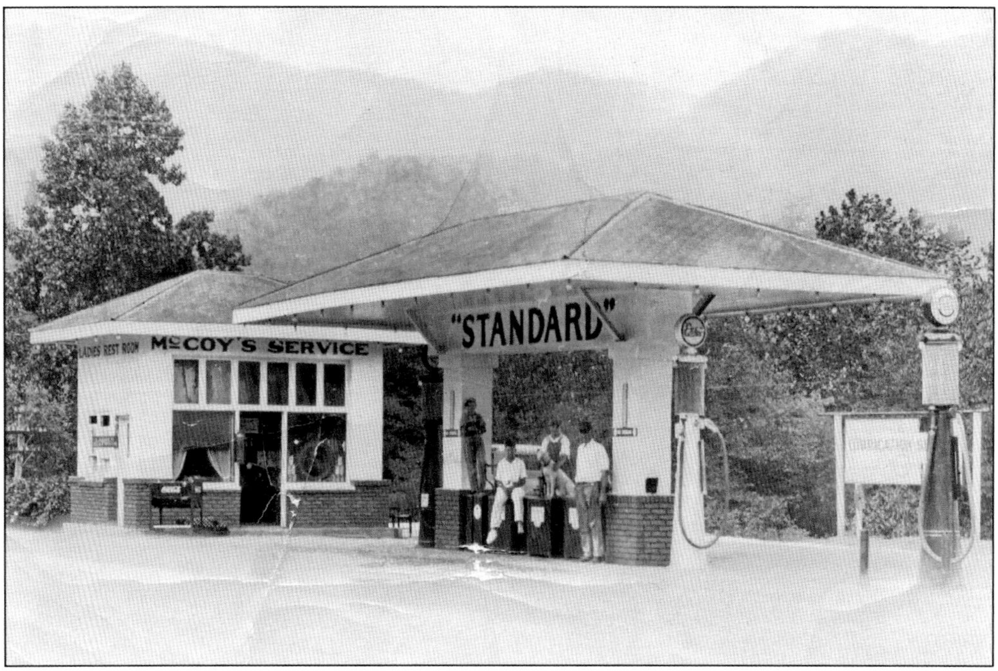

McCoy's Service Station once stood at the west intersection of Main and Mill Streets, near the Jackson County Courthouse. Pictured about 1930 are, from left to right, Tom Kelly, future congressman David Hall Jr., Ernest Wilson Jr., and station owner Mr. McCoy. (Courtesy of Bob Hall.)

U.S. Marine corporal William Horace Bradsher and his new bride, Inez Revis Bradsher, who graduated from Sylva High School in 1940, are shown at right on Main Street in front of Shelton Bradsher's taxi in 1942. Bill Bradsher was later wounded in World War II's Pacific theater. In the photograph below, taken around 1948, longtime Sylva barber Dillard Coward stands on Main Street near his barbershop. Businesses visible across the street include, from left to right, Professional Drug Store, Sylva Supply Company, Stovall's Café, and Belk's. The Esso sign is a reminder that Main Street was once home to several filling stations. (Right courtesy of Benny Bradsher; below courtesy of Jay Coward.)

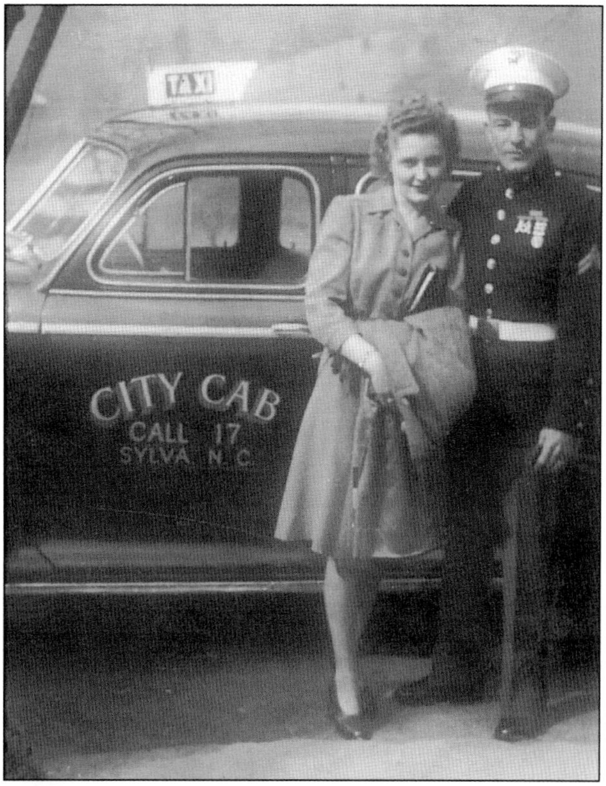

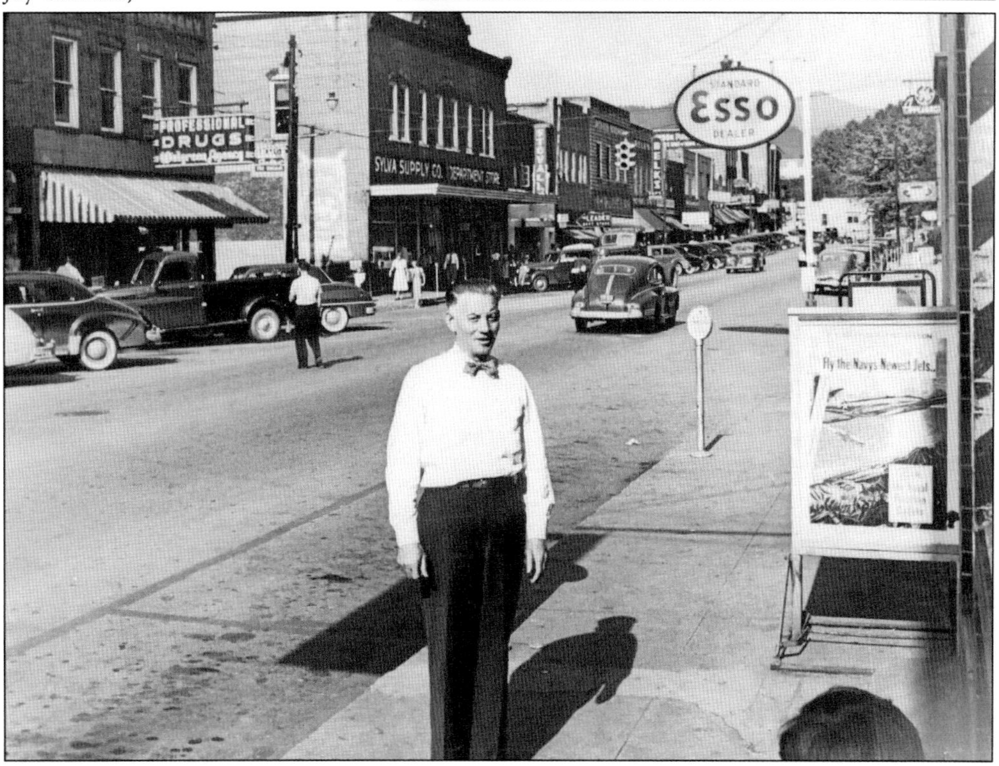

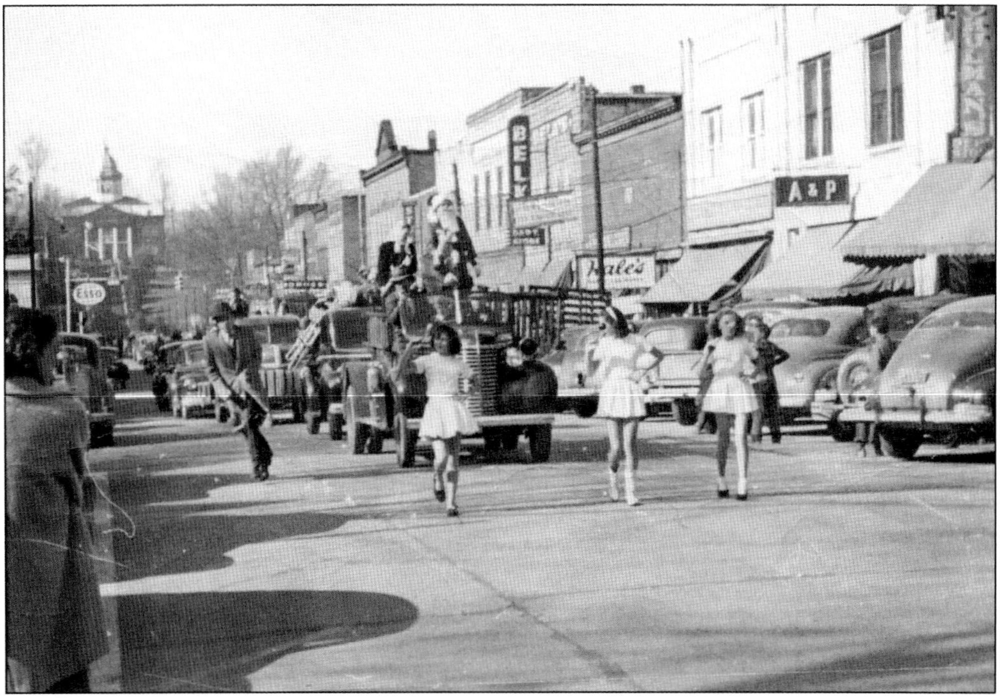

These images from downtown events are both thought to date from the late 1940s. In the above Christmas parade photograph, the trees in front of the courthouse are small, Belk's is in the present Motion Makers location, and the A&P is still across from what was then Allison's and is now the *Sylva Herald*. Other businesses include Sylva Supply Company and Hale's Dress Shop. The photograph below, which may depict a post–World War II celebration, shows the Farmers' Federation and Velt's Café on the left side of the street. Businesses visible on the right side include the former Tuckaseegee Bank building; an Esso station; Massie Furniture, which celebrated its 75th anniversary in 2007; the McGuire dental offices; and Allison's. (Courtesy of Western Carolina University Special Collections.)

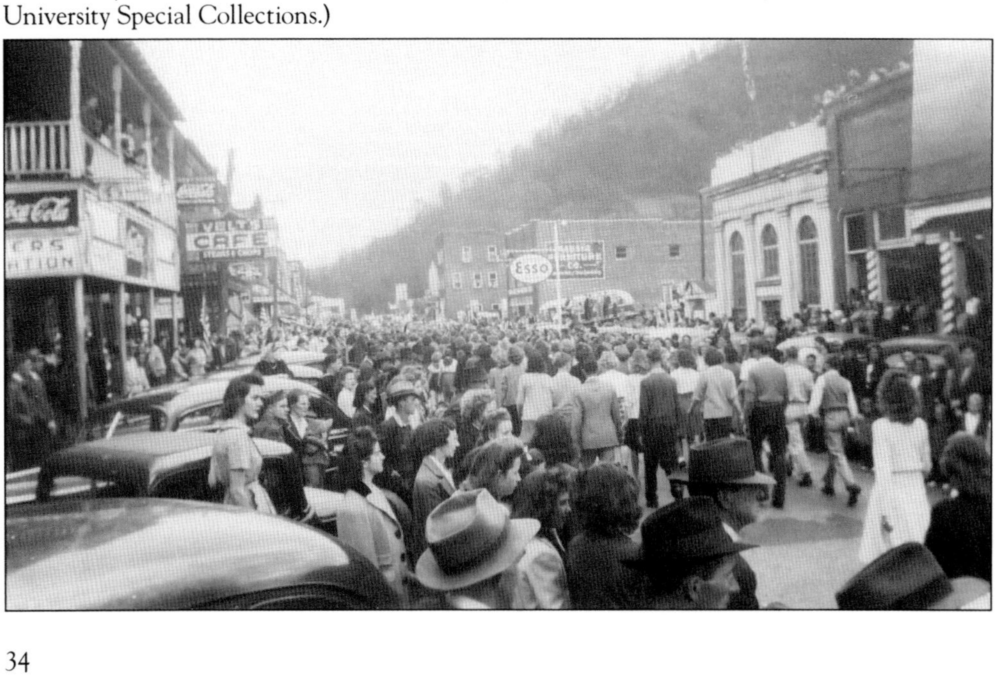

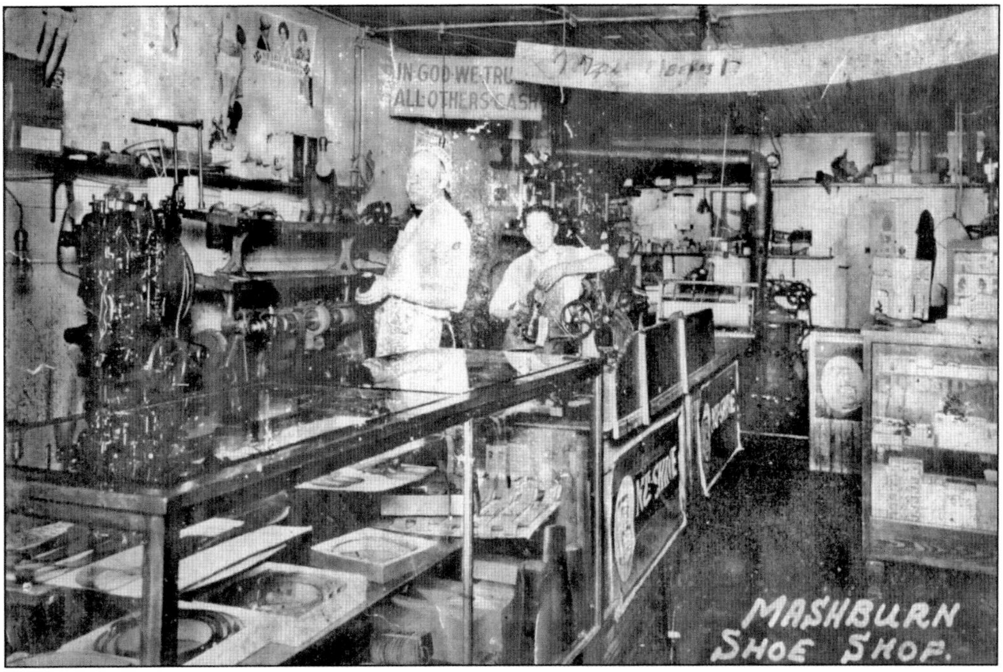

Above, Ed "E. O." Mashburn (left) and employee Garland Parris stand in the original Mashburn Shoe Shop, a shoe repair business located across the railroad tracks from Mill Street on the corner of what is now Grindstaff Cove Road. E. O. opened the shop with his brother Gurley around 1914, but Gurley left after a few years and moved to Asheville. In 1920, Mashburn's moved across Mill Street into the building on the corner of Spring Street that recently housed Bay's Corner and is now Bill's Backstreet Take-out. The first store to specialize in new shoes, Wallin Shoe Store (below), opened in the Hollifield Jewelers building around 1947. Joe Wallin was a teacher, and his wife, pictured with him inside the store, ran the business. (Courtesy of Nancy Browning.)

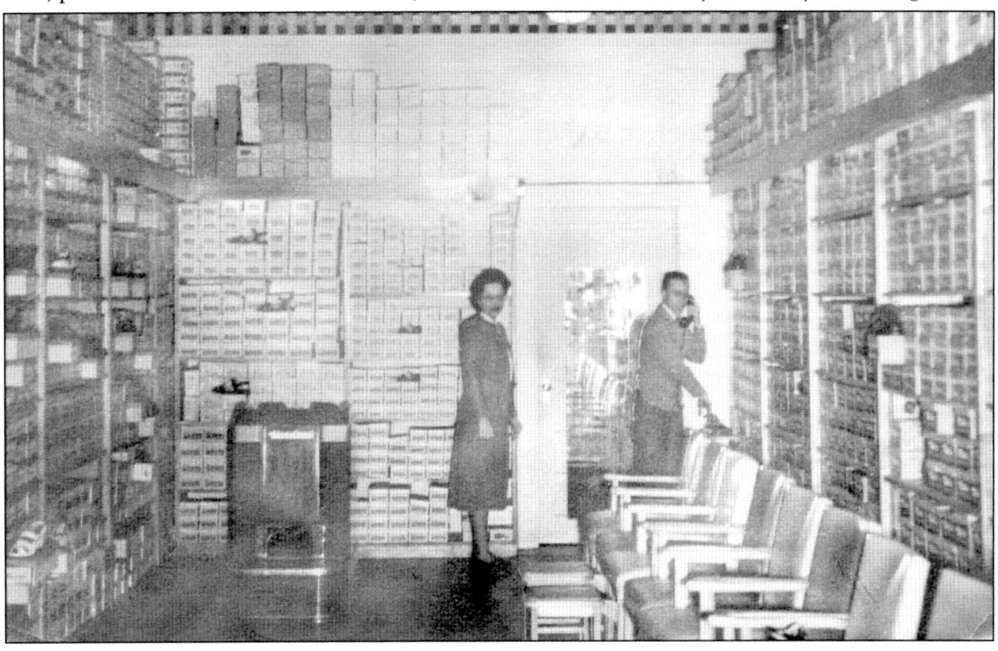

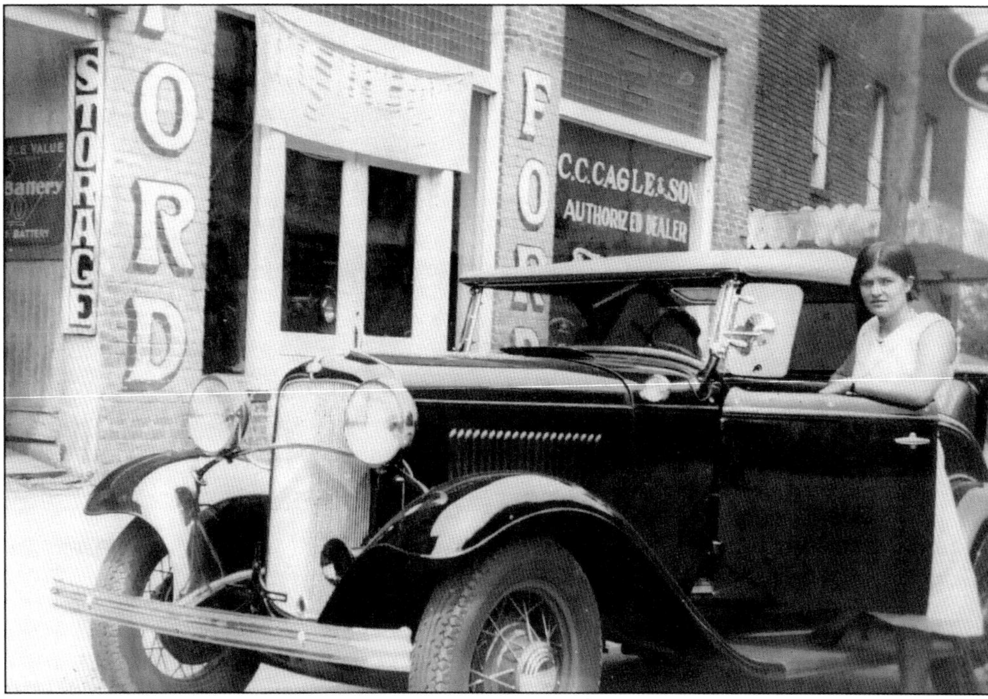

J. S. Higdon's Ford garage (above) was located on Main Street in the building that was Western Auto for years and now houses Arsenal Artifacts and Dodie's Auction. Higdon, a blacksmith, was the first car dealer west of Asheville and also the town's first mechanic. To boost car sales in 1914, he drove a Model T up the courthouse steps. Sam Cogdill, pictured below with his 1917 Dodge, and his son Ray began Sylva's first Dodge dealership, Cogdill Motor Company, in 1929. (Above courtesy of Betty Foxx; below courtesy of Sam Cogdill.)

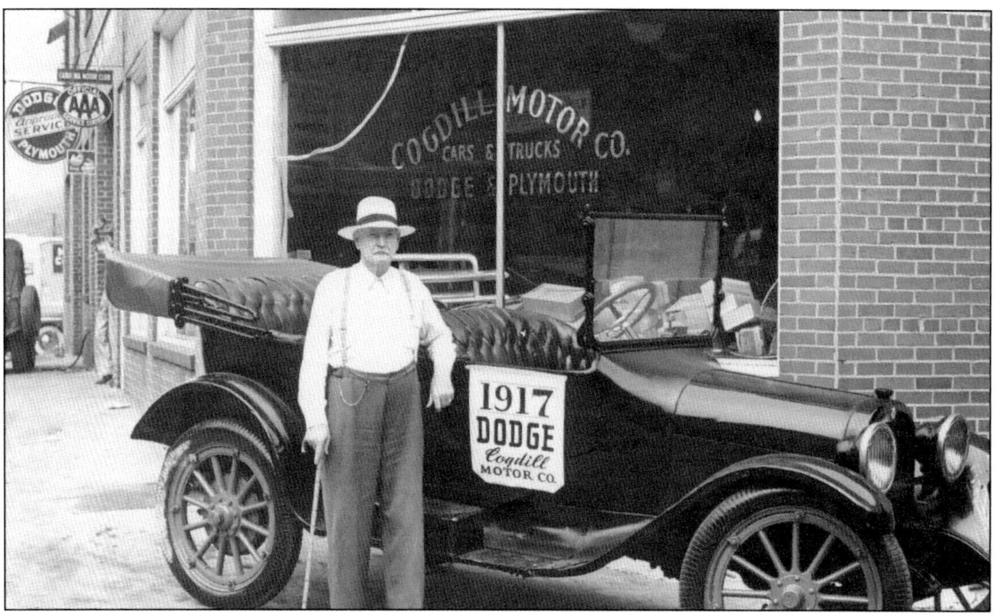

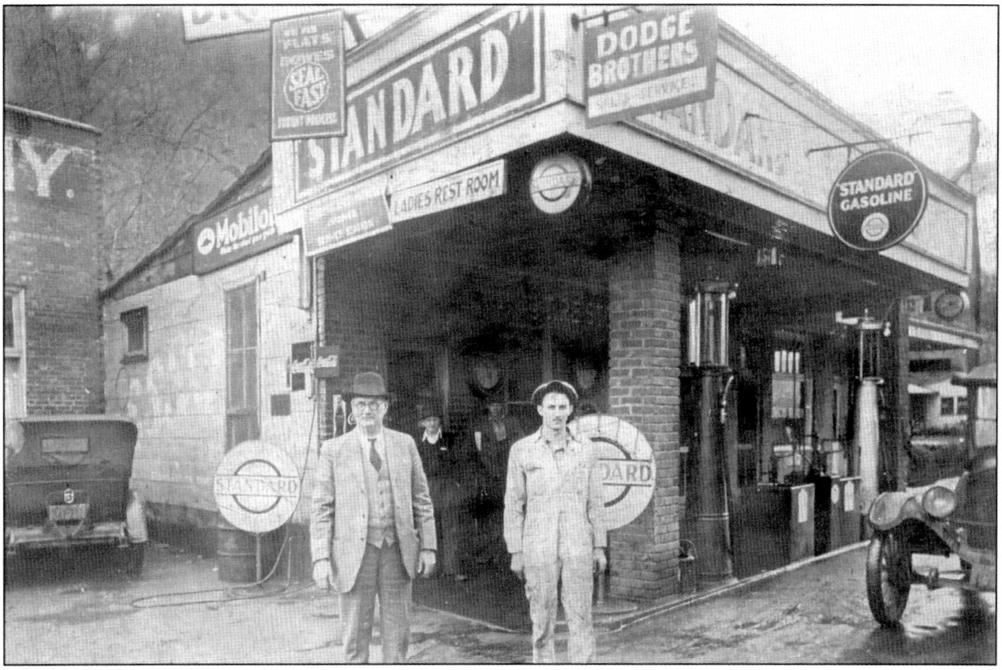

Sam Cogdill (above, left) and his son Ray (right) moved their business downtown, building a Dodge dealership and Standard service station near the eastern intersection of Main and Mill Streets in 1941. Sam died in 1952. Ray's son, also named Sam, joined the operation in 1961; after Ray's death in 1976, Sam continued the operation until 1995. The dealership had the same parts manager, Major Allison, for 45 years. The former Cogdill location was home to Western Carolina Chrysler for about a decade and is now Balsam Creek Designs. (Above courtesy of Sam Cogdill; below courtesy of Jim McGinnis.)

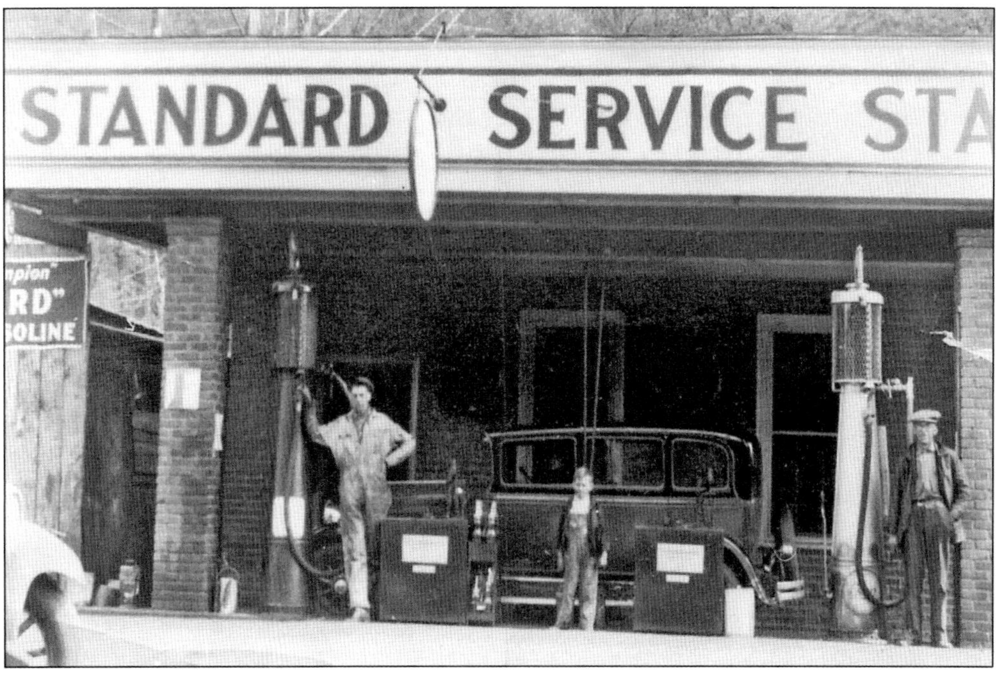

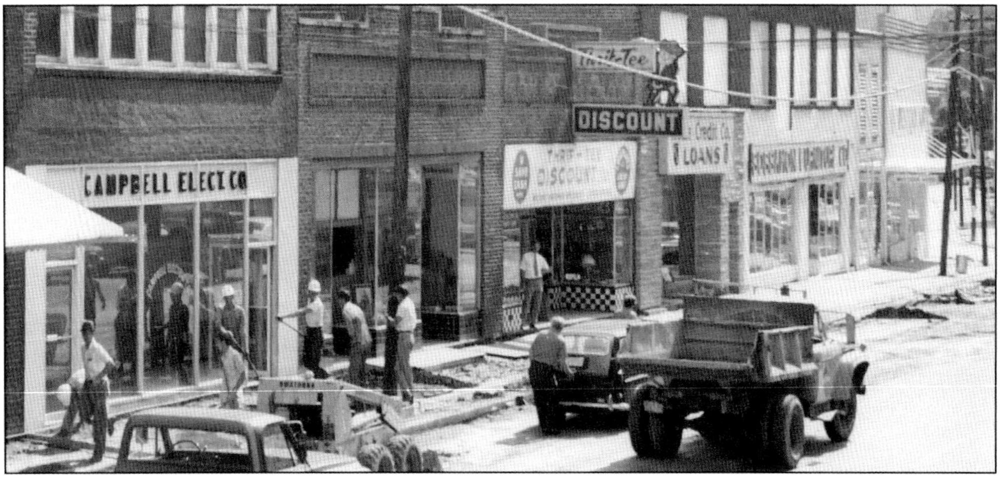

Main Street's east end (above) is undergoing sidewalk construction in 1971. Businesses operating included, from left to right, the Campbell Electric Company, owned by Claude Campbell, which moved to Schulman Street in 1975 (current Mountain Projects) and closed in 1991; David Parker's Blue Ribbon Shoe Store; Thrift-tee Discount; Home Credit; Sossamon Furniture; and Western Auto, which was owned by Ed Wilson and closed in 1989. Businesses in the same buildings in 2008 are Livingston's Photo, Annie's Bakery, Sylva Barber Shop, Simply Elegant and Main Design, Arsenal Artifacts, and Dodie's Auction. David Schulman's clothing store, David's, was located in the former Campbell's and Blue Ribbon buildings from the mid-1970s through about 1990. Sossamon's, seen below in the late 1940s, was owned by Boyd Sossamon, who first moved a few doors west (Used Bookstore location) around 1990 and then to Mill Street before closing about 1998. (Courtesy of the *Sylva Herald*.)

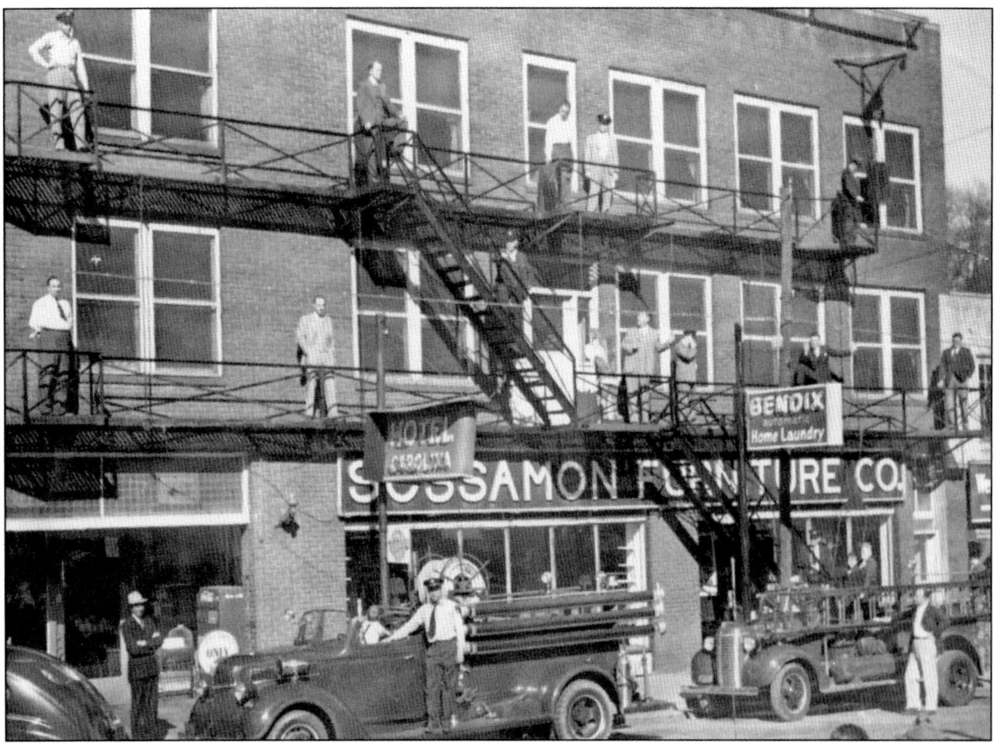

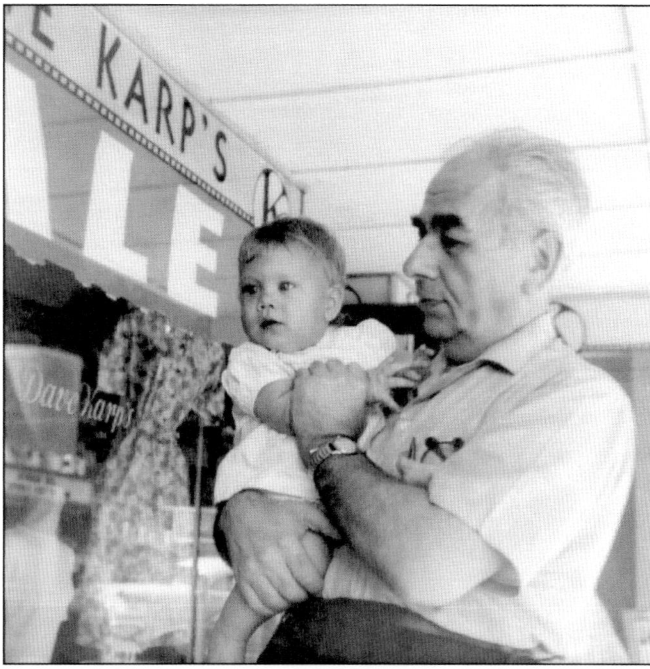

Dave Karp, seen with his granddaughter Sharon Rosenberg, owned Karp's department store from 1932 until 1961. Located across from the Ritz Theater, the store stood where Annie's Bakery is now. Karp and his wife, Rebecca, sold general merchandise such as overalls, dresses, work shoes, ladies' and children's shoes, nylon stockings, socks, and red wagons. (Courtesy of Rachael Rosenberg.)

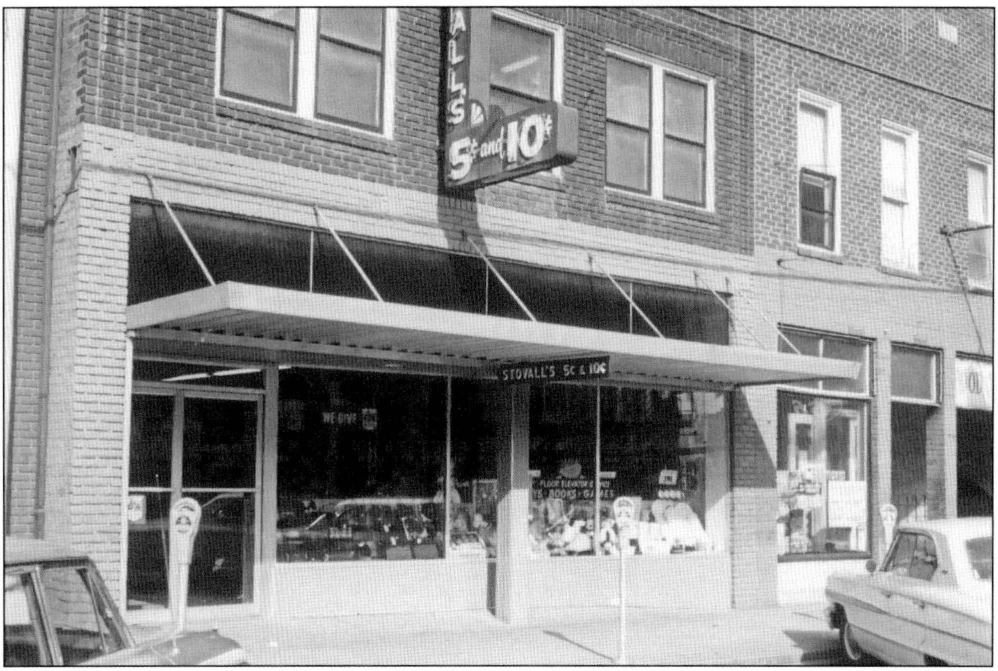

Stovall's 5¢ and 10¢, operated first by Dewey and then Raymon Stovall, was a fixture on Main Street for more than three decades. Dewey opened the store in the 1930s, and Raymon bought it around 1946, when he arrived in Sylva. Stovall's was first located at the current site of the Friends of the Library's Used Bookstore; in January 1960, Raymon purchased the old Farmers' Federation building (now the patio side of Lulu's on Main) and moved his dime store down the street. The three-story Stovall's had the only passenger elevator on Main Street. (Courtesy of John David Stovall.)

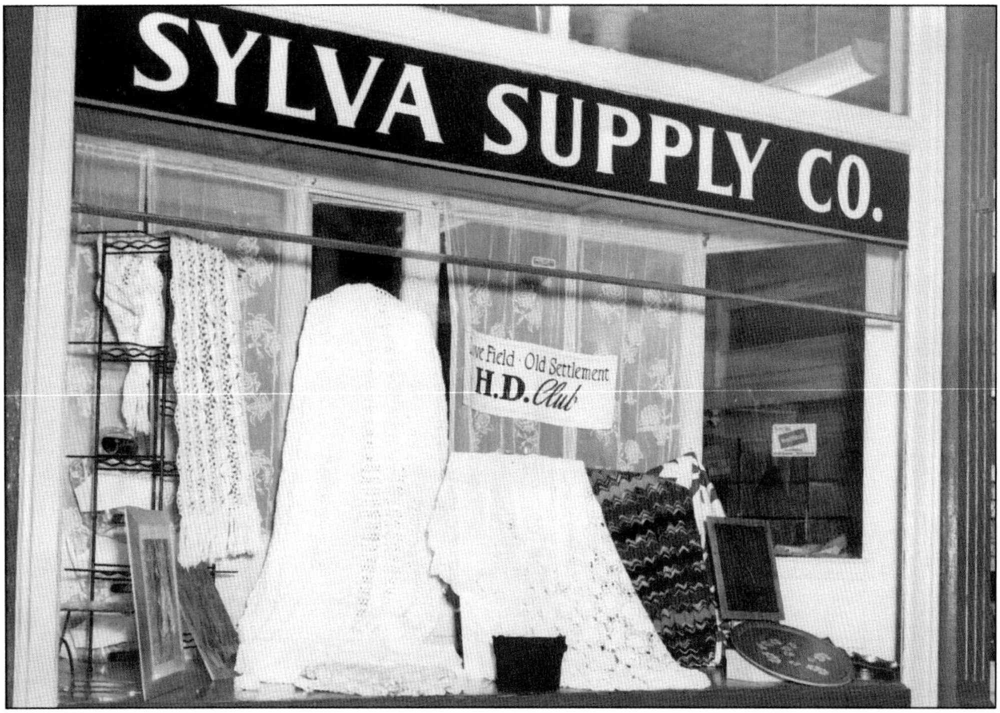

Sylva Supply Company, shown above in the 1960s, closed its doors on June 1, 1999, after 101 years as a Main Street mainstay. Crystal Jones opened Jackson's General Store in the same location a few months later. The building was constructed in 1902 by early entrepreneur C .J. Harris to house Sylva Supply, which had opened in 1898 at the current First Citizens Bank site. Sylva Supply served as a commissary store for the Harris-Reese Tannery, opened by Harris at the present Jackson Paper location in 1901. The Main Street scene below was taken around 1956, when two-way traffic had ended. Businesses operating on the right were, from left to right, Belk's, the Hotel Lloyd, Velt's Café, and Hooper's Drug Store. (Above courtesy of Cleatus Barron; below courtesy of the *Sylva Herald*.)

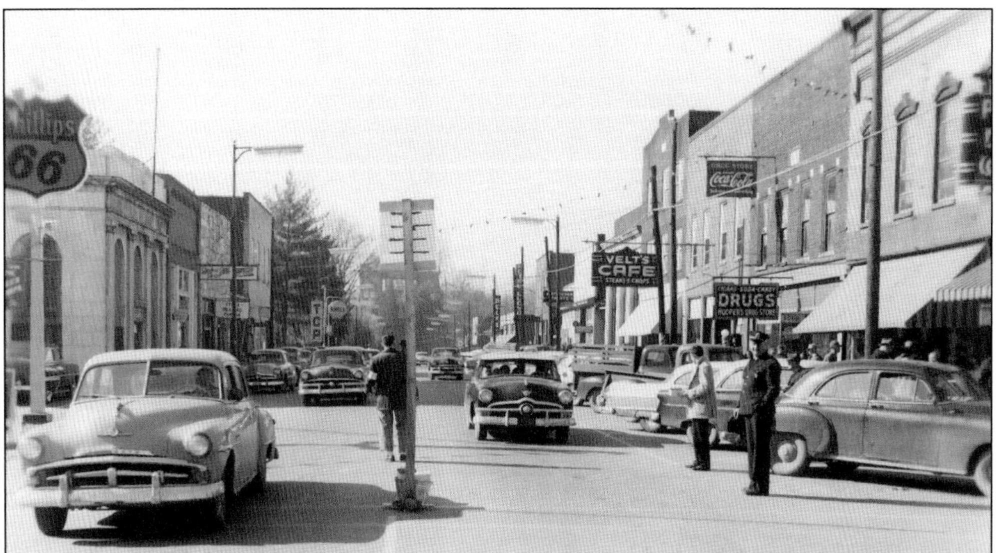

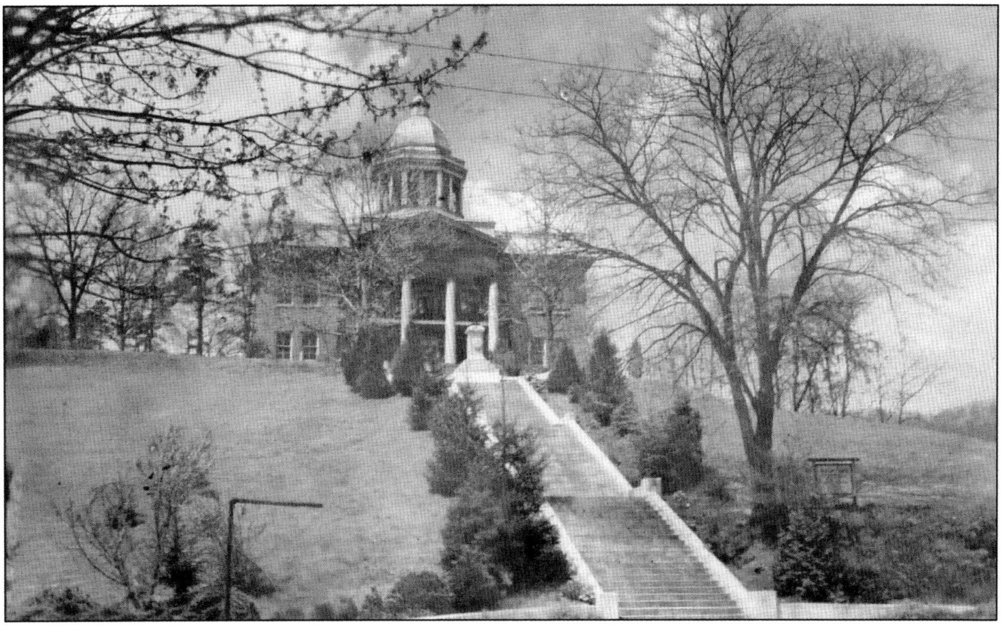

Jackson County's most photographed building—the historic Jackson County Courthouse—has rows of young evergreens beside its steps in the above view, believed to date from the 1940s. Those trees have grown taller in the photograph below, taken a decade later. The Jackson County Courthouse was constructed in 1913 after a special election that moved the county seat from Webster to the then-booming railroad town of Sylva. The original red bricks, still visible in both images, were painted white in the late 1960s, which was about the same time that the trees were removed. Two-way traffic is still in effect below, as evidenced by the road signs signaling motorists to bear right at the west end of Main Street. N.C. 107 no longer runs through downtown as it once did; instead, the Sylva–South Carolina highway now begins farther east, at Kel-Save. (Above courtesy of Diane Buchanan; below courtesy of the *Sylva Herald*.)

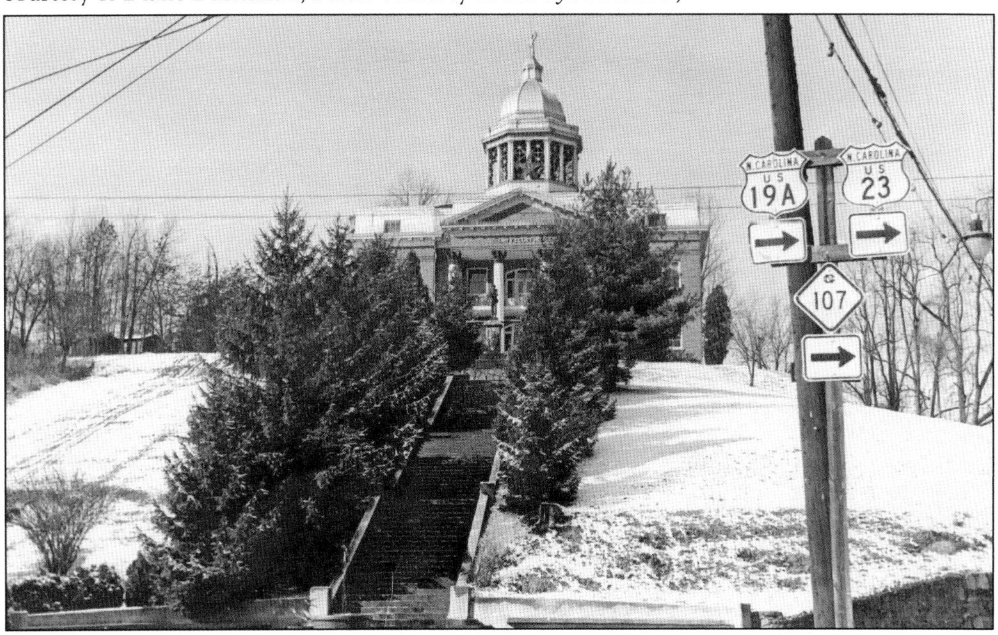

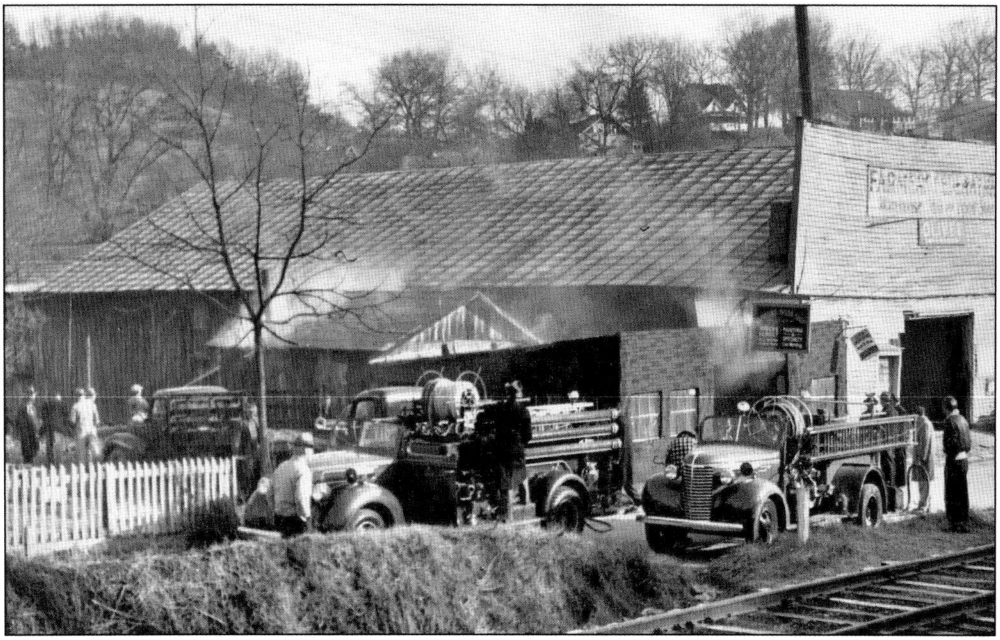

Members of the Sylva Fire Department battle two separate blazes at the old Farmers' Federation warehouse, which stood near what is now the intersection of Railroad Avenue and Grindstaff Cove Road on the lot next to LifeWay Community Church. A specific date for the older fire is not known, but the photograph below shows a January 19, 1967, blaze. It occurred near the time the department switched the trucks' color to yellow. (Courtesy of the Sylva Fire Department.)

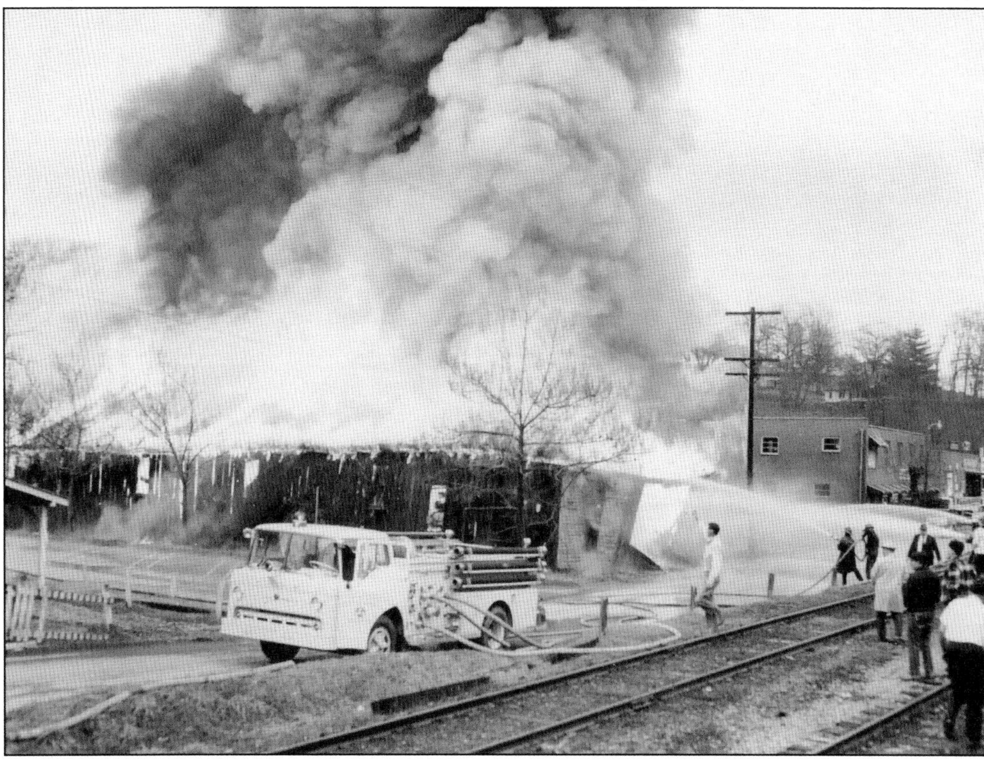

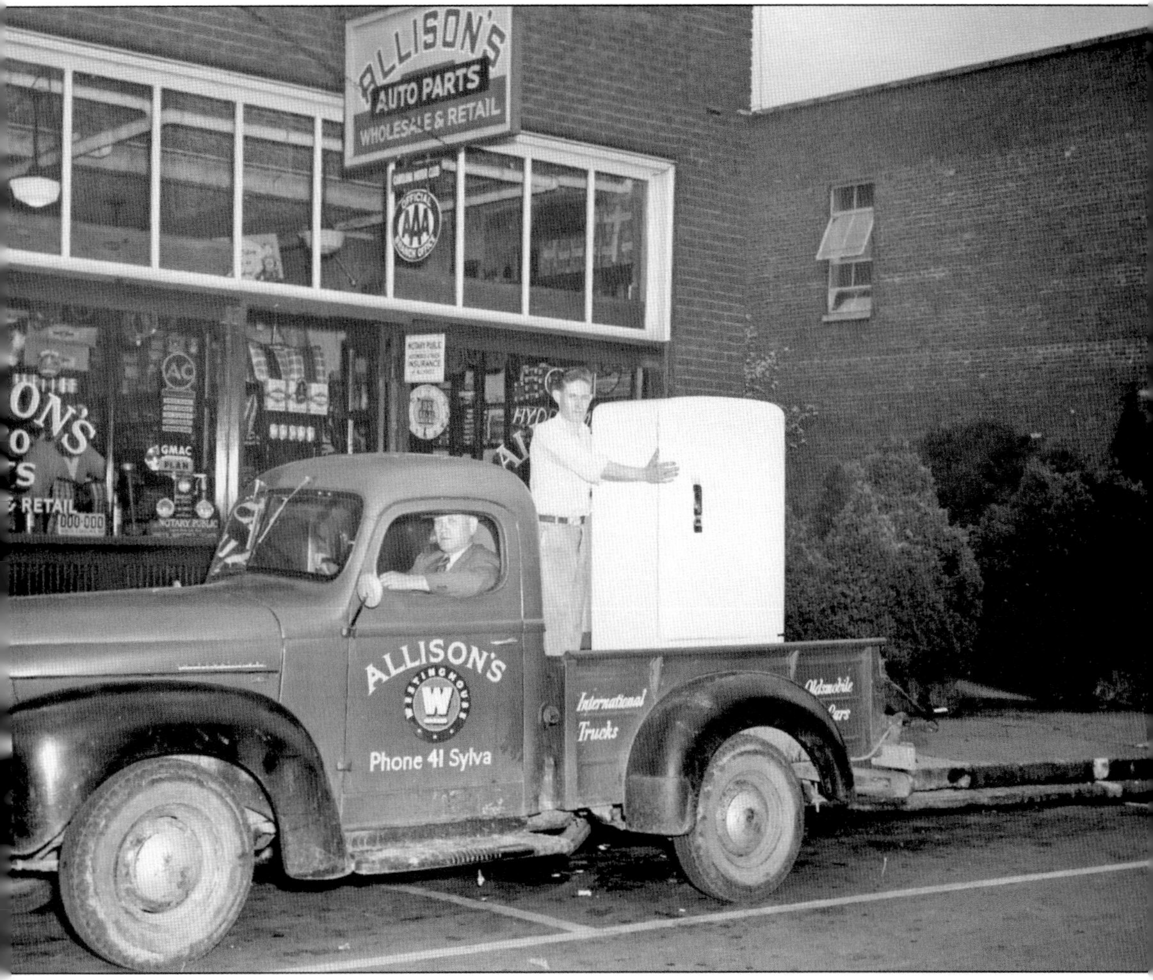

The *Sylva Herald* building had a different look in 1941, when Dan Allison's automobile and appliance business was located in the former McGuire Building's first floor. After Allison's moved down Main Street to the old Sears store in the late 1940s, the downstairs became Elsie Massie's dress shop, which closed in 1980. When that shop moved out, the McGuires moved their dental practice down from the upper stories into the first-floor offices, where they stayed for about a decade until completion of their current building on King Street. Lawyers' offices then occupied that space until the newspaper expanded its operations from the adjacent building in 1997. The Allison's employees shown here are driver Lonnie Jones and Earl Norton. (Courtesy of Daniel Allison.)

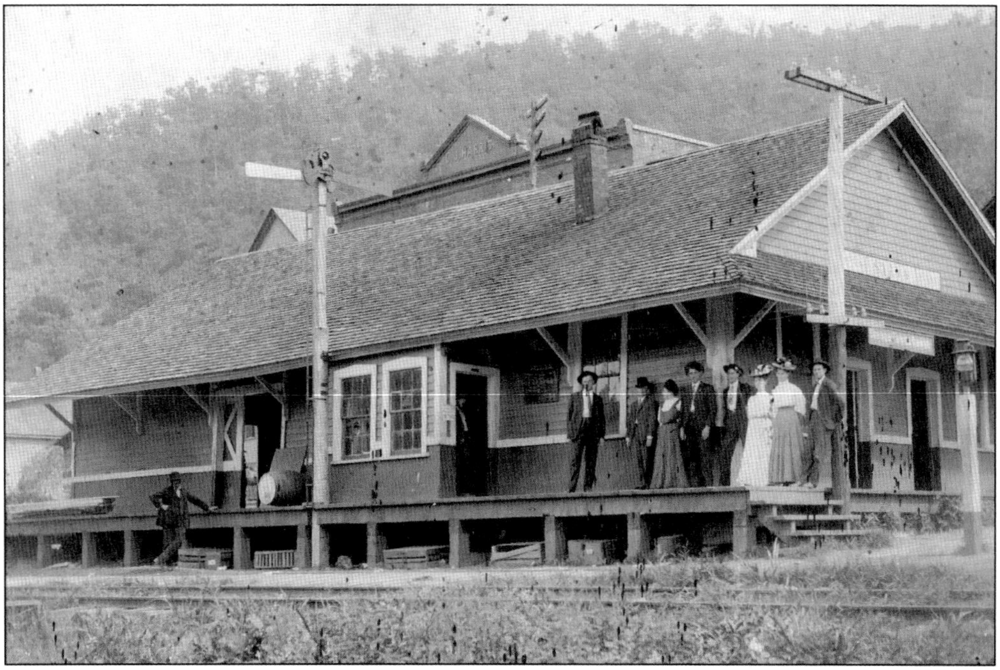

Sylva's train depot stood at the geographic center of the original octagon-shaped town limits and served passengers from the 1890s until 1948. Above, a crowd waits at the depot in the early 1900s; it must have been after 1902, because the peak of the former Sylva Supply Company, which was built in that year, is visible in the background. The photograph below, taken around 1961, shows the depot as it looked after passenger service was discontinued. With the demolition of the depot during the late 1970s, the concrete platform is now used for parking; a surveyor's mark indicating the exact center of town is still visible. (Above courtesy of Claude Jones; below courtesy of the *Sylva Herald*.)

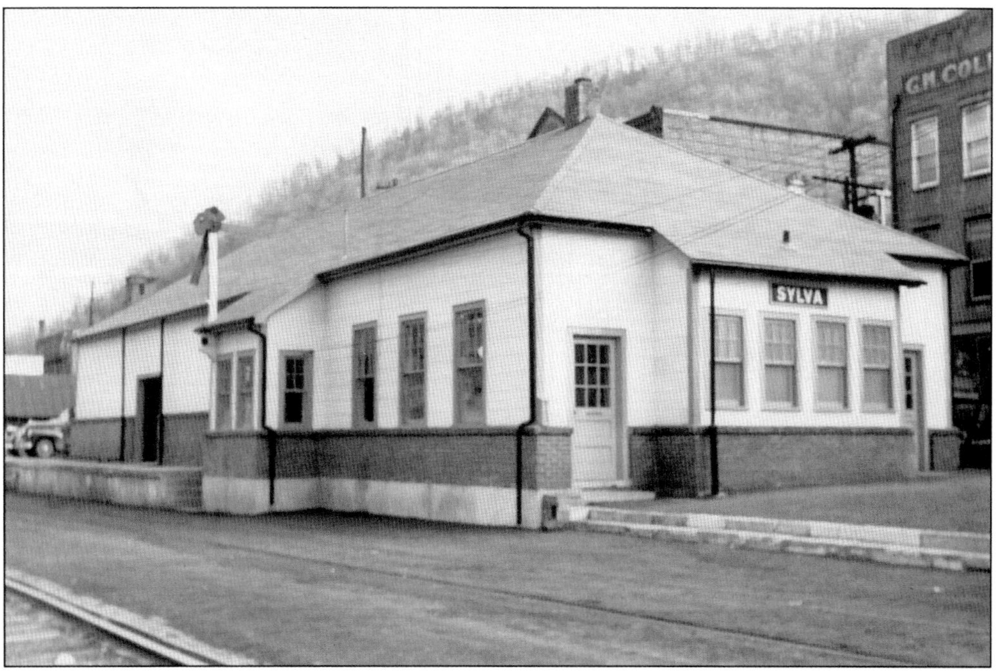

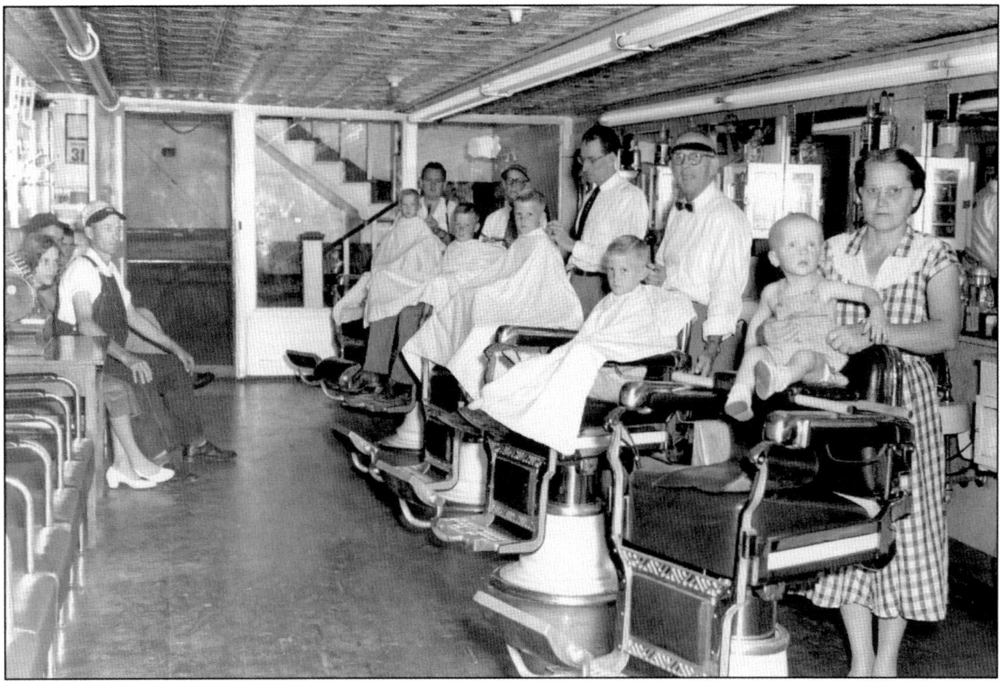

Five Clayton boys get haircuts at Hedden's Barber Shop in downtown Sylva in the mid-1950s. The sons of Terrell (left) and Gertrude (right), the boys include Joe, Bruce, Dickie, Ned, and Neil. The barbers are, from left to right, Wimpy Hyatt, Weaver Hurst, Dillard Robinson, and Jeff Hedden. (Courtesy of Marion Jones.)

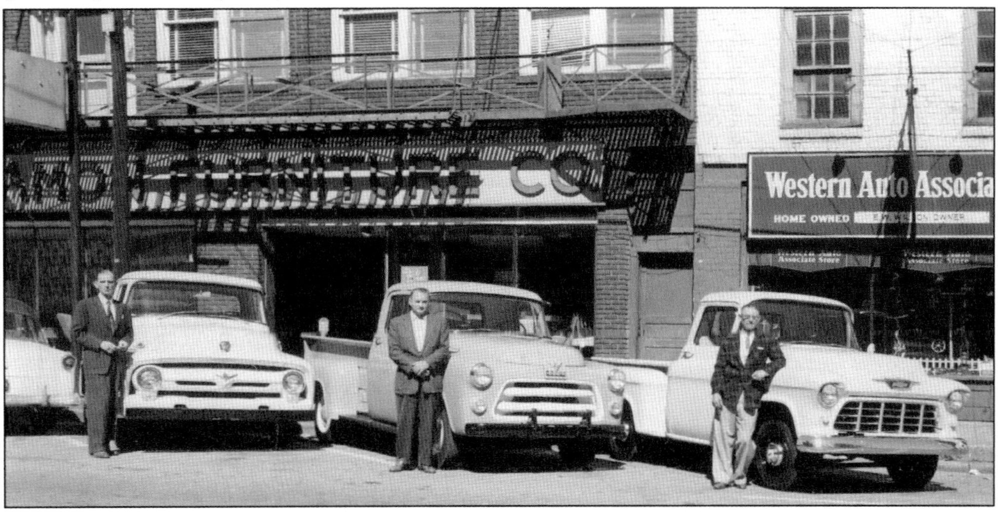

Sylva automobile dealers Woody Hampton (left), with a Ford; Ray Cogdill (center), with a Dodge; and Homer Davis, with a Chevrolet truck, stand in front of the Sossamon Furniture Company in 1955. Boyd Sossamon, who owned and operated Sossamon's from 1944 until about 1998, said he needed three trucks for his business and decided to buy one of each. Cogdill owned Cogdill Motors, which at that time was just down Main Street from Sossamon's. Hampton ran Reece-Hampton Ford, later Cagle and Son, which was located at the current site of Rite-Aid. Davis co-owned Kirk-Davis Chevrolet, which occupied the building where P&M Automotive is today. (Courtesy of the *Sylva Herald*.)

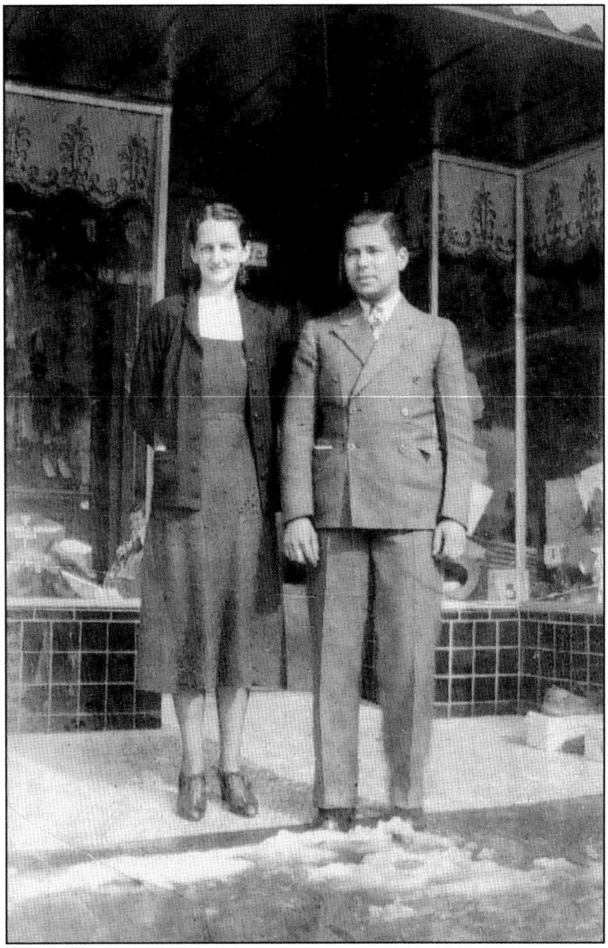

Sol Schulman, pictured at left with clerk Muriel Snyder Mauney, opened his Main Street department store on January 4, 1933, and continued to operate the business for almost seven decades. Penumbra Gallery was established in the former Schulman's location in 2006. The Main Street view below also dates from the 1930s. Businesses visible on the left side of the street include, from left to right, the Poinsett Hotel and Grill (later the Hotel Lloyd), the Park Lunch Room, and Sylva Supply Company. Signs on the right side of the street advertise, from left to right, the Lyric Theater and a Shell service station. (Left courtesy of Bill Fox; below courtesy of June Bess Anderson.)

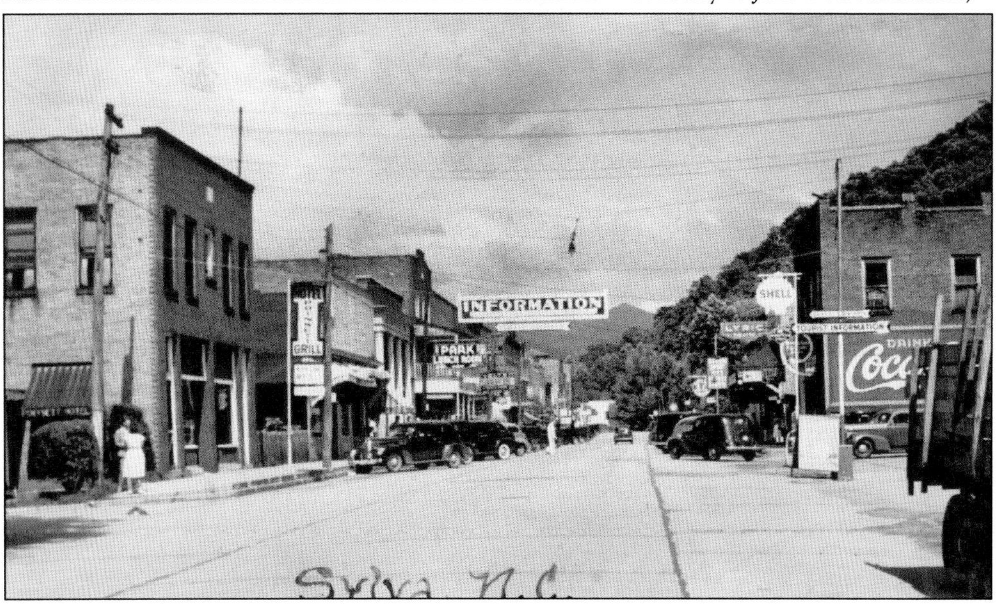

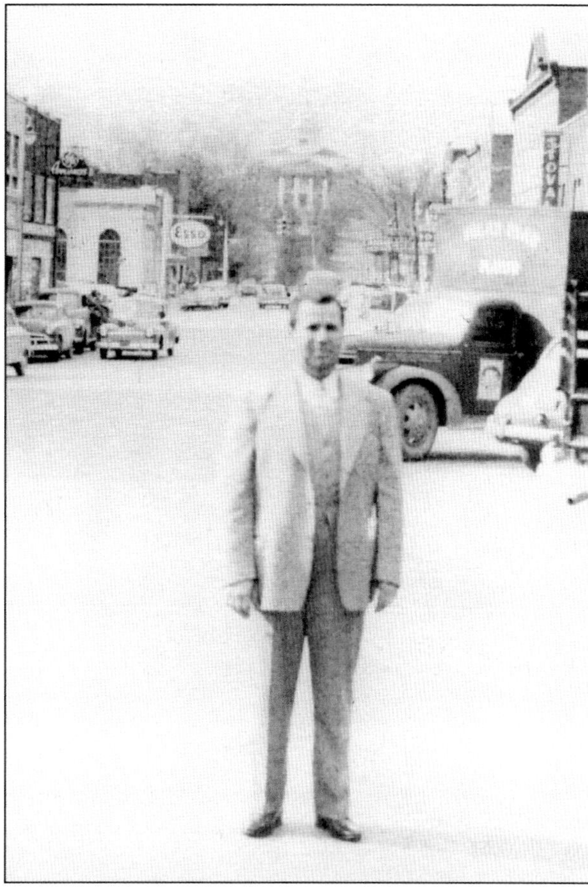

Longtime Sylva merchant Sol Schulman (right) operated his store on Main Street's east end for 69 years. Schulman, who celebrated his 90th birthday at the store in March 2002, died in November 2003. A former member of the Sylva town board who was also instrumental in organizing the local chamber of commerce, Schulman has a downtown street named in his honor. Thought to date from the mid-1950s, the photograph below shows the Leader, a clothing store on Main Street operated by Ben Lessing. Hal Dennis, who opened the adjacent Dennis Men's Store in 1965, expanded into the Leader space with his Ladies' Store after Lessing closed. The former Leader location has housed Blackrock Outdoor Company since December 1999. Schulman's two sons, Herbert and David, are both former Main Street business owners, operating Another World Collectibles and David's, respectively. (Right courtesy of David Schulman; below courtesy of the *Sylva Herald*.)

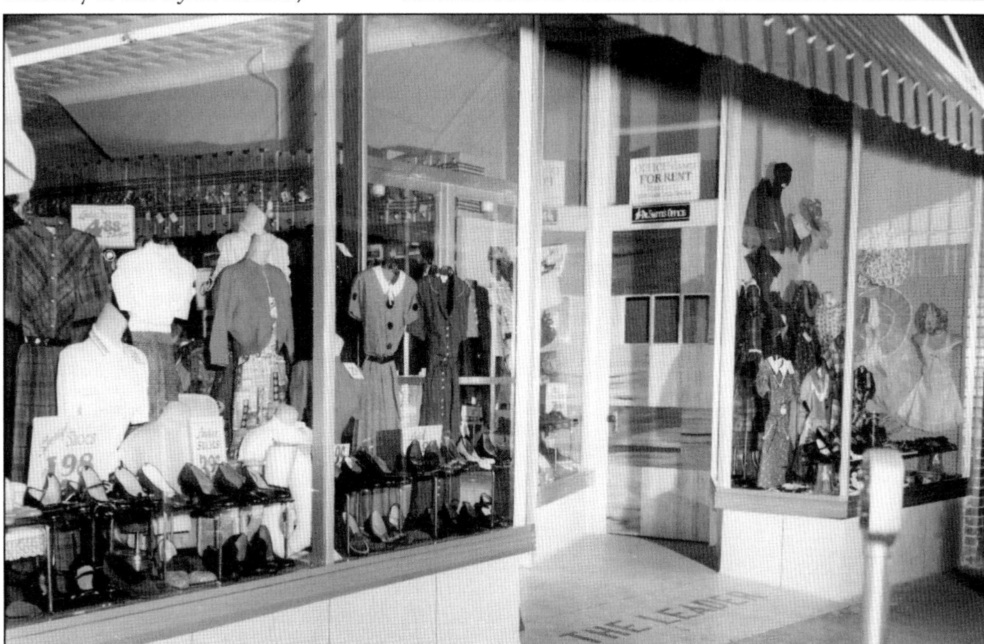

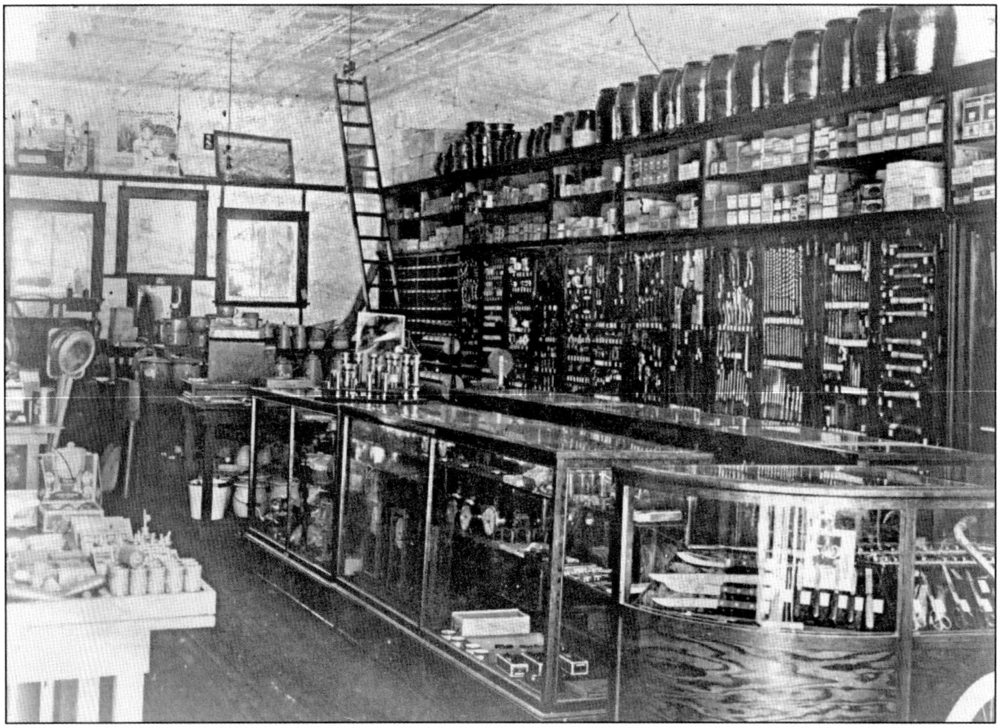

Roy Allison's Jackson Hardware, pictured in 1918, was located in the building that housed Andretti's for a number of years and is now Nick and Nate's. (Courtesy of Western Carolina University Special Collections.)

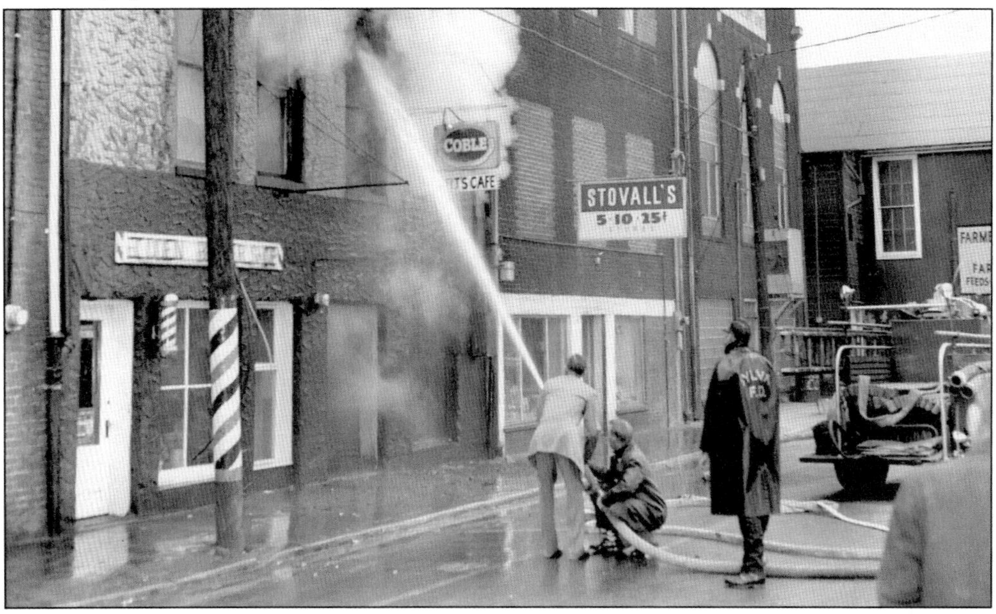

Sylva firefighters battle a blaze from the Mill Street side of Velt's Café on February 28, 1960. The downtown restaurant was started by Velt Wilson in the 1930s, but he had sold it by the time of the fire. Also visible are Jeff Hedden's Barber Shop on the left of Velt's and Stovall's 5, 10, and 25¢ on the right. (Courtesy of the Sylva Fire Department.)

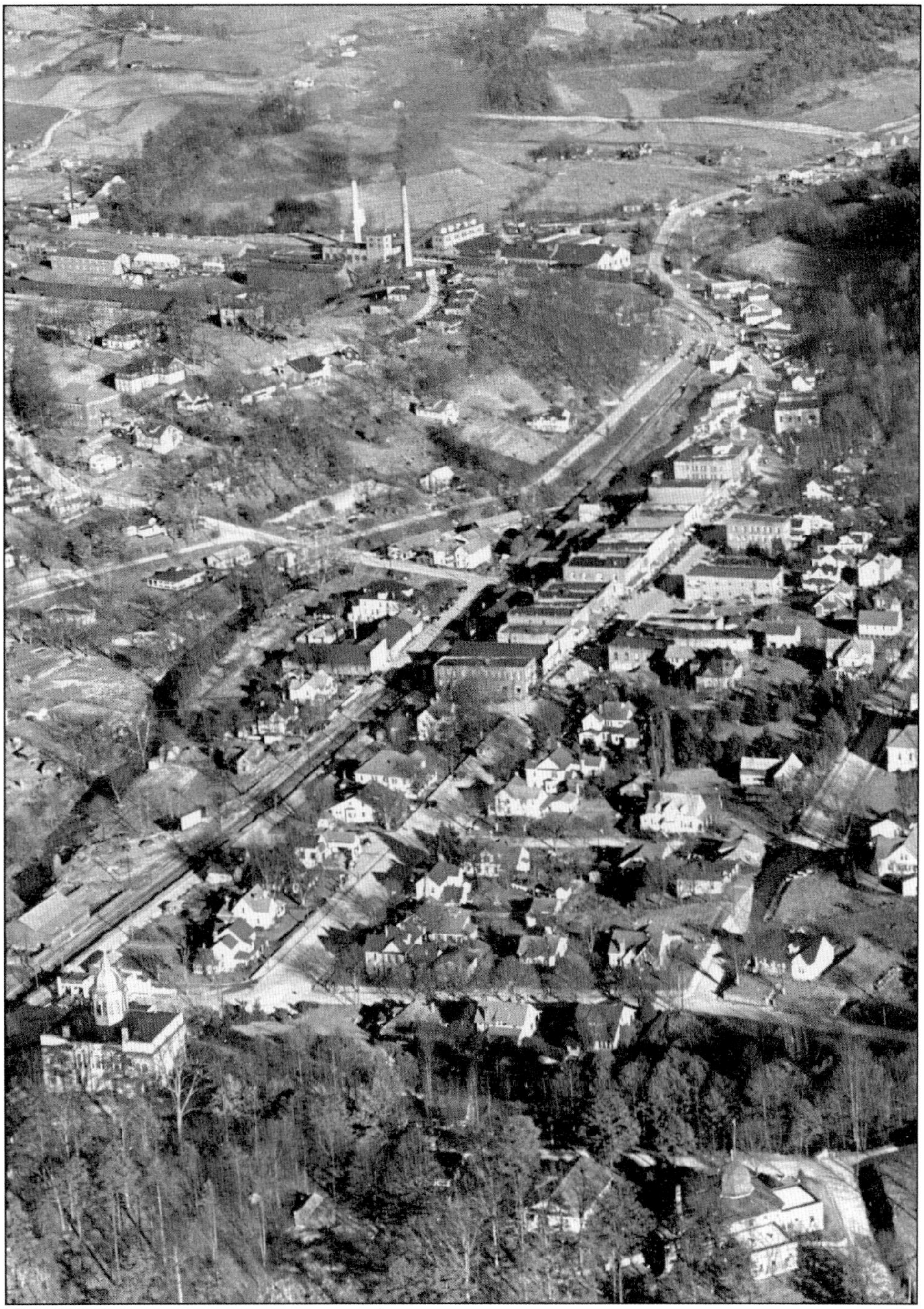

In this c. 1940 view looking south over Sylva's downtown, houses still line both sides of Main Street as far up as Landis (then Walnut) Street. The Jackson County Courthouse is in the left foreground, while the original C. J. Harris Community Hospital is in the far right foreground. The smokestacks toward the back were part of the Armour Leather and Sylva Paperboard Companies and later the Mead Corporation. Those buildings now house the Jackson Paper Company. (Courtesy of the *Sylva Herald*.)

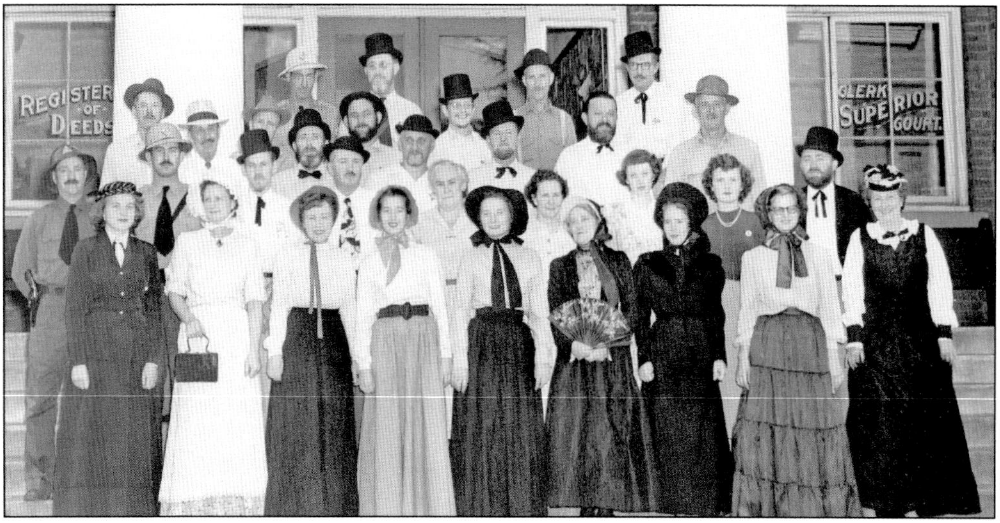

County employees stand on the Jackson County Courthouse steps during the 1951 centennial. Pictured from left to right are the following: (first row) Nell Green Sanford, Wilma Allison Jones, Juanita Phillips, Jane Poteet Buchanan, Hazel Edwards, Sadie Luck, Pearl Henson, Frances Bryson McClure, and Mary Johnson; (second row) Bart Cope, Hayden Ferguson, Tommy Clayton, Carey Henson, Lucille Hunt, Shirley Bryson, Margaret James, Clara Lou Hooper, and Jennings Bryson; (third row) Warfield Turpin, Corsey Buchanan, Frank Allen, Alec Southard, Paul Gibson, Dr. Janowski, Charlie Thomas, John Henson, and Charlie Evans; (fourth row) John Sides, Glenn Hughes, Tommy Cannon, Newt Browning, and Reg Enloe. (Courtesy of Audrey Jones Tritt.)

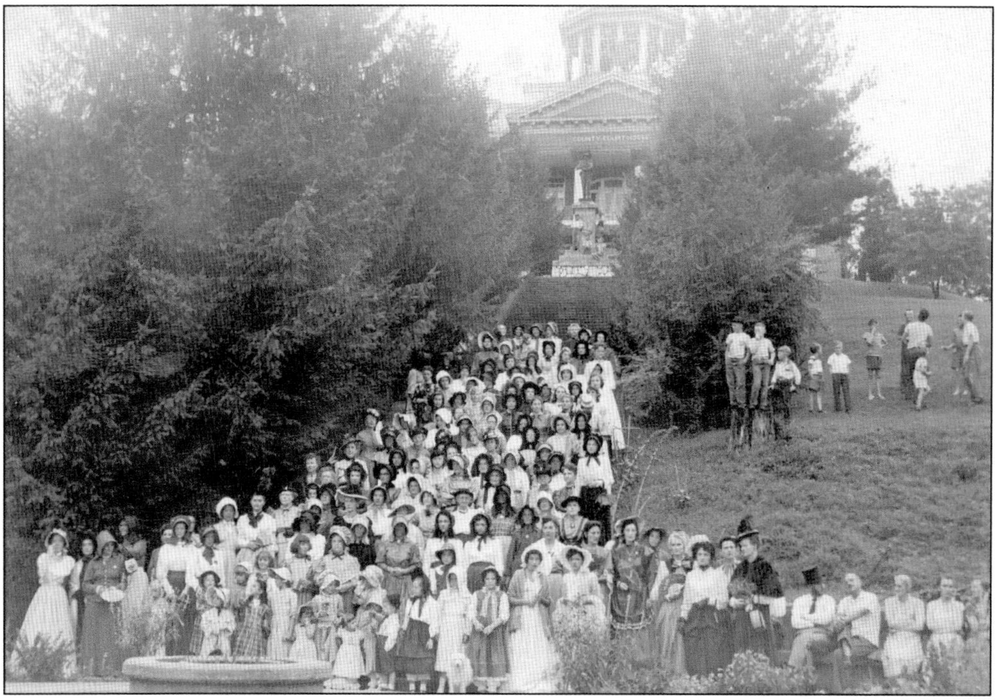

Everyone was encouraged to wear period dress during the weeklong 1951 centennial celebration, which included a parade and pageant. County residents flocked to town to mark Jackson County's 100th birthday. (Courtesy of the *Sylva Herald*.)

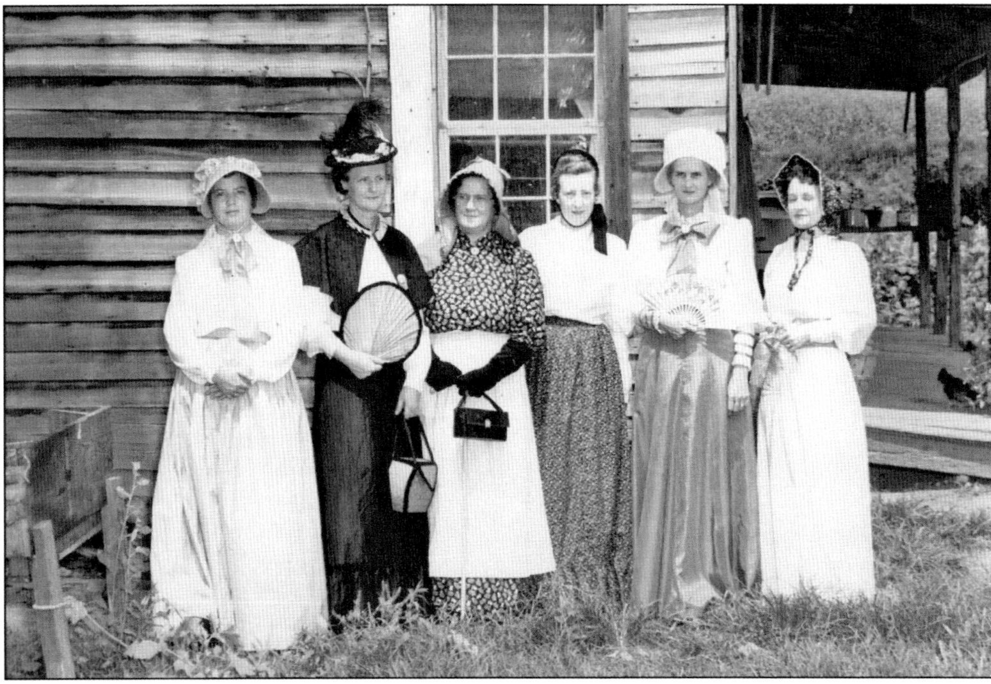

Dressed appropriately for Jackson County's 1951 centennial are, from left to right, Mary Jane Coward Dillard, Wilma Allison Jones, Margaret Sutton, Dallie Fisher, Lenore Bryson, and Juanita Ferguson. (Courtesy of Marion Jones.)

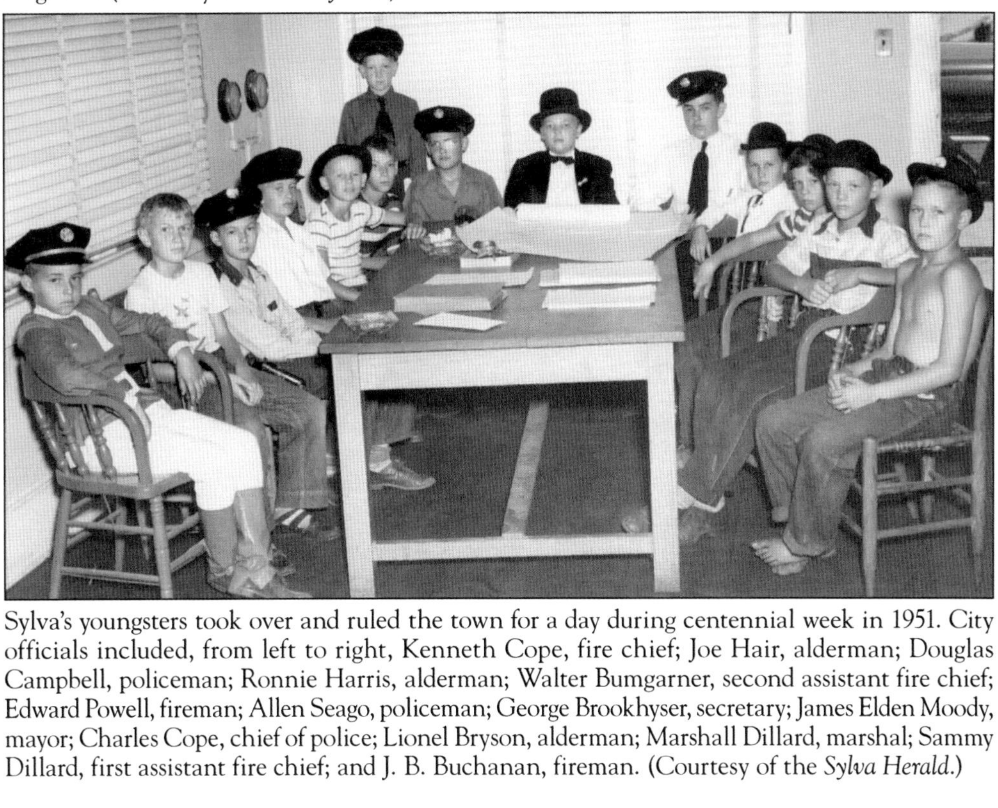

Sylva's youngsters took over and ruled the town for a day during centennial week in 1951. City officials included, from left to right, Kenneth Cope, fire chief; Joe Hair, alderman; Douglas Campbell, policeman; Ronnie Harris, alderman; Walter Bumgarner, second assistant fire chief; Edward Powell, fireman; Allen Seago, policeman; George Brookhyser, secretary; James Elden Moody, mayor; Charles Cope, chief of police; Lionel Bryson, alderman; Marshall Dillard, marshal; Sammy Dillard, first assistant fire chief; and J. B. Buchanan, fireman. (Courtesy of the *Sylva Herald*.)

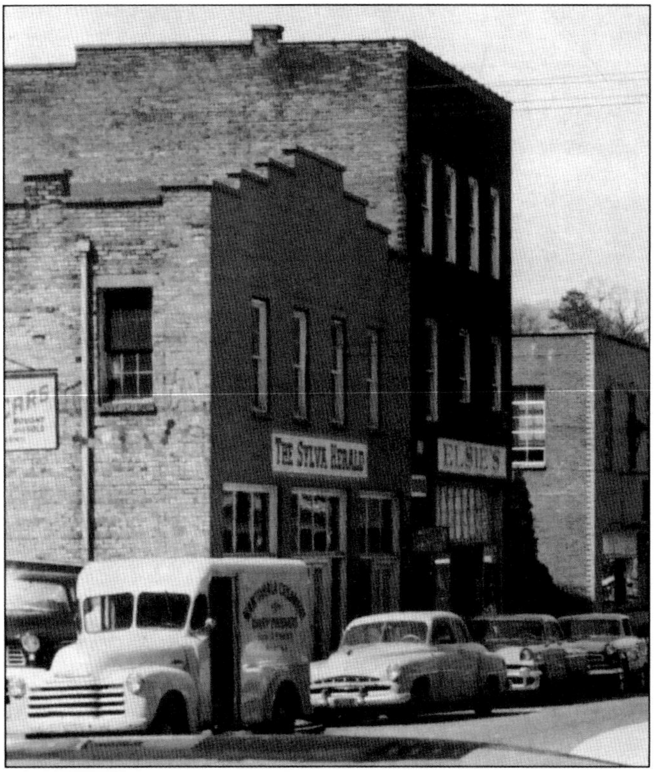

The *Sylva Herald*, Jackson County's oldest newspaper, is pictured here in 1956. Also visible are Rexall Drug and Elsie's, a dress shop owned and operated by Elsie Massie. Elsie's occupied the ground floor of what was at that time the McGuire Building, with the McGuire dental offices upstairs. That building was once three full stories, with a large meeting room on the third floor, but a portion of the top story collapsed after a heavy snow in 1960. Then-*Herald* publisher Jim Gray purchased the McGuire Building in 1997. (Courtesy of Western Carolina University.)

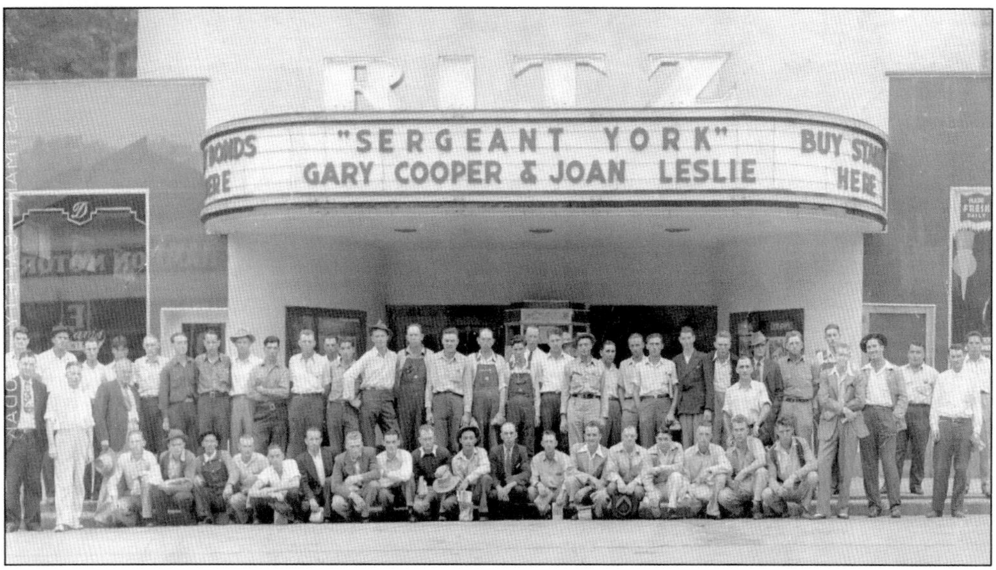

Army recruits gather in front of the Ritz Theater, which was once located in Silva's Main Street municipal parking lot, before departing on September 3, 1942, for World War II. Jim Massie of Waynesville built the Ritz for $100,000 to replace Main Street's Lyric Theater, which he also owned. Massie's son Frank, who had managed the Lyric, was to run the Ritz as well; however, Frank died in a car accident, so instead his widow, Elsie Geisler Massie, became the first manager. The theater opened on April 1, 1942, and closed in 1982. The Town of Sylva purchased the property in 1998. (Courtesy of Nancy Buchanan.)

Looking west down Main Street during the mid-1950s, the view at right shows the shops across from the *Sylva Herald* offices: Schulman's department store (left) and Jackson Furniture. At that time, traffic on Main Street was still two-way; the current one-way traffic pattern did not begin until July 1956. The Jackson Furniture building later housed Livingston's Photo for about three decades and is still part of Livingston Kelley's photograph and framing operation. Penumbra Gallery moved into the former Schulman's location in 2006. The image below depicts Main Street from the opposite direction in June 1946. Massie Furniture (right), which celebrated its 75th anniversary in 2007, remains in the same building. Prominent among the businesses on the left side of the street is Velt's Café, which was located in the building that now houses Lulu's on Main. (Courtesy of the *Sylva Herald*.)

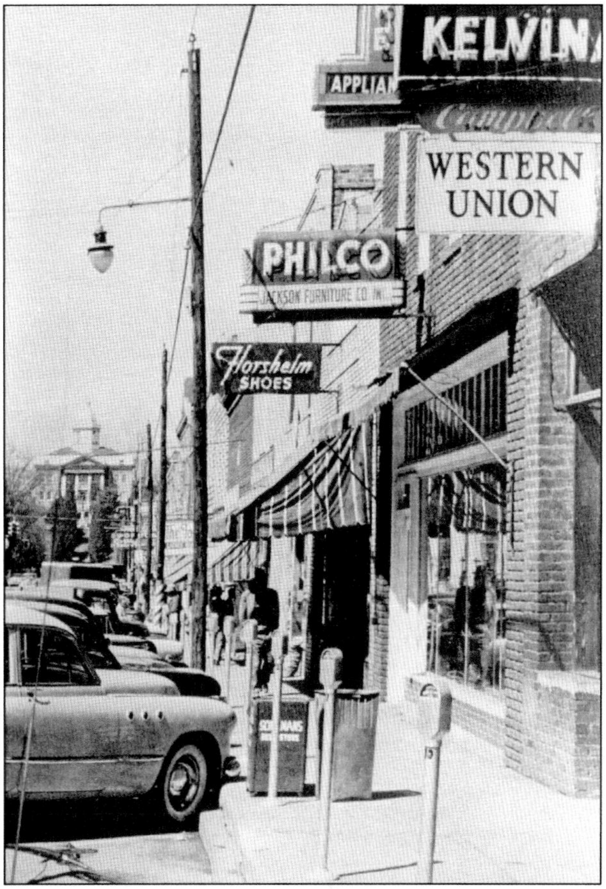

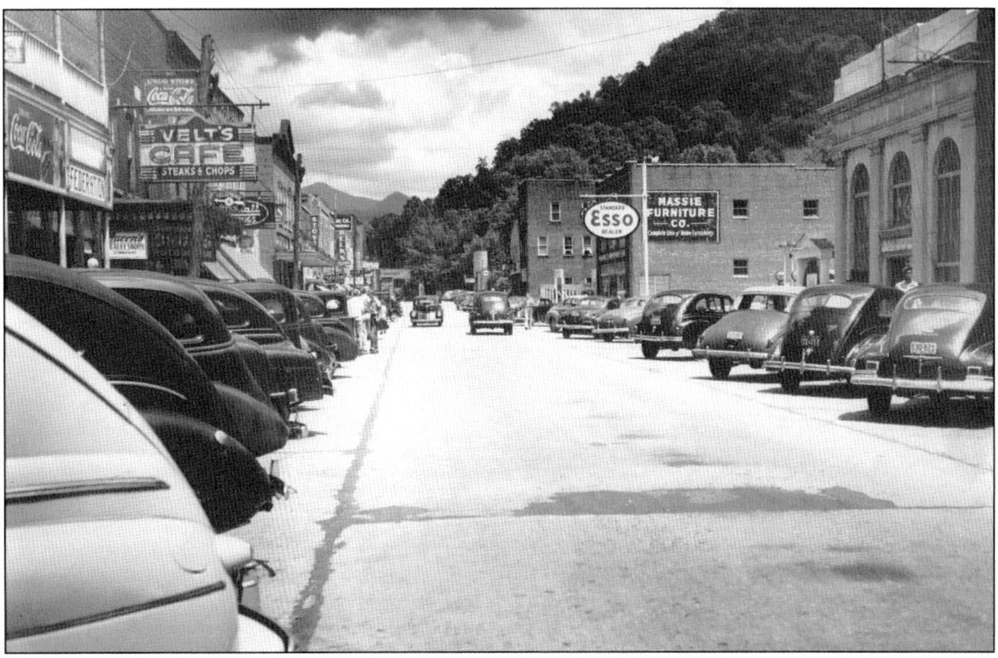

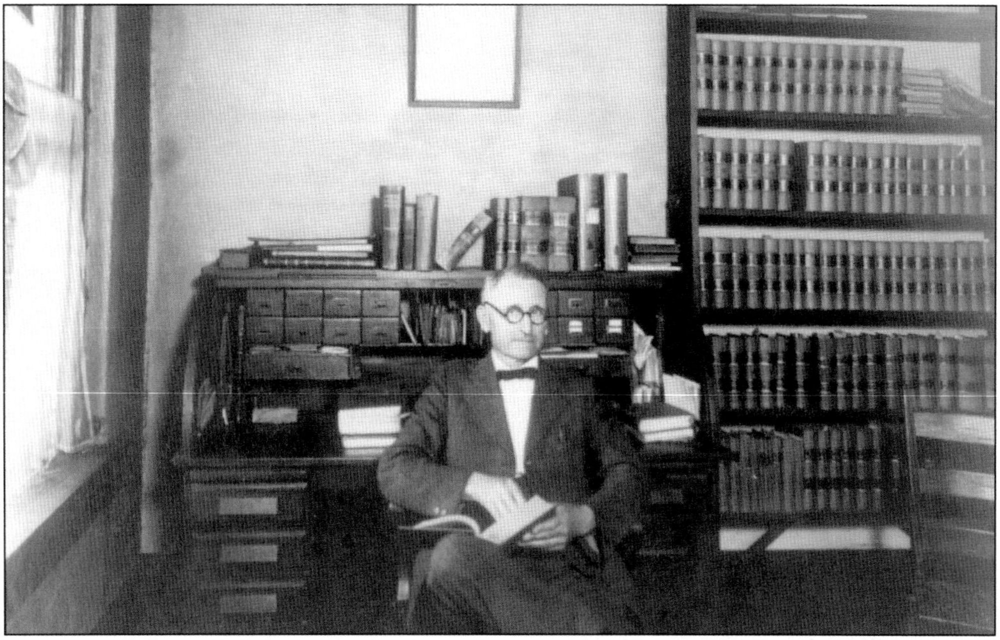

W. R. Sherrill practiced law locally from 1909 until his death in 1950. He constructed the building that now houses Hollifield Jewelers and ran his law practice upstairs; for much of his career, however, his office was upstairs in the Nantahala Building, which is now owned by attorney Jay Spiro. The Killer Creek Company is currently located there. (Courtesy of Ann Melton.)

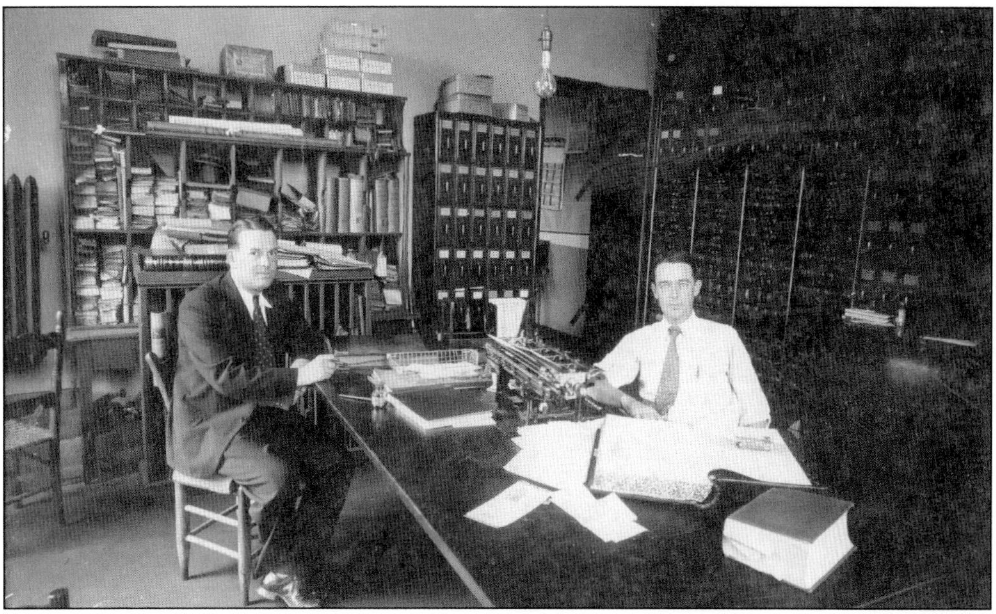

Dan Allison (left) sits with J. H. Morris, then a justice of the peace, in Morris's office on August 11, 1931. Allison was a downtown car dealer for many years, and Morris founded the Sylva Insurance Agency in 1925. Both Allison's car dealership, now located near Sylva's western city limits and operated by grandson Daniel Allison, and Sylva Insurance remain open. The insurance company is Main Street's oldest business to operate continuously under the same name. (Courtesy of Betty Foxx.)

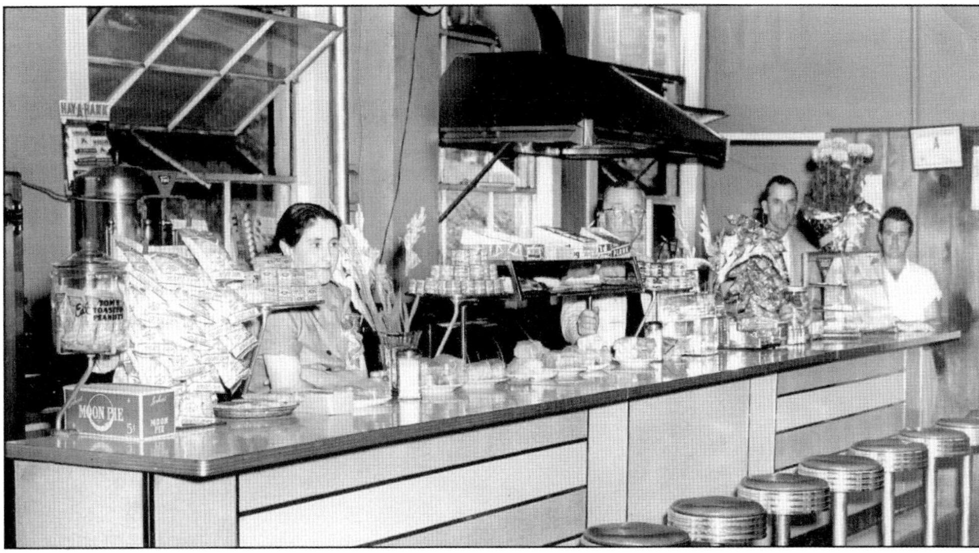

Ella Mae Davis (left) and her husband, Don Davis (second from the left) once operated a lunch counter in the bus station on Mill Street. (Courtesy of Marion Jones.)

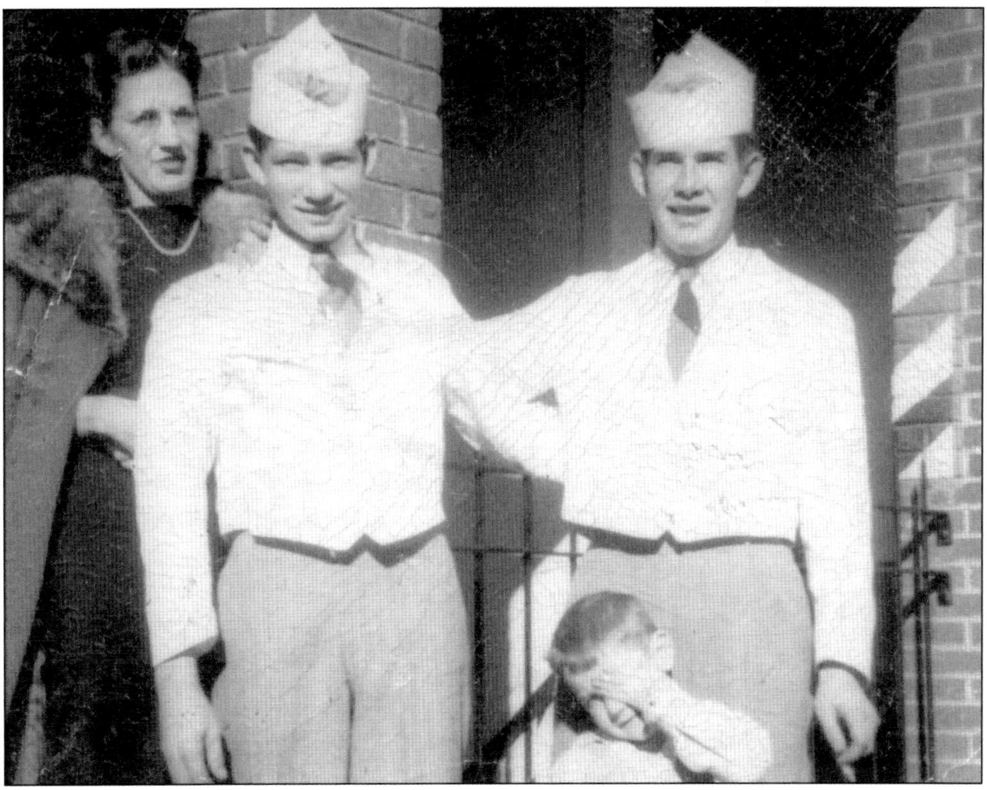

Nancy Canipe (left), Hugh Moon (center), and Bill Childers stand in front of Velt's Café in 1950. Moon was the restaurant's night manager at the time. Velt Wilson bought the building, opened his café there in the 1930s, and ran the business until 1957. A series of owners operated restaurants there, mostly under the Velt's name, until Stovall's 5¢ and 10¢ expanded into the building in the late 1960s. (Courtesy of Hugh Moon.)

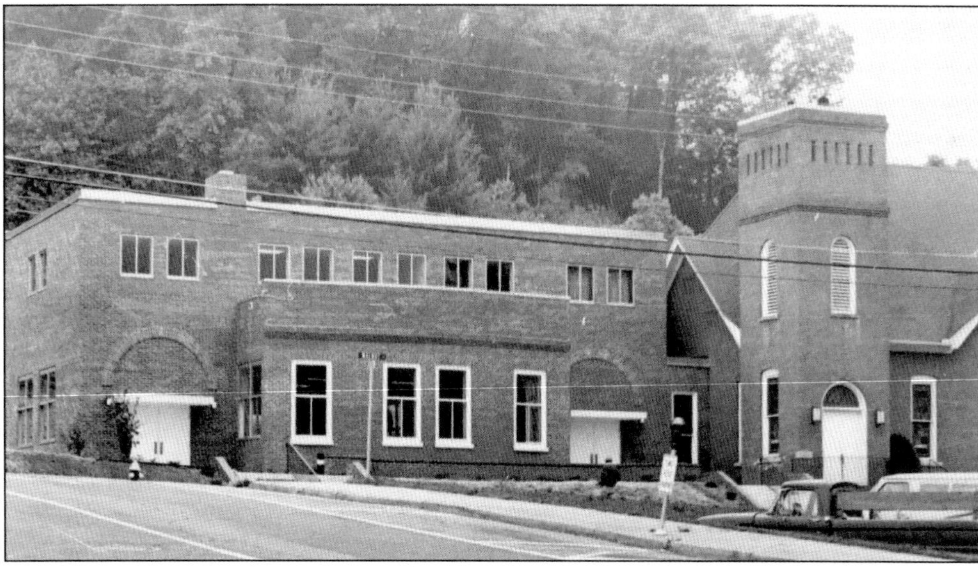

Established in 1888, Sylva First United Methodist Church completed its first brick sanctuary (right) in 1917. The Charles L. Allison Educational Building, named for the church's longtime Sunday school superintendent, was built in 1942. The 1980 addition that contains the Asbury Room (front) was named for Asbury Carden, who oversaw its construction. In 2005, the church added the Christian Life Center, which includes a gymnasium. (Courtesy of the *Sylva Herald*.)

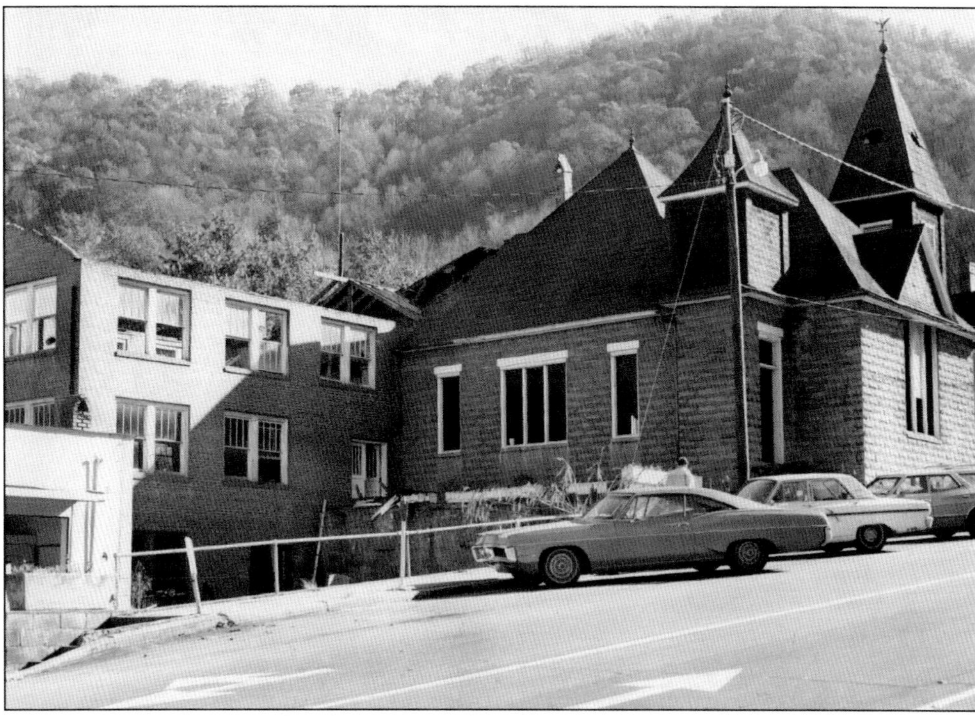

The old Sylva First Baptist Church, which stood in part of what is now the SunTrust parking lot, was razed around 1972 after the church, which was established in 1888, built first an education building and then a sanctuary across Walnut (now Landis) Street. The above sanctuary and education building were constructed in 1908 and 1938, respectively. (Courtesy of the *Sylva Herald*.)

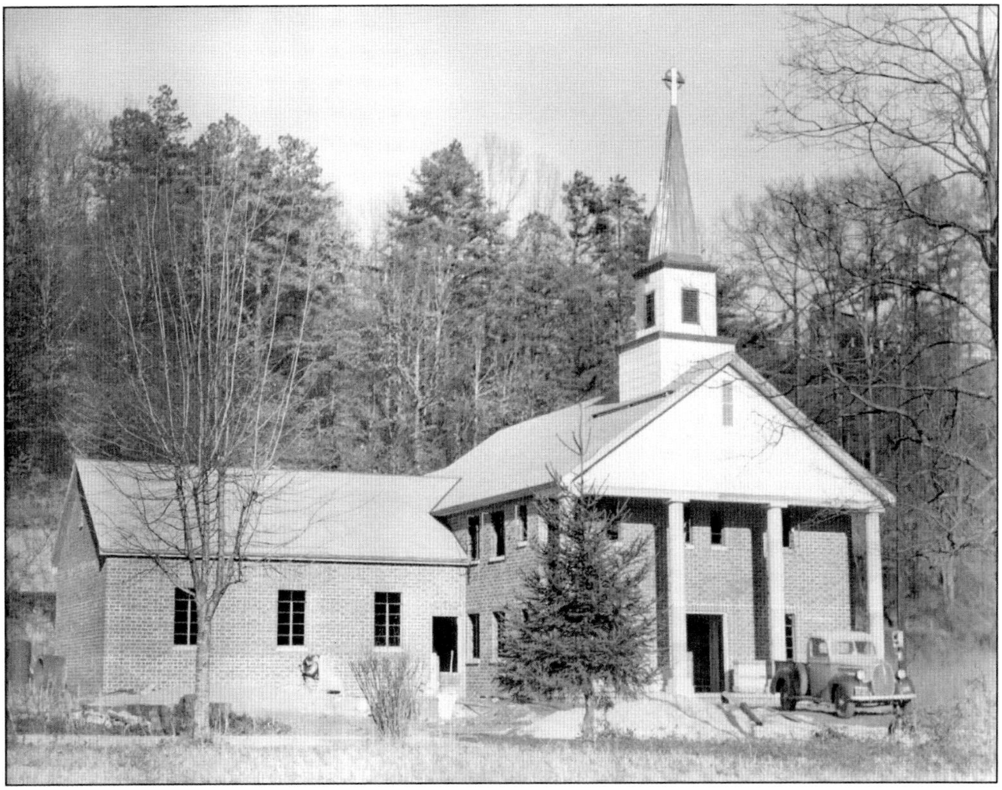

Sylva First Presbyterian Church, pictured above under construction in 1949, was formally organized in 1941, though Presbyterians had worshipped together in the county since the 1870s. The building was extensively renovated in 1989, and additional improvements were made in 2005. St. John's Episcopal Church, shown at right at its current Jackson Street location in 1940, traces its beginnings to an 1879 congregation in Webster, according to *The History of Jackson County*. The church moved to Sylva around 1912 and had a church and school at the Dillard and Mollie Love house, which stood on Main Street in the current Peeble's location. St. John's present building was completed in 1955. (Above courtesy of the *Sylva Herald*; right courtesy of Jim Madison.)

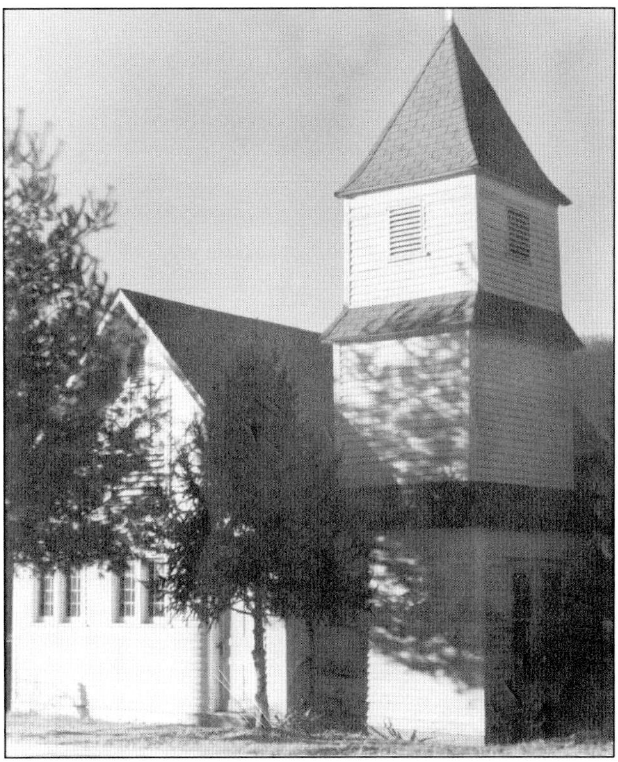

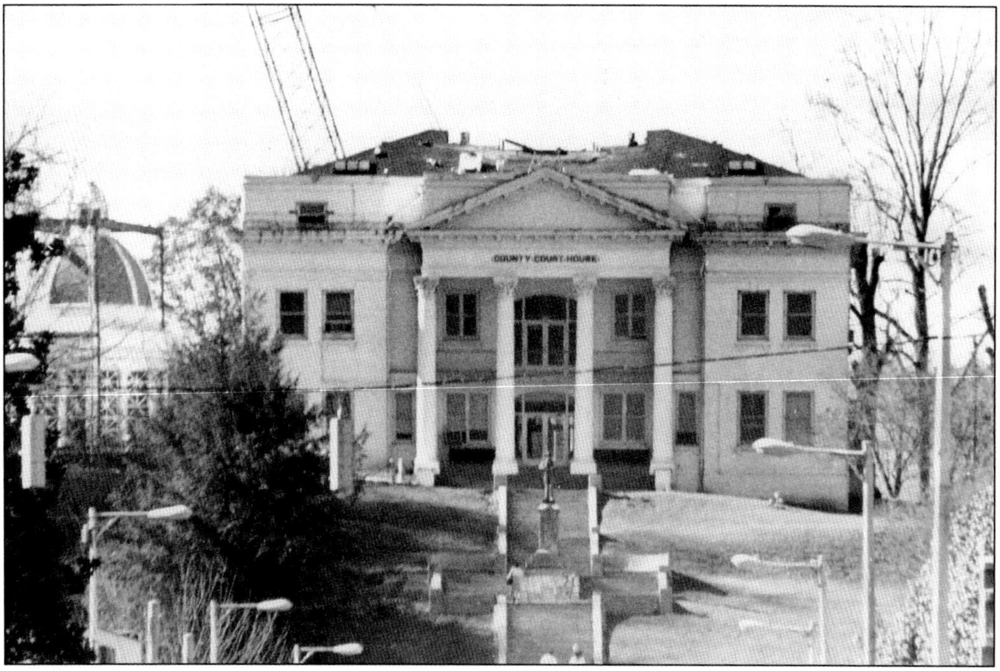

The famed Jackson County Courthouse appears topless in the above November 1994 photograph, taken just after the cupola was removed for repairs. Once restoration was complete, the former green dome was painted white and replaced in May 1995. A complete paint job during the summer of 1997 dressed the Jackson County Courthouse in ice-cream colors of lemony cream and lime. More renovations and paint in 2004–2005 restored the building's familiar white walls and dark green dome. The structure was built in 1913–1914 by entrepreneur C. J. Harris, who had promised local voters he would construct a courthouse in Sylva for a sum not to exceed $30,000 if they approved a referendum that would move the county seat. The measure passed after a contentious campaign. After the resolution was approved by voters, Harris submitted the low bid and was awarded the building contract. The Jackson County Courthouse was back in the news in 2007, when commissioners voted to incorporate the historic structure into a new county library on Courthouse Hill. An architect's sketch of the planned facility, as viewed from Keener Street, is below. (Above courtesy of the *Sylva Herald*; below courtesy of McMillan Smith and Partners.)

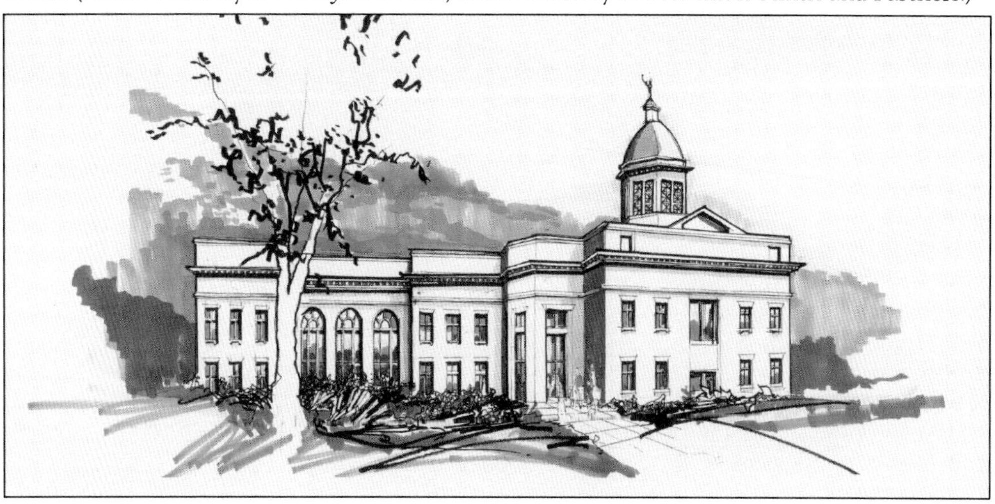

Two

Community Life

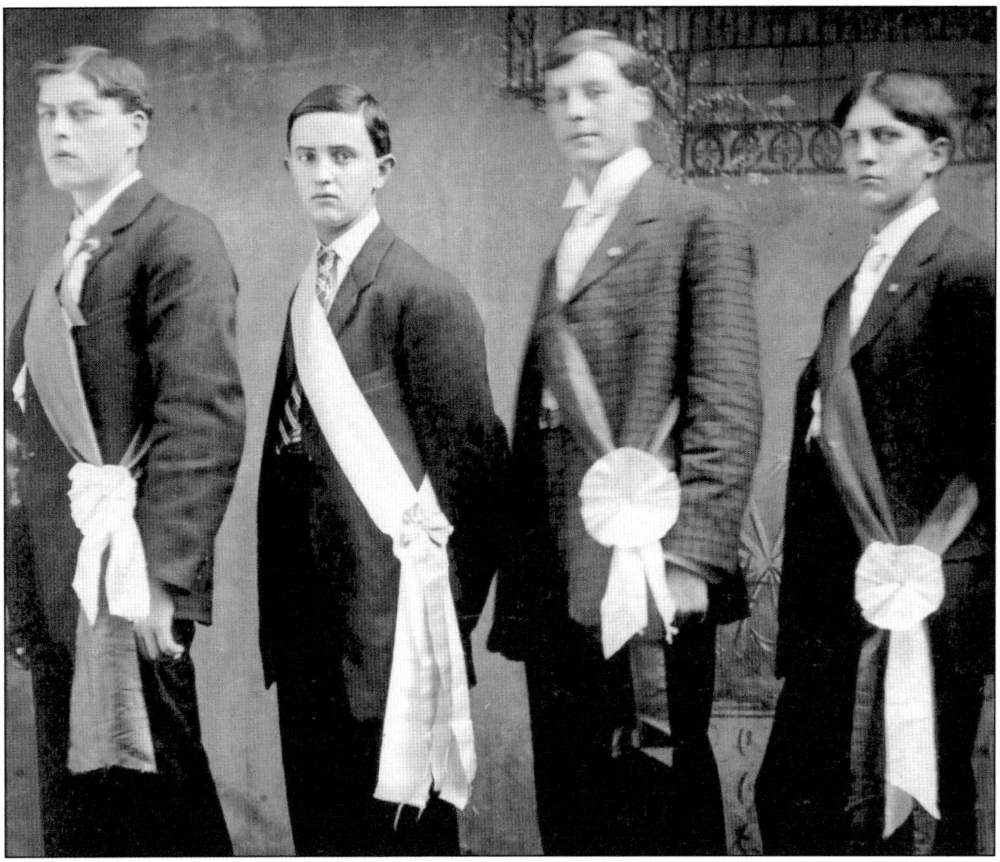

Marshals for a Sylva Collegiate Institute graduation in the early 1900s include, from left to right, unidentified, Brag Keener, unidentified, and Everette E. Brown. The Baptist-run boarding school operated in Sylva from 1898 until 1931. At one time, it had 229 students and 10 teachers. (Courtesy of Rachel Phillips.)

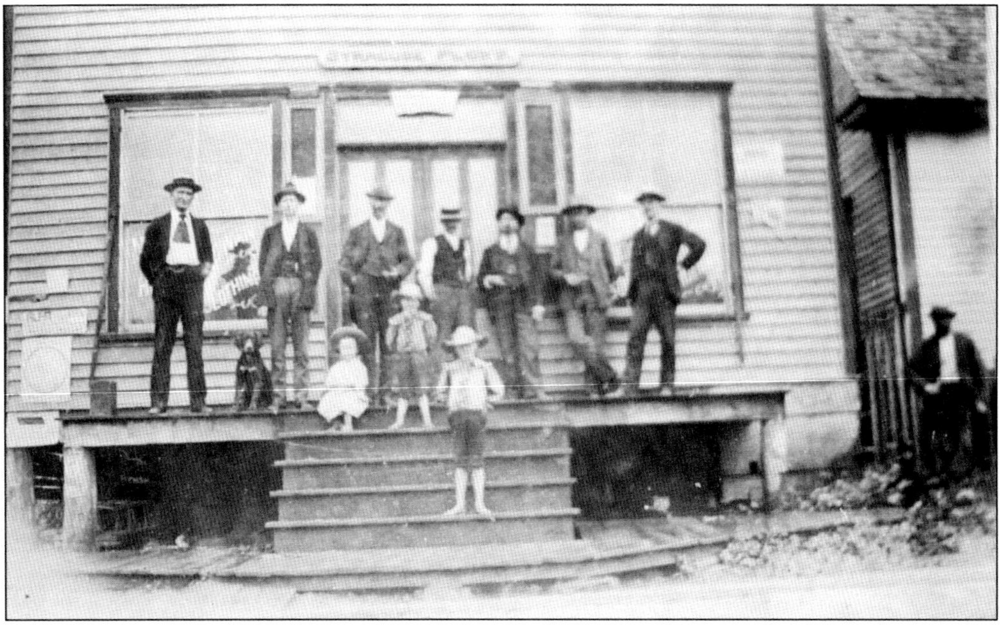

This store, pictured prior to 1898, once stood on Main Street and is thought to have been at the current site of the First Citizens parking lot. It was owned by E. L. McKee and M. D. Cowan. This may have been the shop McKee co-owned in 1898 with Oscar Coward; when C. J. Harris bought out Coward's share of that business, Harris and McKee formed the Sylva Supply Company, a Main Street landmark for a century. (Courtesy of Dorris Beck.)

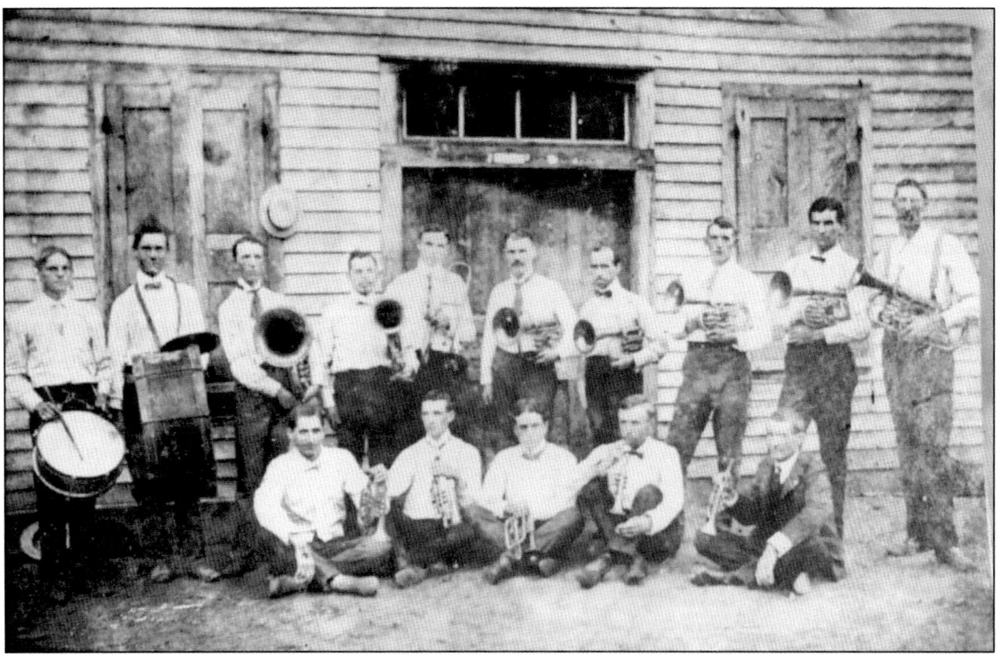

The first Sylva band is shown here around 1900. Members include, from left to right, (first row) A. J. Dills, George Bryson, Alex Baum, James R. Love, and instructor Walter F. Crause; (second row) Graham Grindstaff, Bill Smith, Fred McLain, Ed Tustin, Wade Hill, Dr. J. H. Knight, W. W. T. Sorrells, Ed Bryson, Charles L. Allison, and L. P. Allen. (Courtesy of Dorris Beck.)

Important figures in Sylva's past include William Demetrius Sylva (above right), who gave the town its name; Col. Charles Joseph "C. J." Harris (below left), who spearheaded the county seat effort; and Gertrude Dills McKee (below right), the first woman to serve in the North Carolina Senate. A wayfaring Dane from Texas, Sylva was a handyman for Gen. E. R. Hampton, who once owned most of the land where the town now sits. Harris, an early industrialist and entrepreneur, operated clay mines at Hog Rock (near Webster), constructed the Dillsboro Dam, and founded the Harris-Reese Tannery and Sylva Supply Company. McKee, one of North Carolina's pioneer women in politics and social legislation, was the daughter of Dillsboro founder William Allen Dills. She was elected to the state senate in 1931, 1937, and 1941, serving three terms. She was also elected in 1948 but died before serving. (Above right courtesy of the Town of Sylva; below left courtesy of *Sylva Herald*; below right courtesy of Ann McKee Austin.)

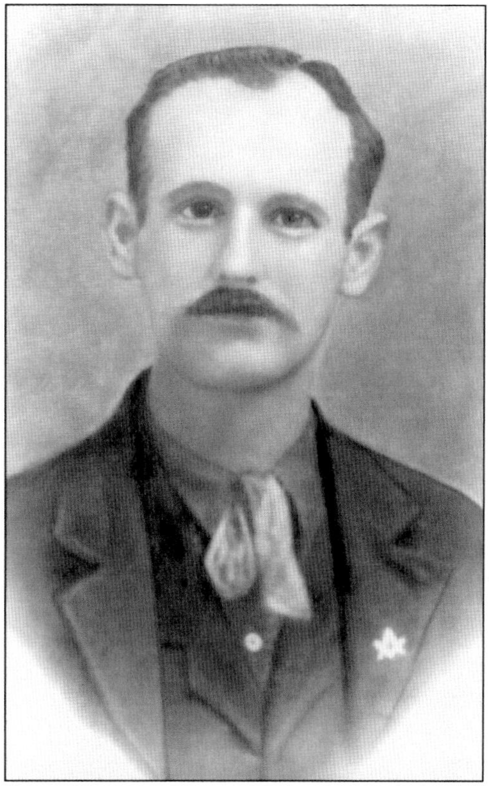

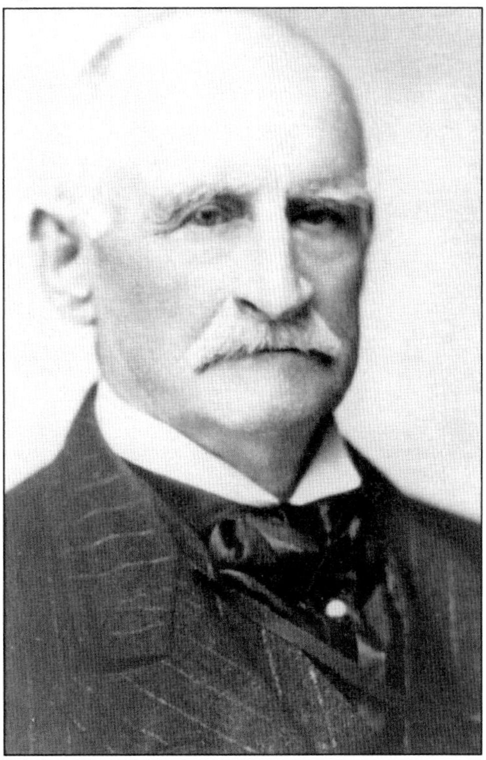

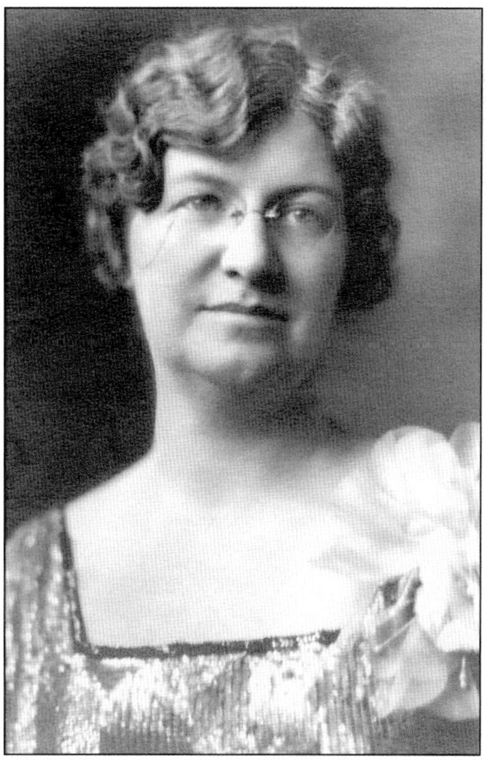

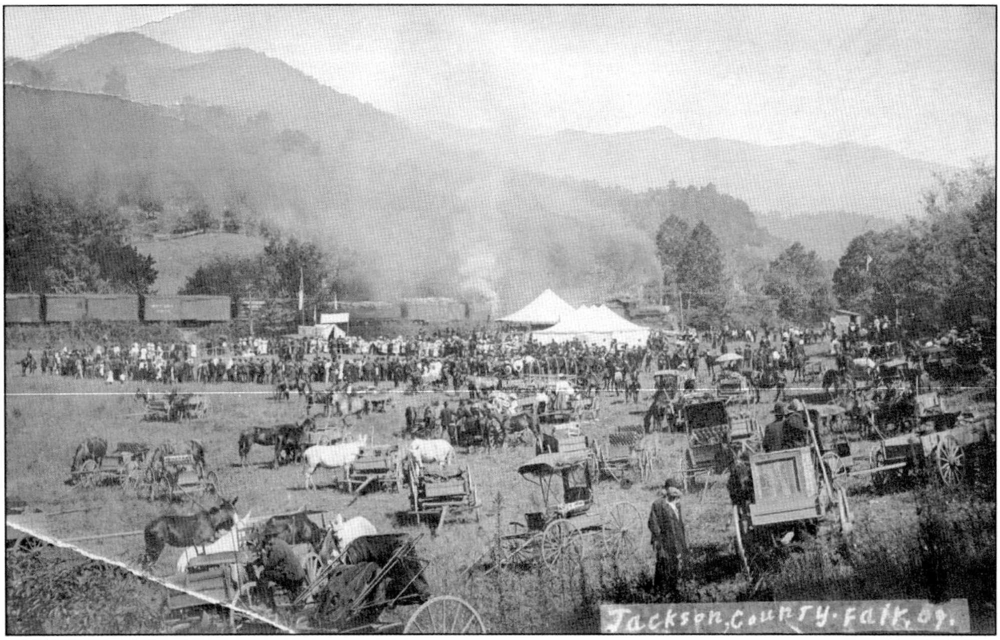

In the early 1900s, the Jackson County Fair was an annual event held on the Baum property, which became the site for Sylva High School in 1924 and then Sylva Elementary School in 1929. Hundreds turned out for the fairs, which included livestock, events, and parades. The above photograph was taken in 1909; the below photograph is undated. The fairs were a casualty of World War I. After the opening of Sylva-Webster High School in 1960 and Fairview Elementary in 1973, the area became Mark Watson Park. (Courtesy of Rachel Phillips.)

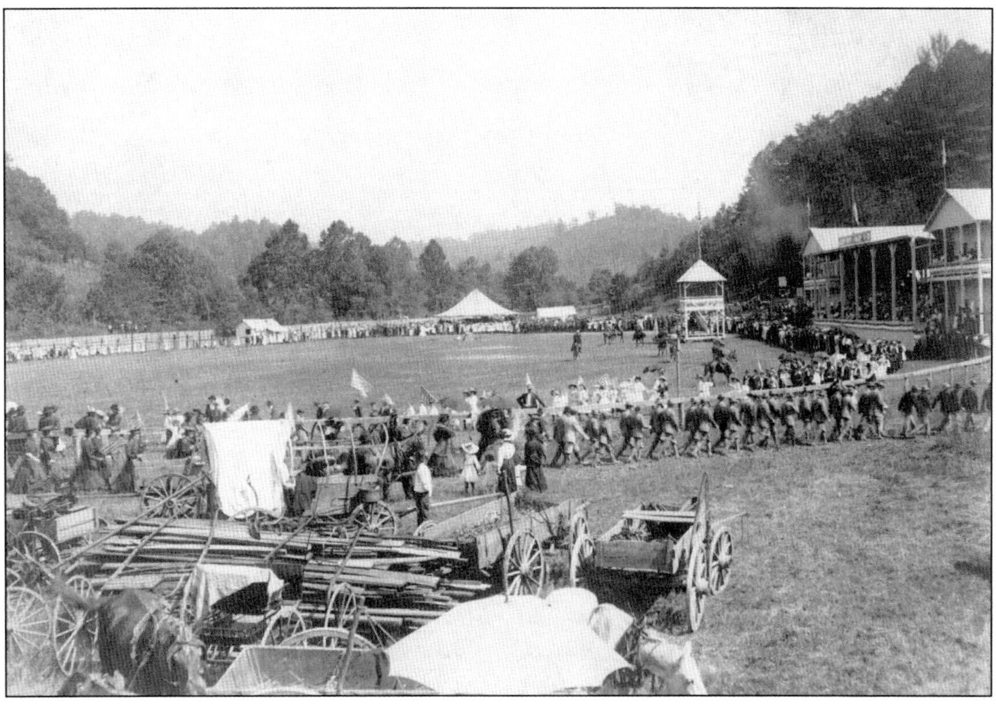

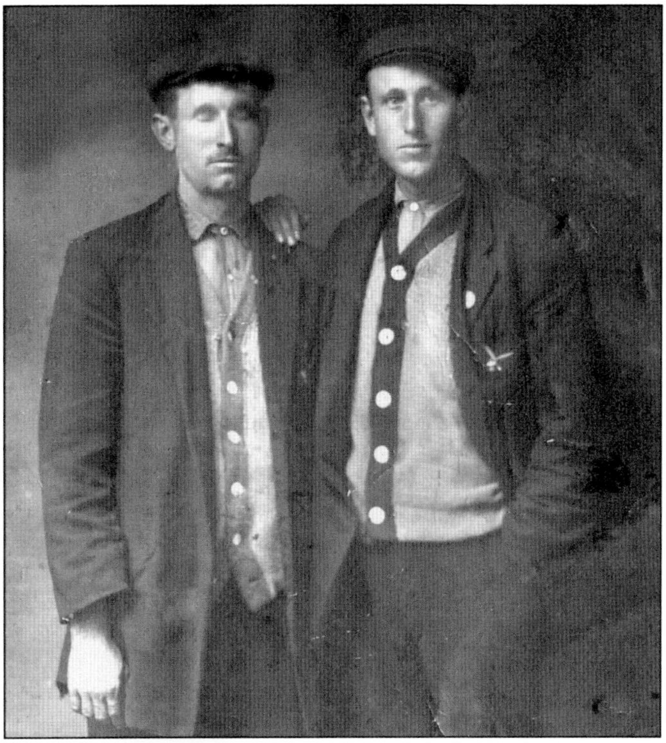

Brothers Gurley (above, left) and Ed Mashburn came to Sylva around 1914 to open a shoe store and livery stable just across the railroad tracks from Mill Street at the corner of what is now Grindstaff Cove Road. Ed made and repaired shoes and harnesses, while Gurley rented out horses. The brothers took two Reece sisters from Macon County as their brides, with Ed marrying Alice (below left) and Gurley marrying Minnie. (Courtesy of Nancy Browning.)

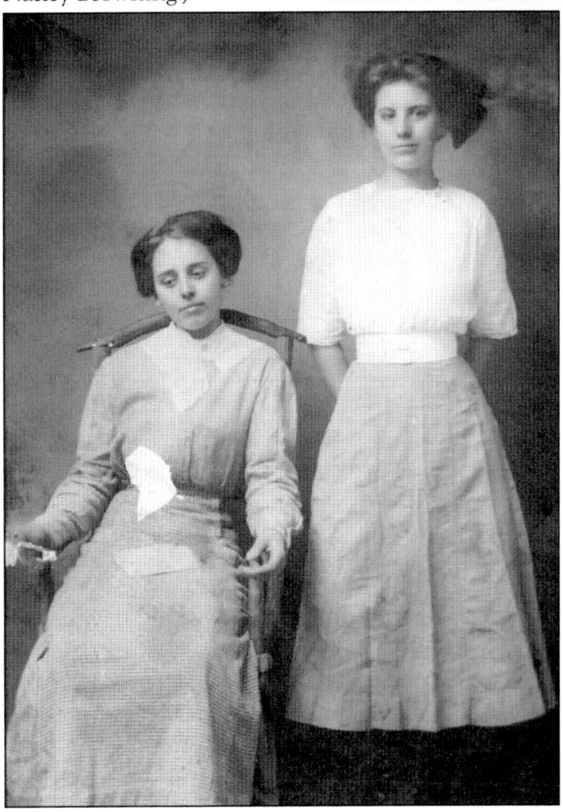

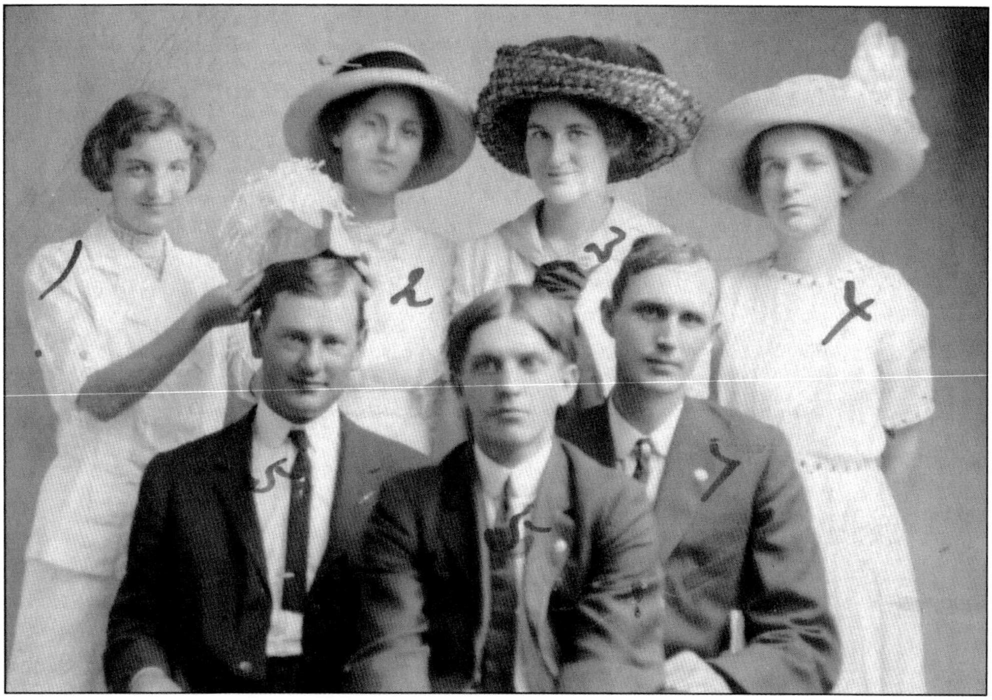

This group posing around 1910 includes the parents of Rep. David M. Hall Jr., the only person from Jackson County ever elected to the U.S. House of Representatives. Congressman Hall died in office in 1960. The gathering also includes Everette E. Brown, who founded the *Herald* forerunner *Ruralite* in 1926. Upon Brown's death in 1932, his wife, Attie Bridges Brown, continued to publish the paper until 1943. Pictured from left to right are (first row) David M. Hall Sr., Everette E. Brown, and Malcolm Bridges; (second row) Stella Broyles Hall, Attie Bridges Brown, Edith Moore Hall (Congressman Hall's mother), and Hannah Moore. (Courtesy of Rachel Phillips.)

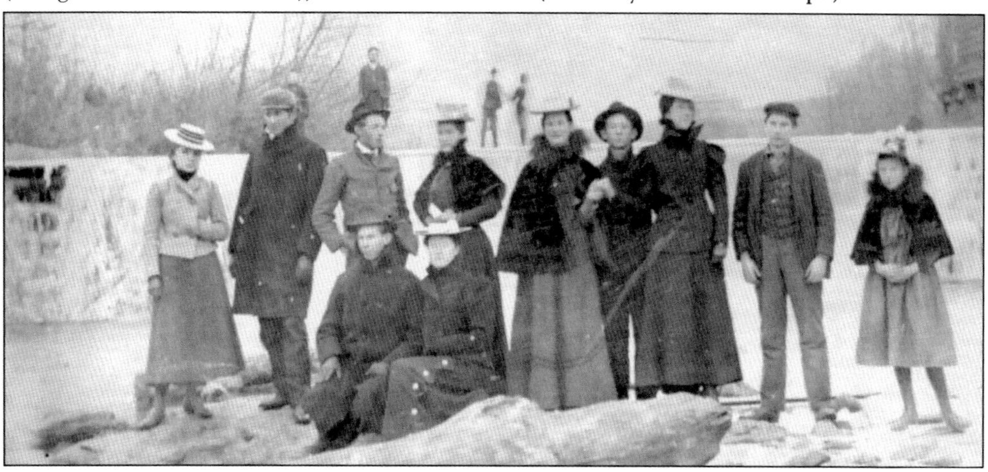

Ice on Scotts Creek measured 15 to 18 inches thick in 1888, when area residents enjoyed skating for 11 weeks. The dam in the background was located near the east intersection of Main and Mill Streets, behind Balsam Creek Designs, according to the late Willa Mae Scroggs. Shown from left to right are (first row) Mack Fowler and Dicus Dills; (second row) Maggie Long, A. J. Dills, Ed Bryson, Sadie McClain, Cora Henson (Dills), Buren Fowler, Ethel Leatherwood, Edgar Lewis, and Bertie Henson. (Courtesy of Dorris Beck.)

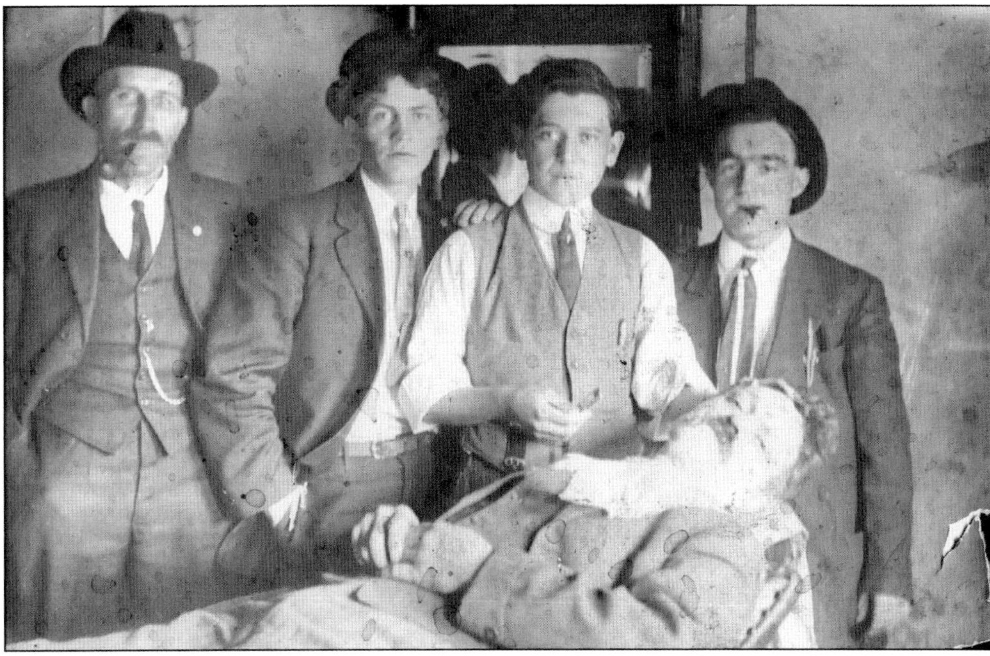

Getting a shave around 1915 is J. S. Higdon, who built the Hotel Carolina building (initially called the New Jackson Hotel) and owned the first Ford dealership in Sylva. Behind him, from left to right, are Landrum Gidney, Everette Brown, barber Noah Ledford, and an unidentified man. (Courtesy of Rachel Phillips.)

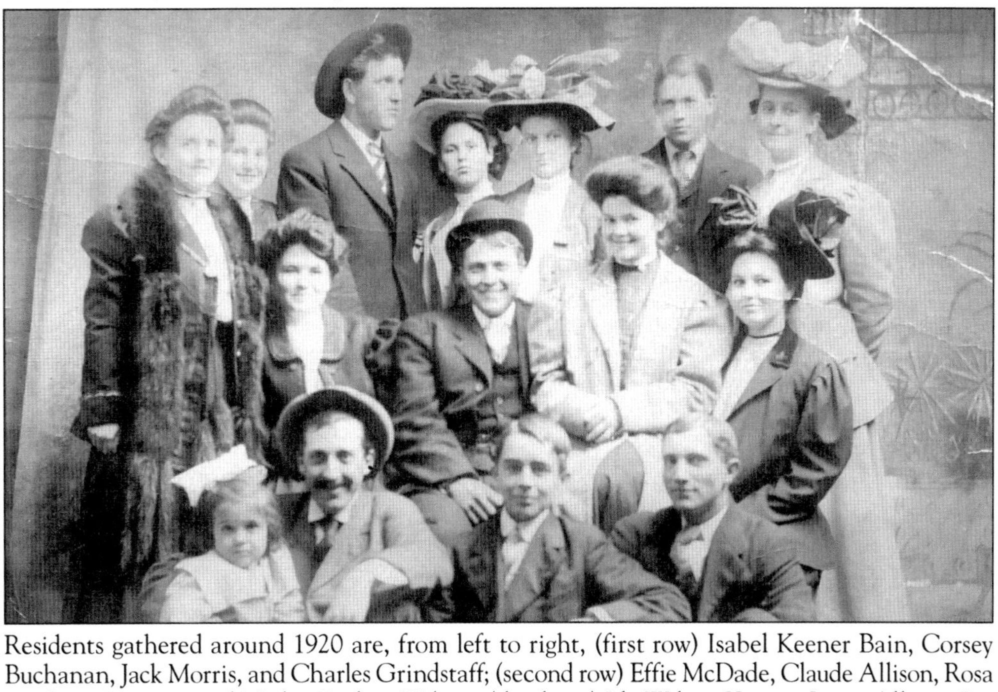

Residents gathered around 1920 are, from left to right, (first row) Isabel Keener Bain, Corsey Buchanan, Jack Morris, and Charles Grindstaff; (second row) Effie McDade, Claude Allison, Rosa Watkins Cannon, and Madge Bridges Wilson; (third row) Ida Wilson Keener, Lucia Allison, Pat Pressley, Attie Bridges Brown, Bonnie McConnell, Ben Cathey, and Louetta Buchanan Wilson. (Courtesy of Rachel Phillips.)

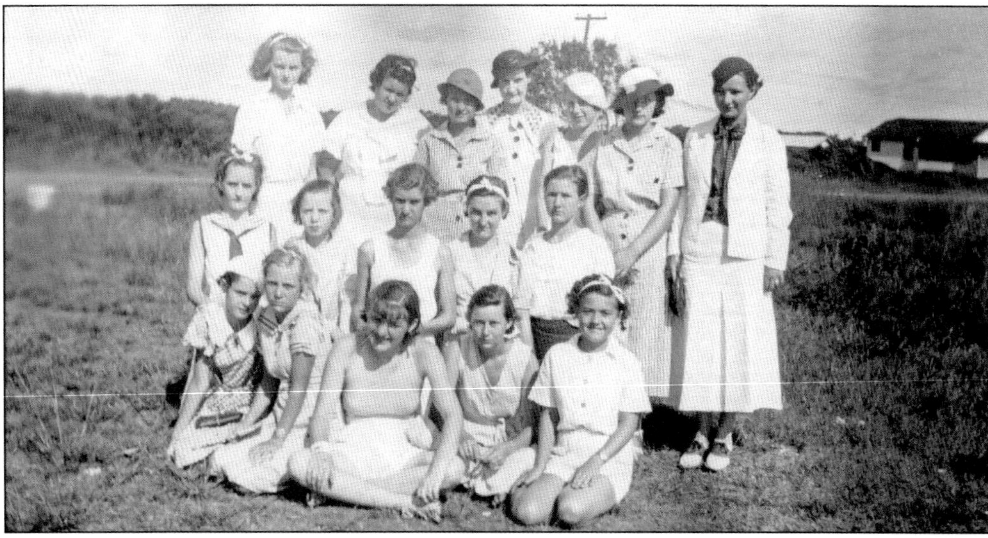

Sylva's first Girl Scout troop traveled to Carolina Beach in 1934. Scouts and leaders included, from left to right, (first row) Audrey Buchanan Goddard, Ruth Dietz Mills, Dot Higdon Owens, Bonnie Fleeman Wachter, and Betty Bain Poteet; (second row) Kathleen Hooper Nash, Mary Jane Coward Dillard, Edith Garrett Jenkins, Matilda Wilson Lavange, and Hattie Hilda Sutton Allison; (third row) Rachel Brown Phillips, Frances Allison Whitt, Isabel Dillard Griffin, leader Docia Garrett, Maggie Dillard Anderton, Elsie Geisler Massie, and assistant leader Margaret Hall Dowdle. (Courtesy of Edith Garrett Jenkins.)

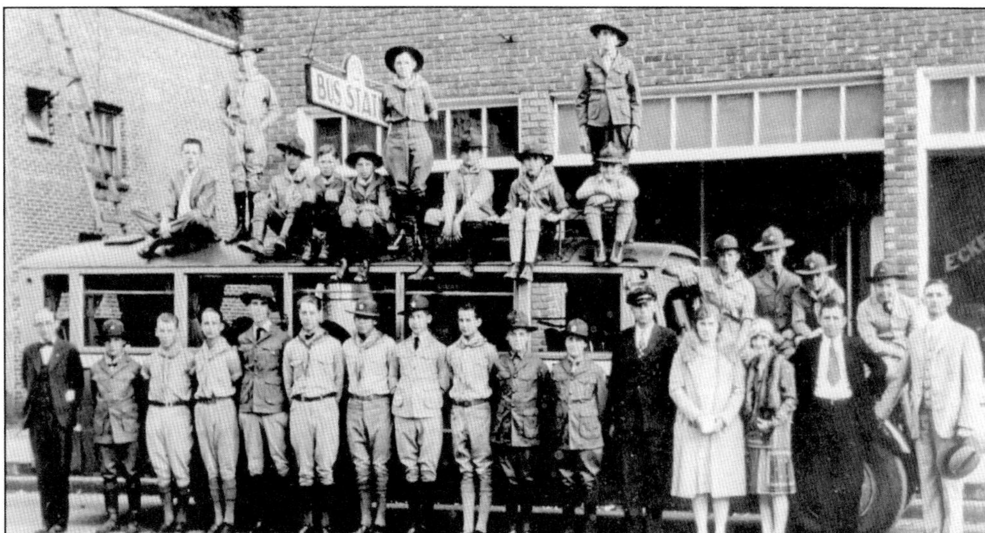

The first Boy Scout troop poses for a photograph before leaving for Washington, D.C., around 1926. Pictured from left to right are (first row) Assistant Scoutmaster Hugh Monteith, T. K. Guthrie, Bill Edwards, Johnny Wilson, Marshall Cooper, Herbert Bryson, Alvin Sutton, Edwin Brown, Tom Wilson, Roscoe Askey, Johnny Parris, bus driver Harry Sorrells, Clara Clemmer, Dorcas Allen, Assistant Scoutmaster Walter Allen, and Rev. George Clemmer; (second row) Alden Coward, William Curtis, Lyndon Carden, Frank Watson, Malcolm Brown, Tom Kelly, Ernest Wilson, Ralph Morgan, David "Buddy" Hall, Mack Hooper, James Moody, Frank Askey, J. T. Gribble, and Clyde Brown. (Courtesy of Rachel Phillips.)

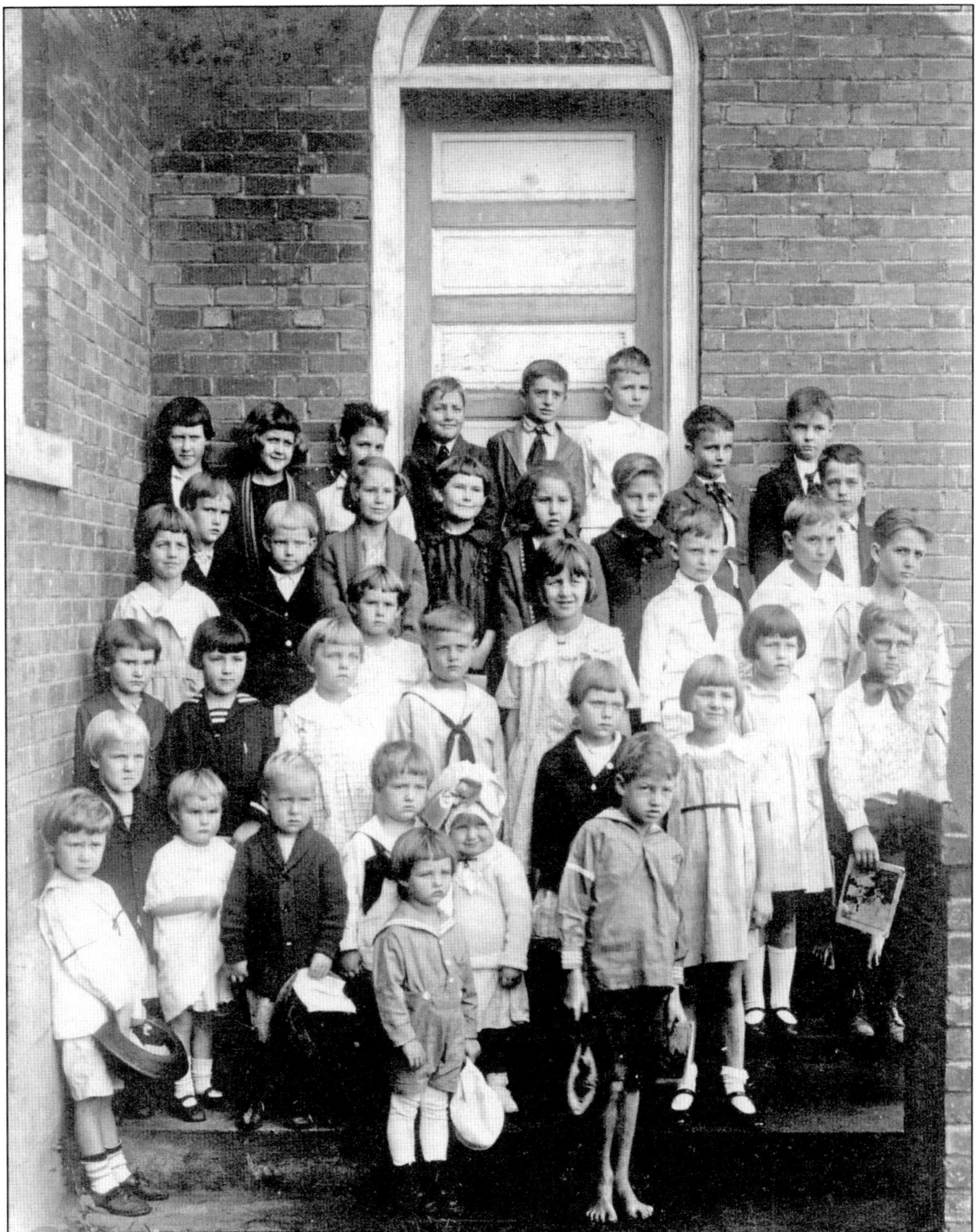

Sylva Methodist's Sunday school class gathers on the steps of the church around 1924. Shown from left to right are (first row) Jess Dillard, Mary McLain, Kitty Dean McGuire, John McLain, Joe Ted Wilson, Andrew Wilson, Maggie Dillard, and unidentified; (second row) ? Sherrill, Nimmo Geisler, Hazel Allison, Ernest Wilson, Katherine Grindstaff, Margaret Hall, Madge Wilson, and William Curtis; (third row) unidentified, Patsy McGuire, unidentified, Lyndon McKee, Robert Potts, and Burch Allison; (fourth row) Katherine McLain, unidentified, ? Sherrill, Noracella McGuire, Leona Dillard, Earl Collins, Johnny Wilson, ? Jones, and Tom Wilson; (fifth row) unidentified, Helen Allison, unidentified, John Parris, Mack Hooper, and William McKee. (Courtesy of Ann McKee Austin.)

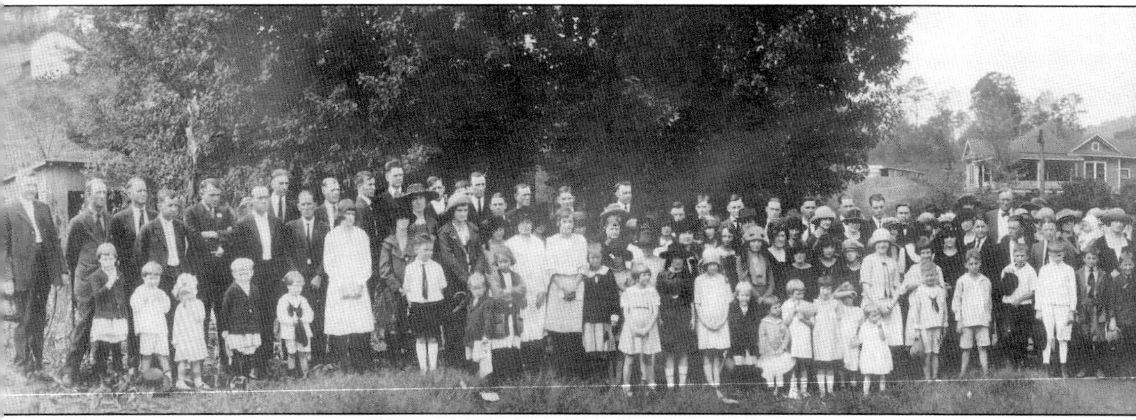

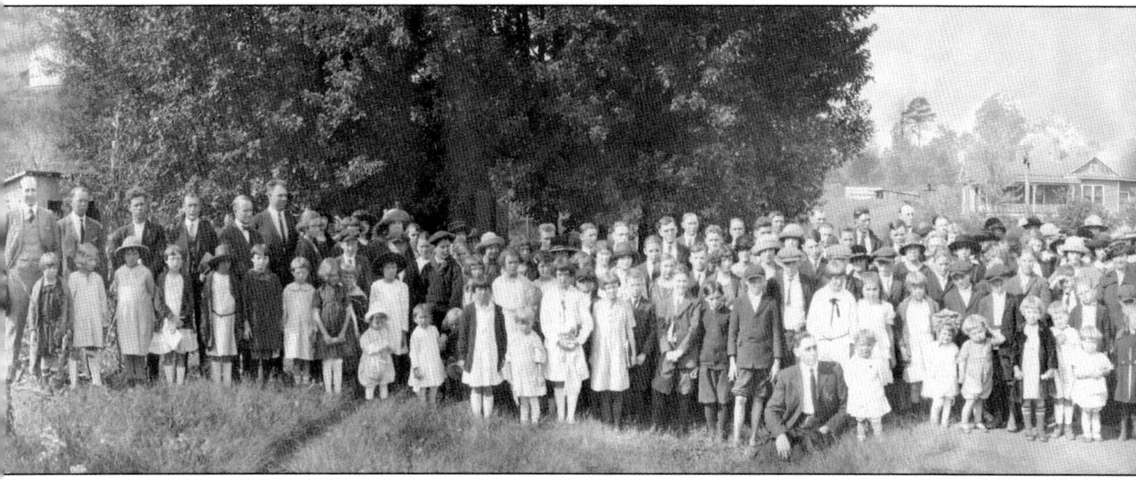

The congregations of Sylva's two largest churches (Baptist, top; Methodist, center), both established in 1888, met at the same spot near the Methodist church around 1924. The Jackson County Courthouse appears in the center of the above photographs; the home closest to it is still standing as the Ernest Burch residence. The Methodist church (lower right) and the Baptist church (above and slightly

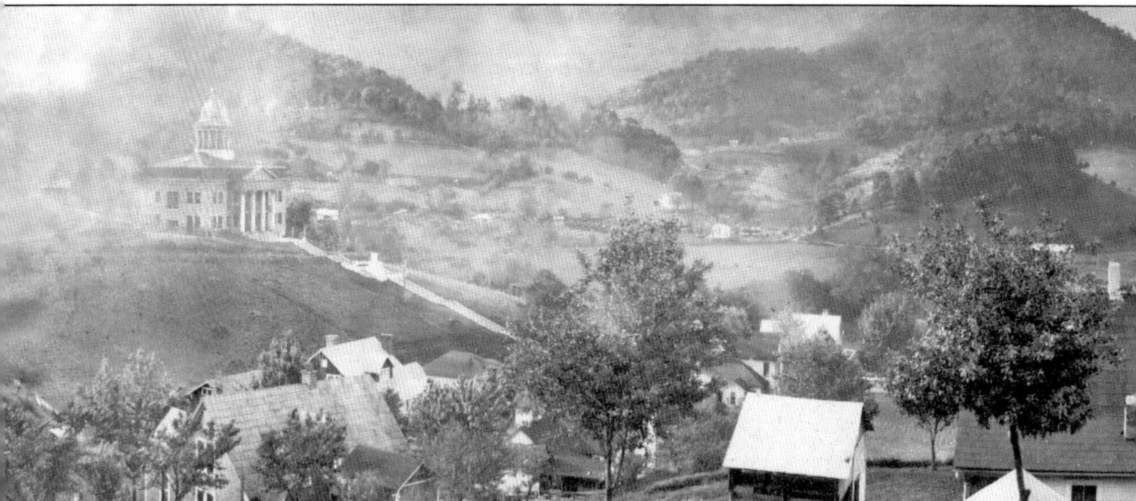

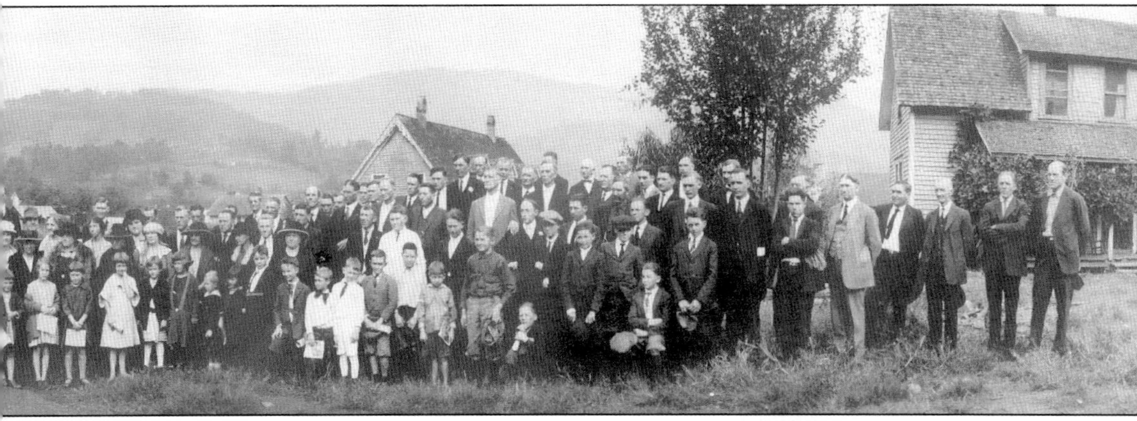

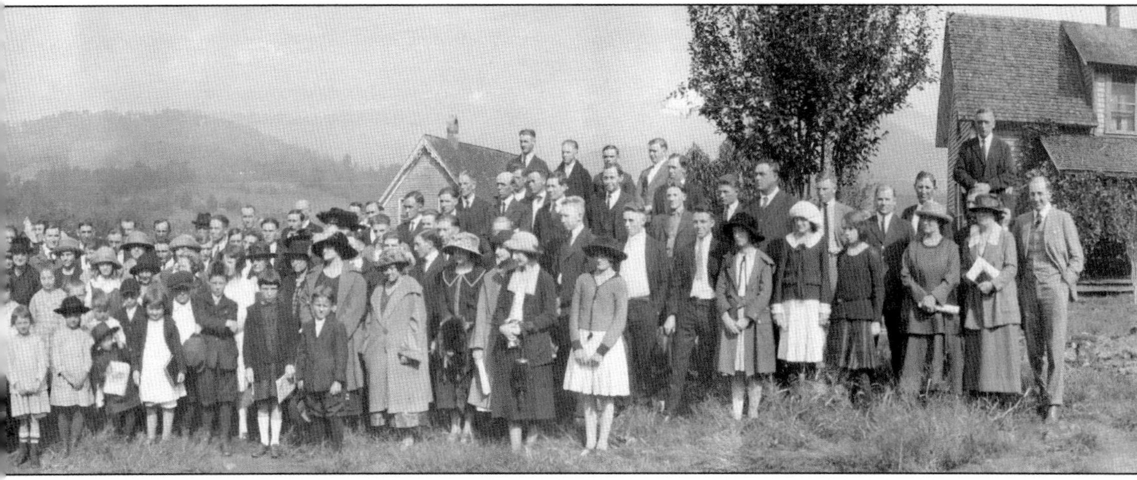

left, with steeple showing) are visible in the panorama below, taken between 1920 and 1923. The white-roofed Commercial Hotel, to the right of the Baptist church, burned to the ground in April 1923. The Jackson County Courthouse is on the hill at left. (Above courtesy of David Trantham; center courtesy of Sylva First United Methodist; below courtesy of Livingston Kelley.)

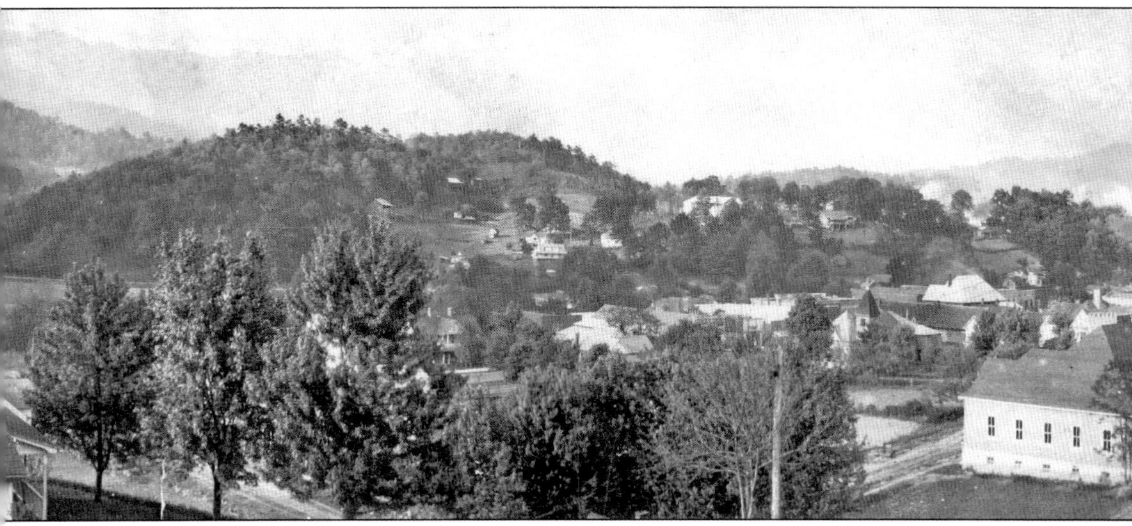

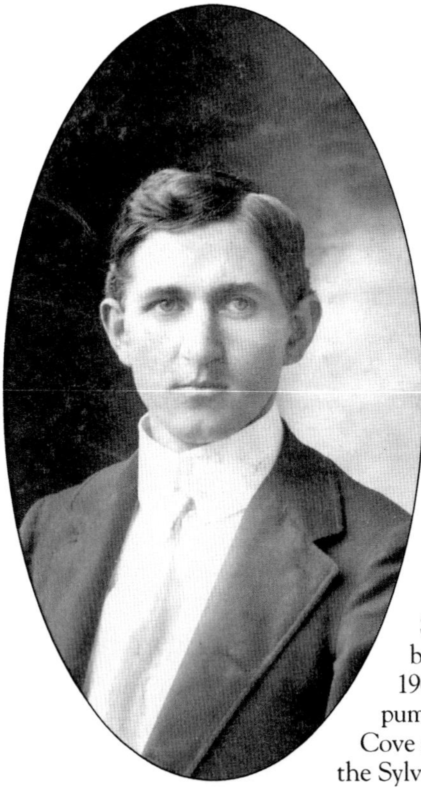

A. J. "Jonah" Dills (left) organized the Sylva Bucket Brigade in 1899 in order to fight fires in town. By 1919, with E. E. Brown as chief, that group had evolved into the Sylva Fire Department. A new city hall and firehouse was built in 1927, and the current city hall was constructed in 1960 to house the fire department. Below, Sylva firefighters pump water from a stream to battle a 1940s blaze in the Dills Cove area. (Left courtesy of Lynn Hotaling; below courtesy of the Sylva Fire Department.)

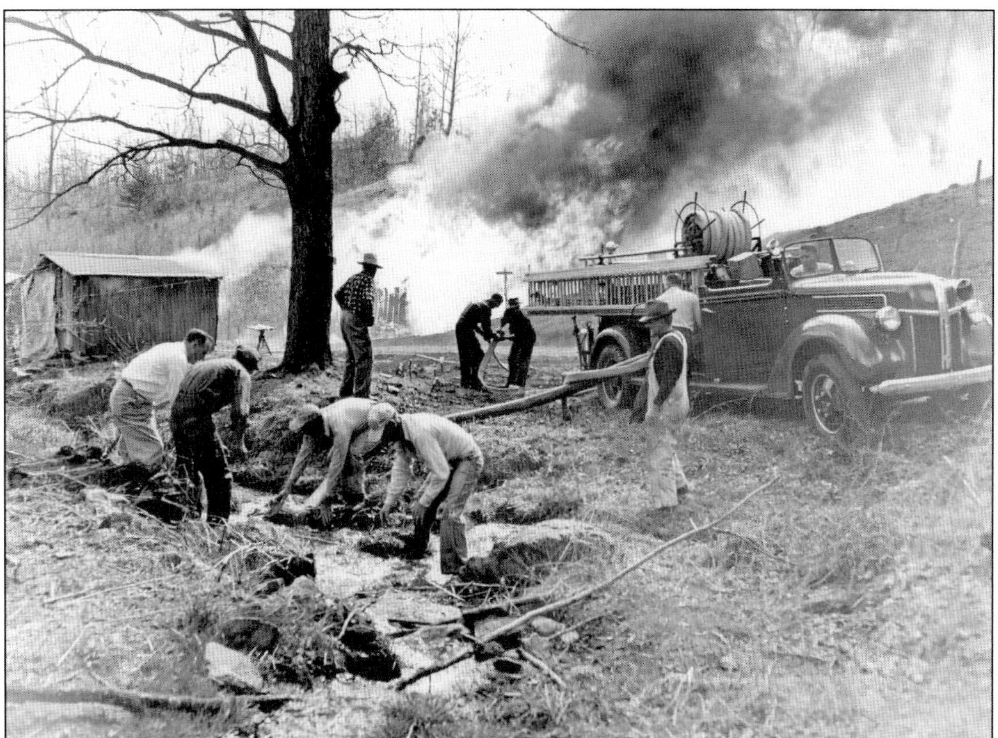

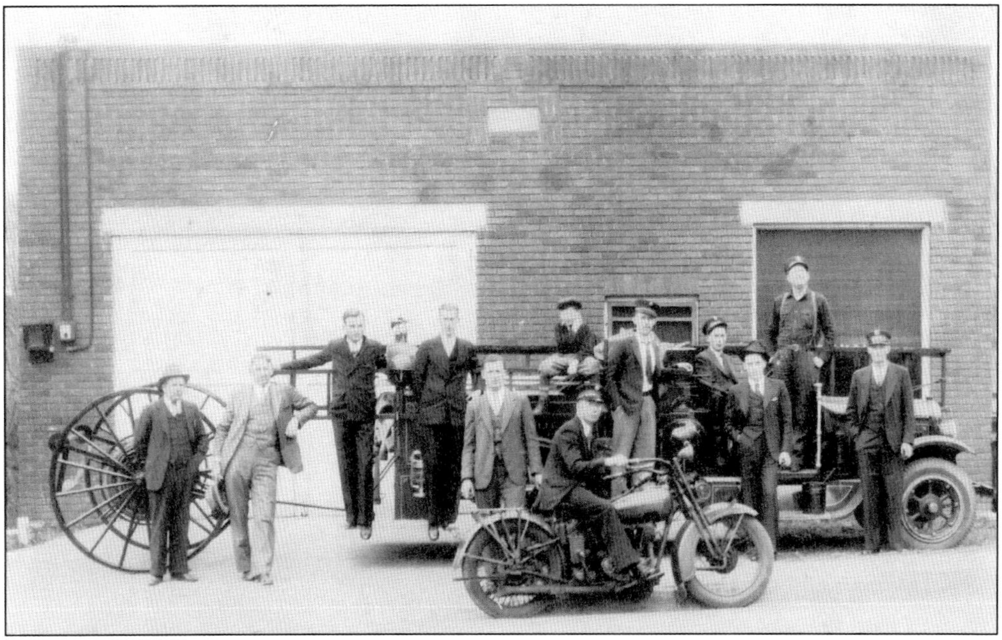

The Sylva Police Department is now housed in the original home of the Sylva Fire Department. Early firefighters (above) included, from left to right, Charlie Price, A. J. Dills, Gordon Dillard, Roscoe Dills, Dick Wilson, ? Eckenrod, Felix Picklesimer, Paul Womack, David Dills, Theodore Mashburn, E. O. Mashburn, and D. M. Tallent. Constructed in 1927 by Mike Brown, this building initially served as both firehouse and city hall. The department's second fire station, completed next door in 1960, was the first separate firehouse for Sylva and was built by the Southern Lumber Company; the firefighters themselves finished the interior. That structure was remodeled for Sylva's town hall after the fire department moved into its present quarters in 1980. "Old Red," a 1940 Ford still drivable in 2008, is shown below when it was new. (Above courtesy of the Town of Sylva; below courtesy of the *Sylva Herald*.)

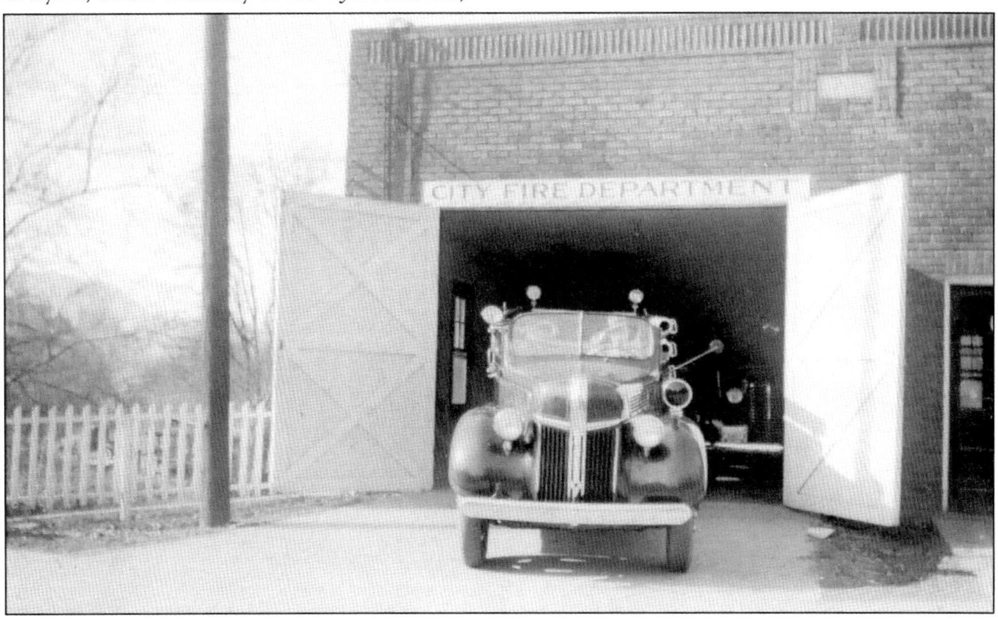

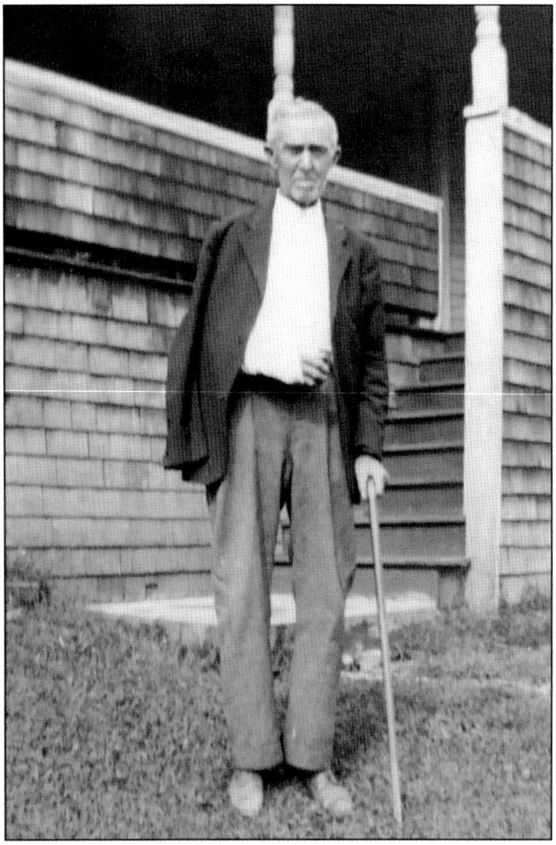

Allen Bartlett Dills (left) once owned most of north Sylva, including Dills Cove, the area encompassing the Presbyterian church and the residential property that surrounds St. Mary's Catholic Church and the Sylva Church of Christ. He married Josephine Brendle, and the streets in that section—Josephine, Bartlett, Brendle—bear family names, as does Dills Cove. At one time, a Dills Street also existed, but its name was changed to Storybook Lane to avoid confusion with Dills Cove. Dills's son A. J. founded Sylva's fire department and served as the town's first real estate broker. Below, Dills family members pose at a family reunion. Pictured from left to right are (first row) Laura Higdon, Della Foster, Tina Bryson, Joyce Garrett, and A. J. Dills; (second row) J. S. Higdon, R. O. Garrett, and Thad Bryson. The children on the left are unidentified. (Courtesy of Edith Garrett Jenkins.)

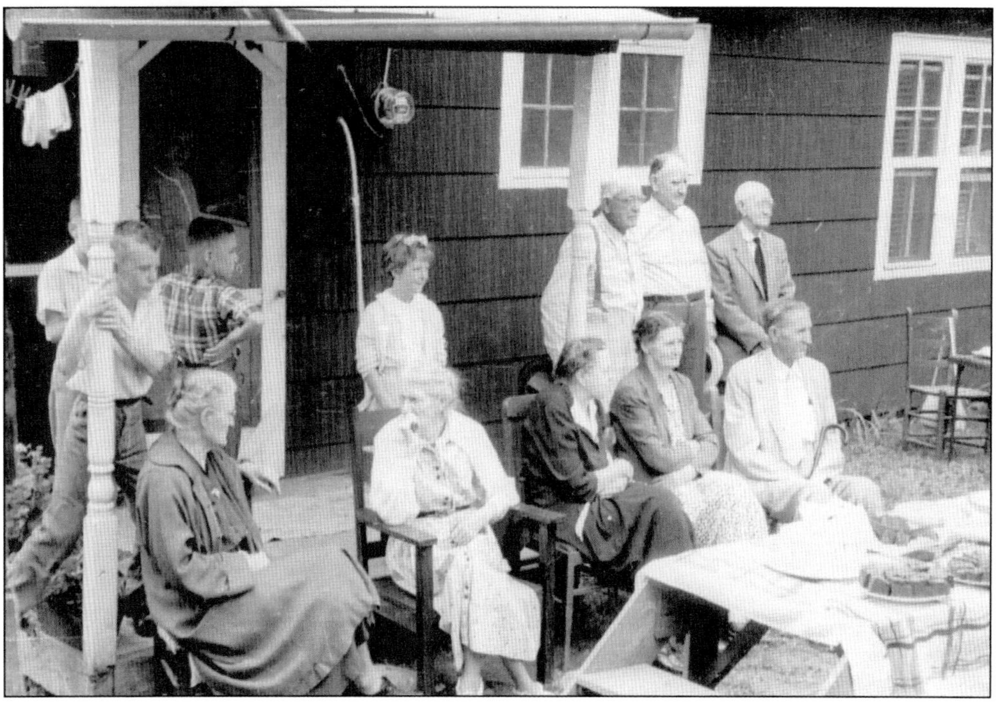

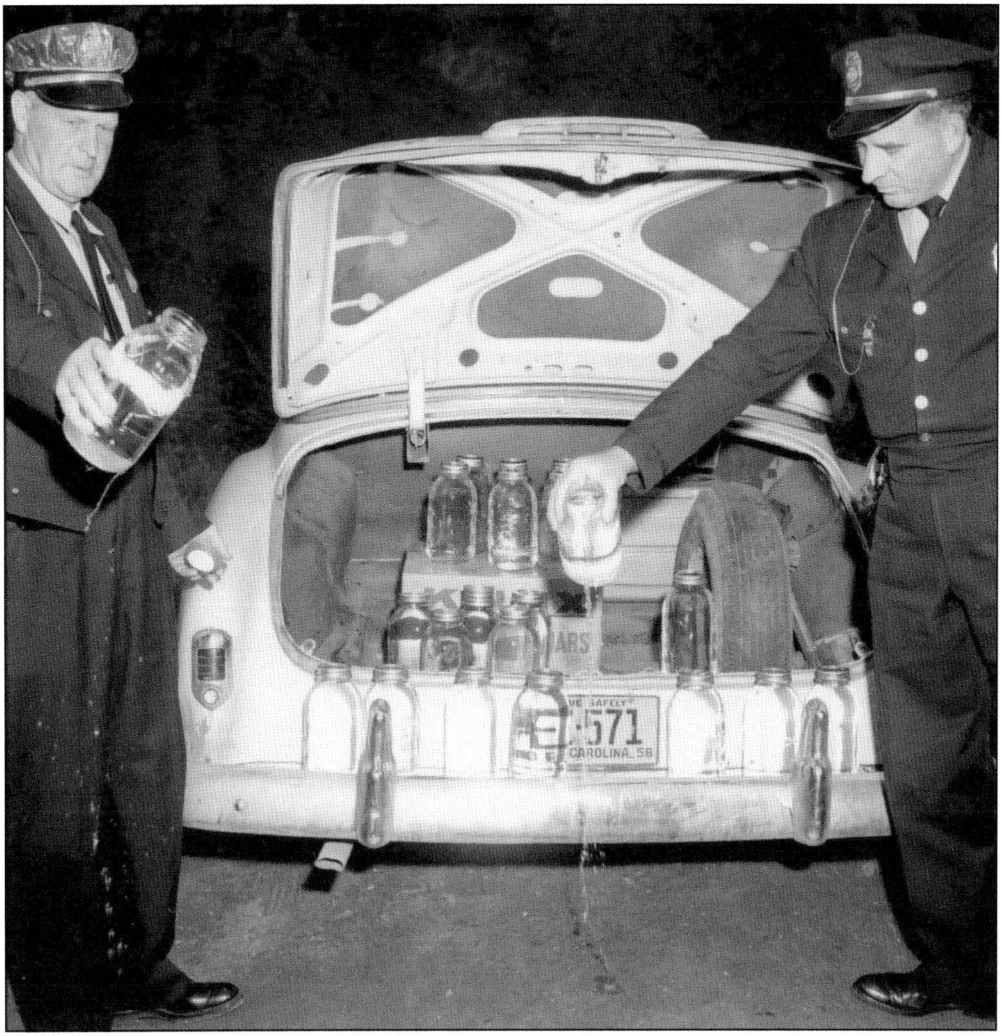

Police chief George Evans (left) and officer Burt Wilkey pour out 12 gallons of moonshine confiscated near city hall in April 1958. According to the issue of the *Sylva Herald* in which this photograph first appeared, Wilkey arrested Jimmy Arrowood and Henry Barnes on charges of transporting and possessing non-tax-paid whiskey. Following a hearing, they were "bound over" to the superior court, the newspaper said. (Courtesy of the *Sylva Herald*.)

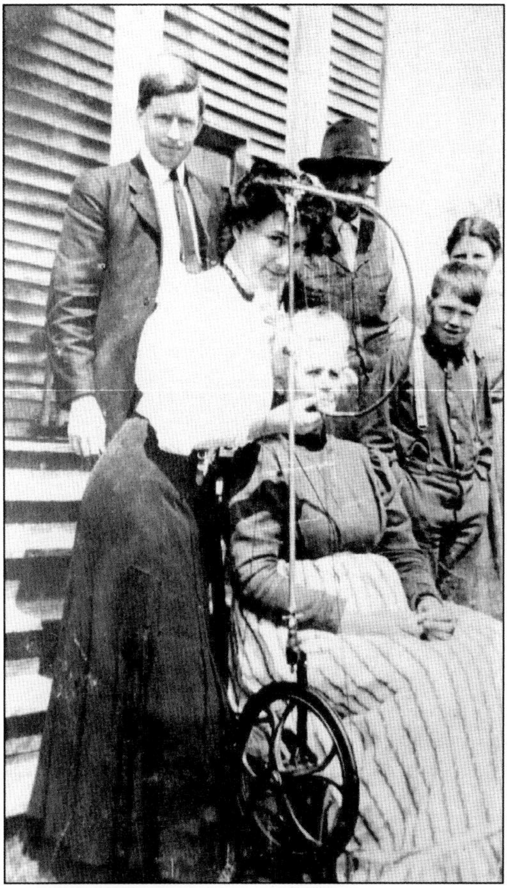

Dr. Daisy Zachary McGuire was the first woman to graduate from Southern Dental College (now Emory University School of Dentistry) in 1908. In the early years of her Sylva practice (left), she treated patients using a portable chair and engine operated by a foot pedal. She often worked outside to take advantage of natural light because electricity was not yet available. Her husband, Dr. Wayne McGuire, also a dentist, stands behind her. Both McGuires worked into their 90s, as shown below, and for a time were the two oldest practicing dentists in the state. Dr. Daisy's patient is Rosser Taylor of Cullowhee. Katie Wood of Sylva sits in Dr. Wayne's chair while her son Denny looks on. At the time of this photograph, Dr. Daisy was 95 and Dr. Wayne 92. All three of the couple's daughters—Noracella Wilson, Patsy McGuire, and Kitty Dean Gamewell—became dentists, and both Patsy and Kitty Dean married dentists. Patsy and her husband, Harold McGuire, and Noracella practiced with their parents in Sylva for decades; Patsy and Harold's two sons, Patrick and David, continue the family tradition in their King Street office overlooking Main Street. (Courtesy of Patrick McGuire.)

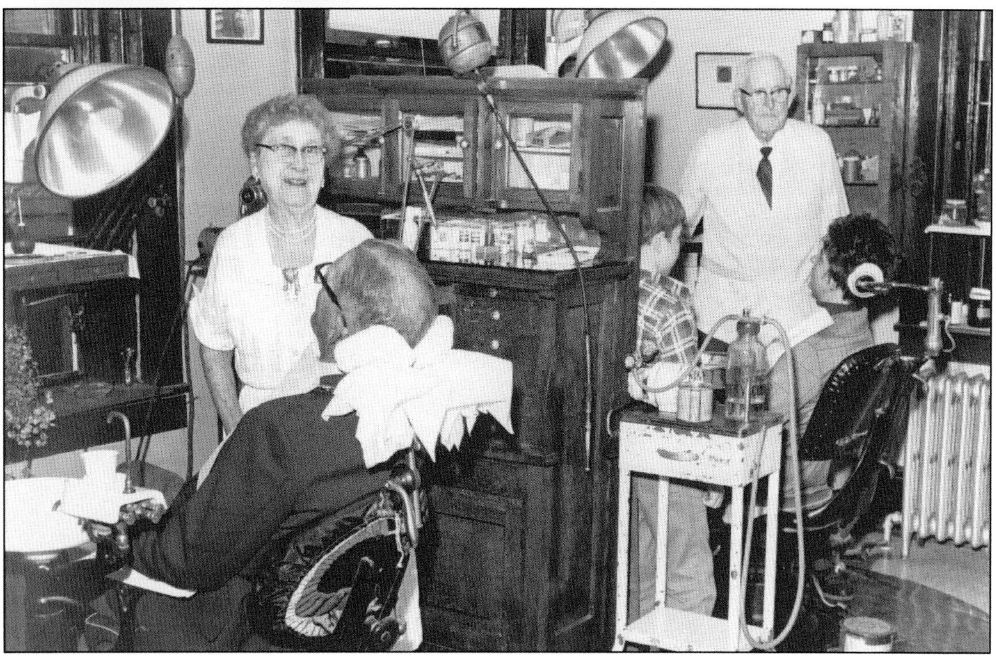

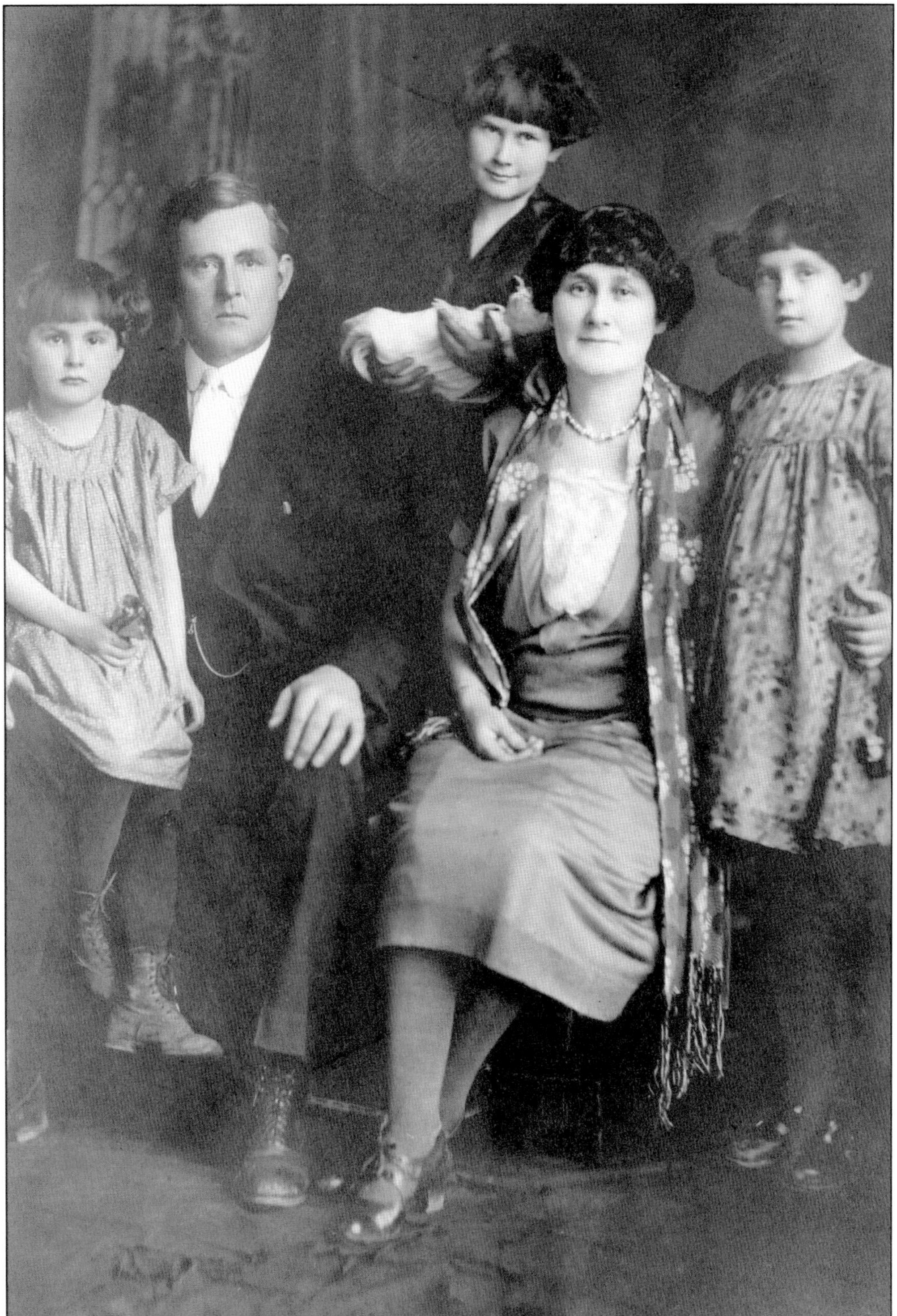

Sylva's "first family" of dentistry includes, from left to right, Kitty Dean, Dr. Wayne, Noracella, Dr. Daisy, and Patsy McGuire. (Courtesy of Patrick McGuire.)

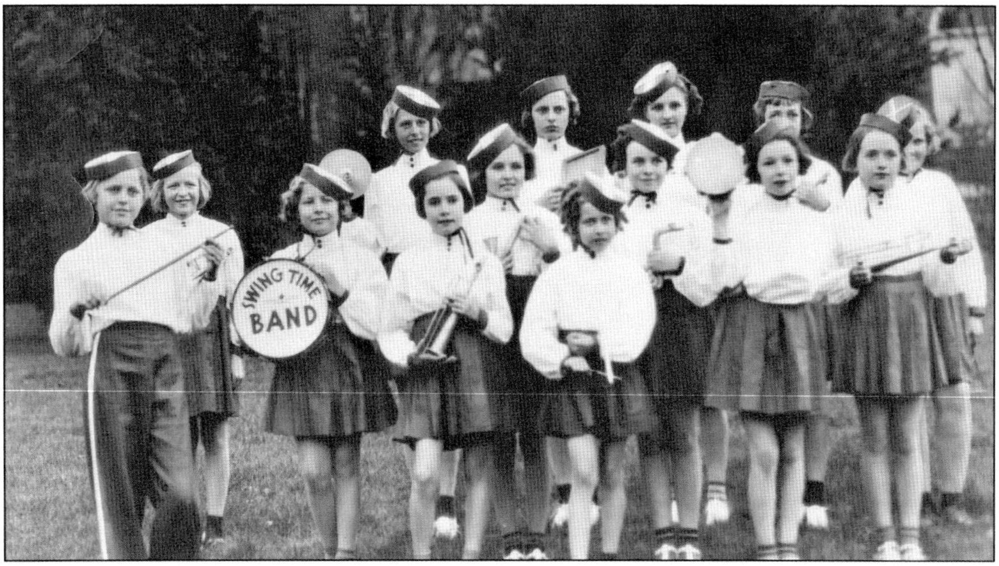

The Sylva Swing Time Band was one of some 20 toy bands, made up of children 12 and younger, organized in 17 western North Carolina counties as part of the Works Progress Administration's recreational division. The group competed in the district-wide finals in Asheville on April 17, 1936. The members of the band are, from left to right, Annie Nell Brown, Ethel Reed, Mary Turpin, Myrtle Bowen Brown, Dorothy Mae McKee, Doris Glenda Bryson, Madge Brown, Peggy Ramsey, Peggy Robinson, Agnes Wilson, Dorothy Sue Tallent, June Bess, Jackie Gaylor, and Nancy Allison. (Courtesy of Annie Nell Rector.)

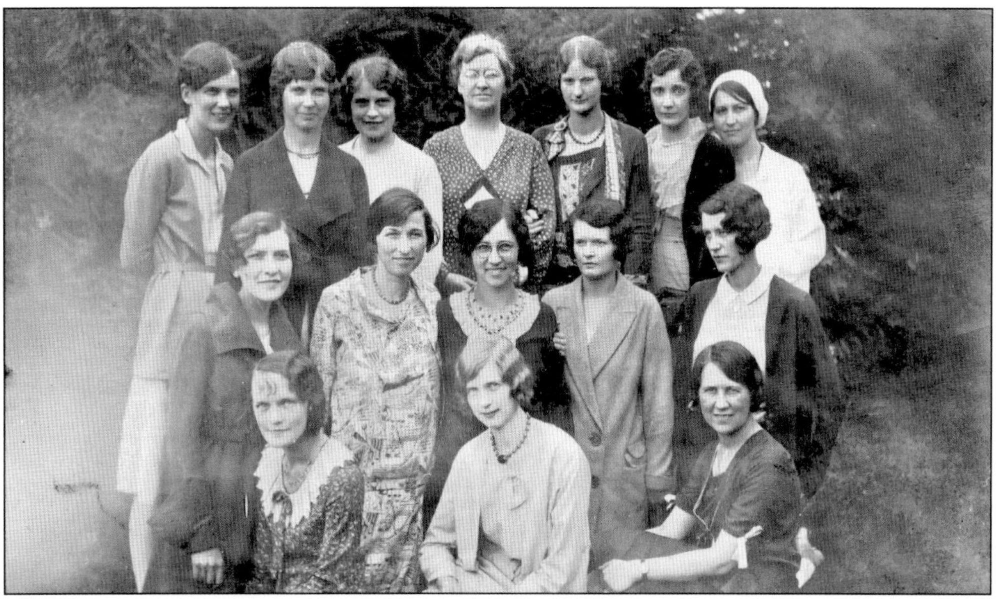

The Sylva Woman's Club was organized in 1926, and this photograph was taken a year or two later. Shown from left to right are (first row) Alma Fisher, Katie McKee Nicholson, and Sadie Hale Reed; (second row) Nell Cowan Jordan, Eloise Bain, Edith Geisler Moody, Maude Leatherwood, and Myrtle Henson Buchanan Cole; (third row) Ruth Oliver Hinds, Lewellyn Rhodes Patrick, Helen Cathey Dillard, Gertrude Dills McKee, Wilma Allison Jones, Pauline Miller, and Edith Alley. (Courtesy of Betty Foxx.)

The Sylva High School Marching Band (below) poses on the school steps in 1950. Members include E. P. Stillwell, Tommy Ginn, Barbara Vance, Betty Blanton, Kenneth Sutton, Audrey Jones, Edith Moore, Pat Montague, Ann Cathey, Jimmy Stovall, Dennis Monteith, Janese Holden, Kenneth Sutton, Tom Morris, Lloyd Kirk, Leah Sutton, Loqueta Holden, Mack Monteith, Charles Baker Reed, Richard Ginn, Herrin Cabe, Bruce Carden, Eddie Buckner, Patsy Buckner, Linda Moody, Melba Elders, Dorothy Ashe, and Neil Wilson. Pictured at right are majorettes Ravena Queen (left), drum major Eddie Lou Terrell (center), and Libby Dillard. (Right courtesy of Frank Crawford; below courtesy of Audrey Jones Tritt.)

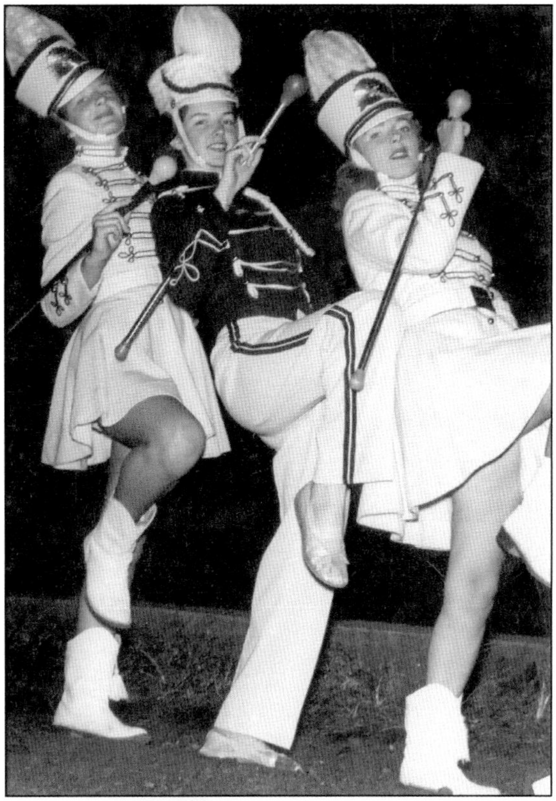

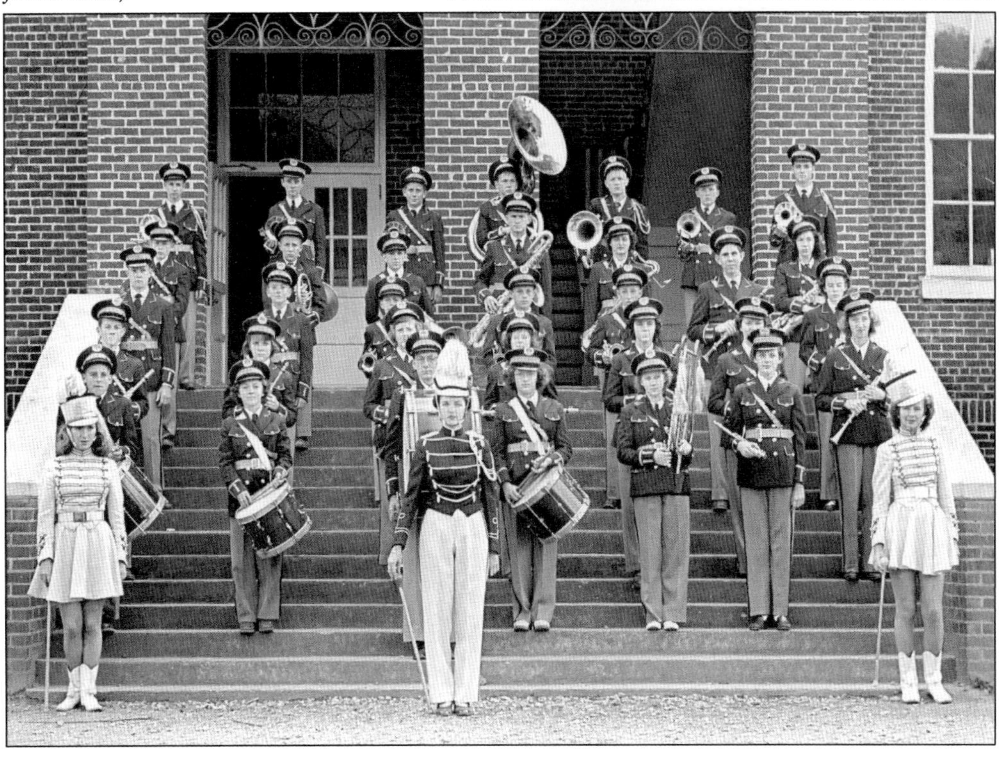

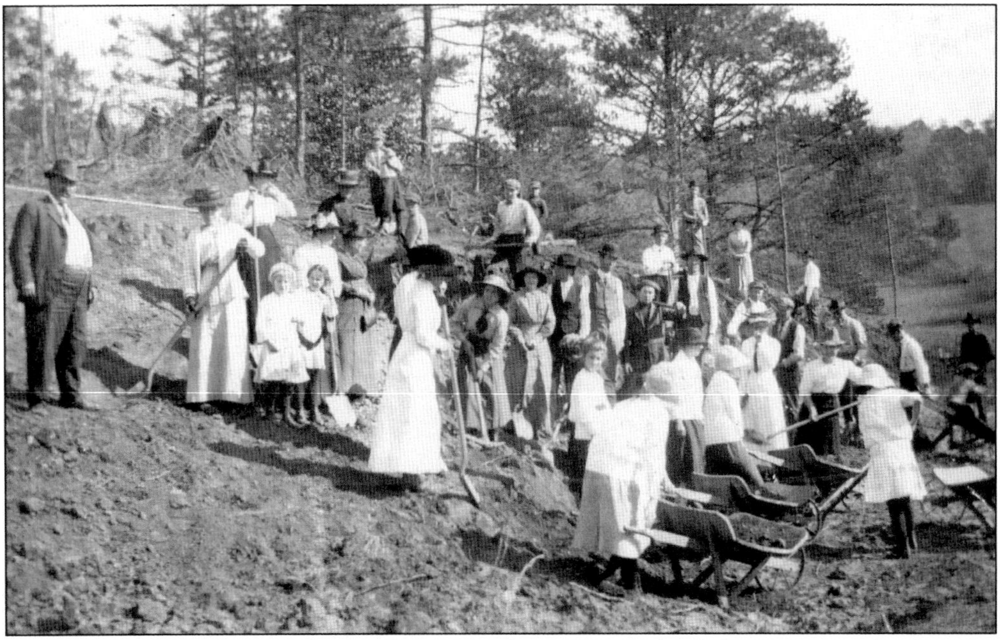

In the early 1900s, all those who lived near a road were required to help maintain it for about six days each year. This group is working in the Lovesfield area. According to *The History of Jackson County*, local roads were poor at best, and much of the fault lay in the "antiquated system of localized maintenance." Work days like the one above often turned into social occasions; in fact, the *Tuckaseigee Democrat* stated in an editorial that the crews "did just enough work to keep from being indicted for neglect." (Courtesy of Rachel Phillips.)

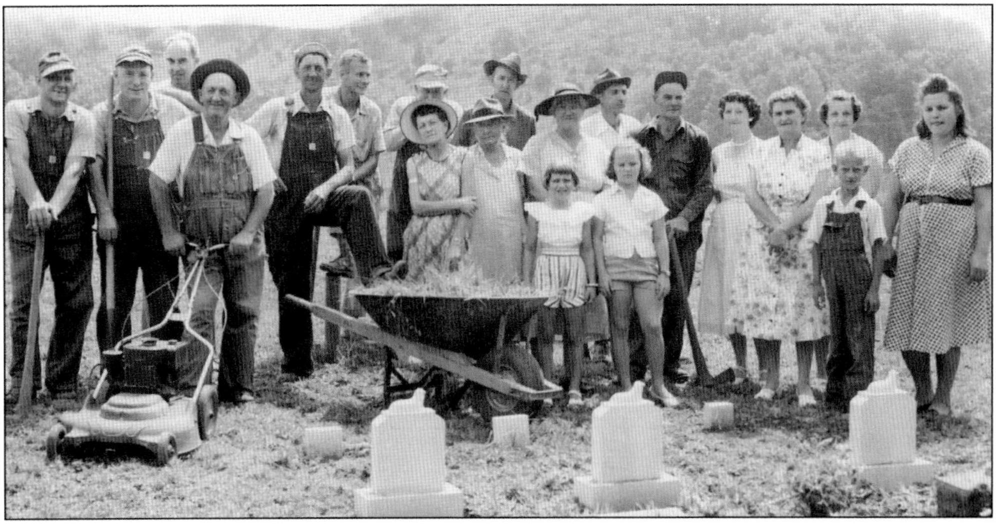

Area residents have also typically maintained community cemeteries. Participating in a mid-1950s cleanup effort at Dills Cemetery on Fisher Creek are, from left to right, (men) Roy Fisher, Newt Dills, Edward Parris, Clyde Fisher, Lloyd Fisher, Joe Cash, Charlie Dills, unidentified, Harold Cooke, and Guy Fisher; (women and children) Blanche Ridley, Ida Dills, unidentified, Judy Howell Edwards, Mary Sue Fisher Mason, Nannie Fisher Howell, Gursie Fisher, Eunice Fisher Parris, Carroll Bradley, and Faye Dills. (Courtesy of the *Sylva Herald*.)

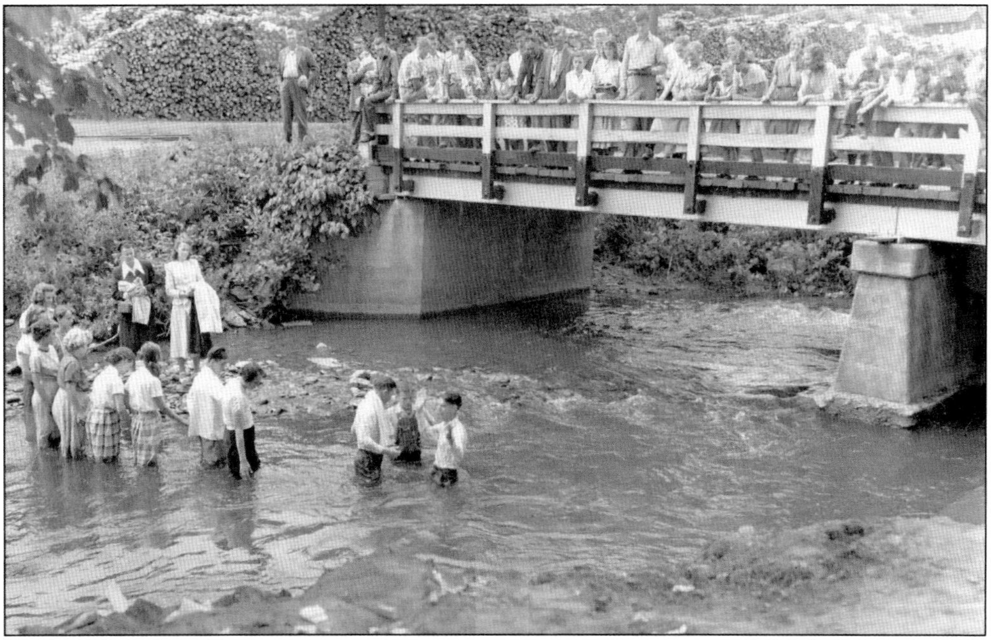

Members of the Sylva Church of God gather in the late 1940s for a summer baptizing in Scotts Creek. At that time, the church stood on the corner of Business 23 and N.C. 107 where Bogart's is today; it is now in Sunrise Park. The preachers are Brother Woodrow Wilson (left) of Alarka and Brother Arvle Nations of Whittier, and those receiving baptism are, from left to right, Annie Crane, ?, Jones, Annie Henry, Marie Crane, Soyrieta Wiggins, Ruby and Helen Jones, Ivery Crane, and Bessie Henry; Junior Jones is with the preachers at right. Ethel Jones, the mother of Helen, Ruby, and Junior, stands by the creek bank holding towels; another daughter is behind her. (Courtesy of Annie Crane Moore.)

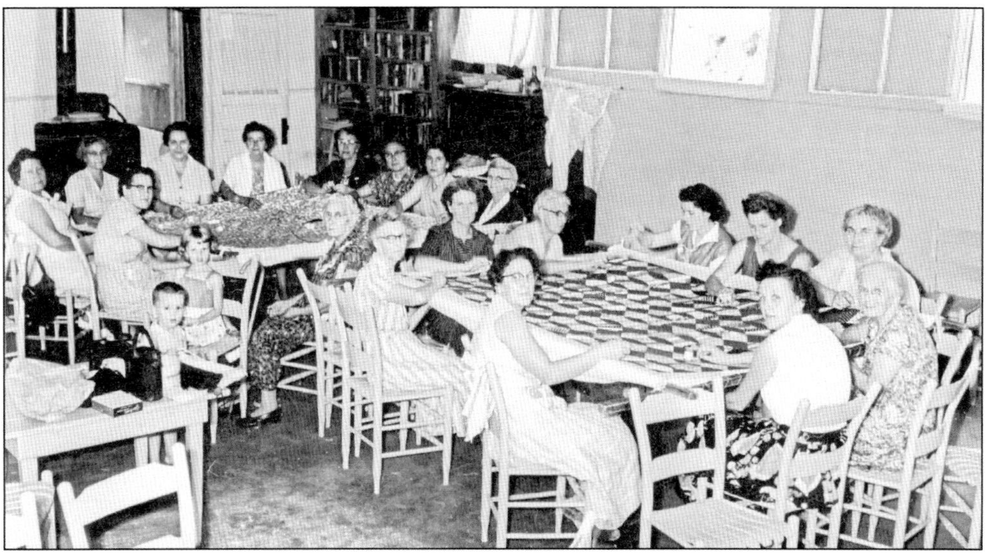

Community members meet around 1955 for a quilting at the Addie Community Building. Quilters include Gladys Henson, Dorcas Parris, Viola Jones, Martha Bryson, Mrs. Garland Dillard, Audrey Springer, Evie Parris, Lou Cogdill, Sue Cogdill, Essie Mull, Lou Johnson, Helen Bryson, Edith Jones, Mrs. Mull, and Nettie McClure. (Courtesy of Joe McClure.)

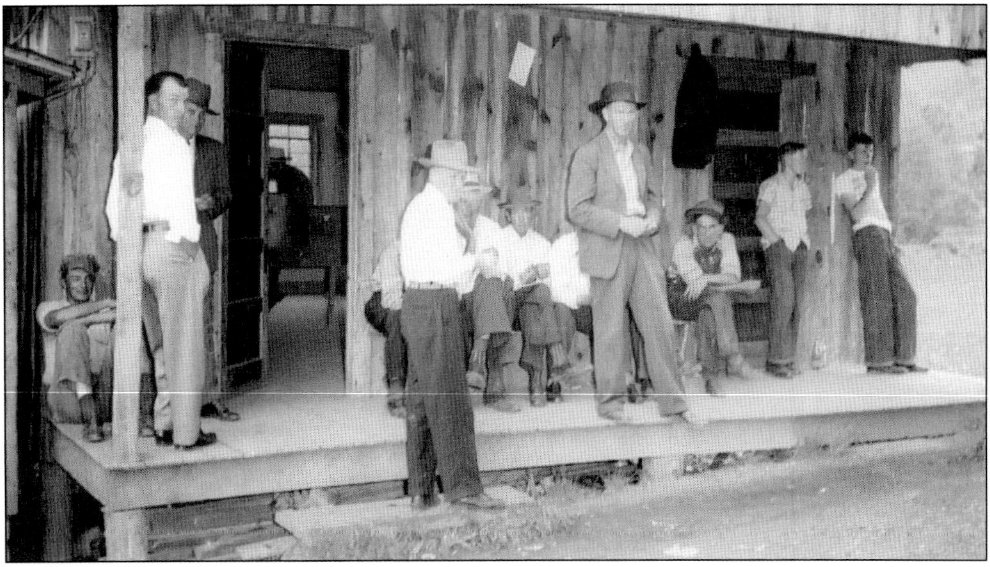

Residents congregate outside the old Gay Community Center on a late-1940s election day. The structure was still in use as a polling place into the mid-1970s. Pictured from left to right are George Webb, Roy Buchanan, Joe Bishop, Coot Turpin (inside), Earl Hughes, Chunk Cowan, Sam Buchanan, and John Deitz. The men to the right are unidentified. (Courtesy of Leo Cowan.)

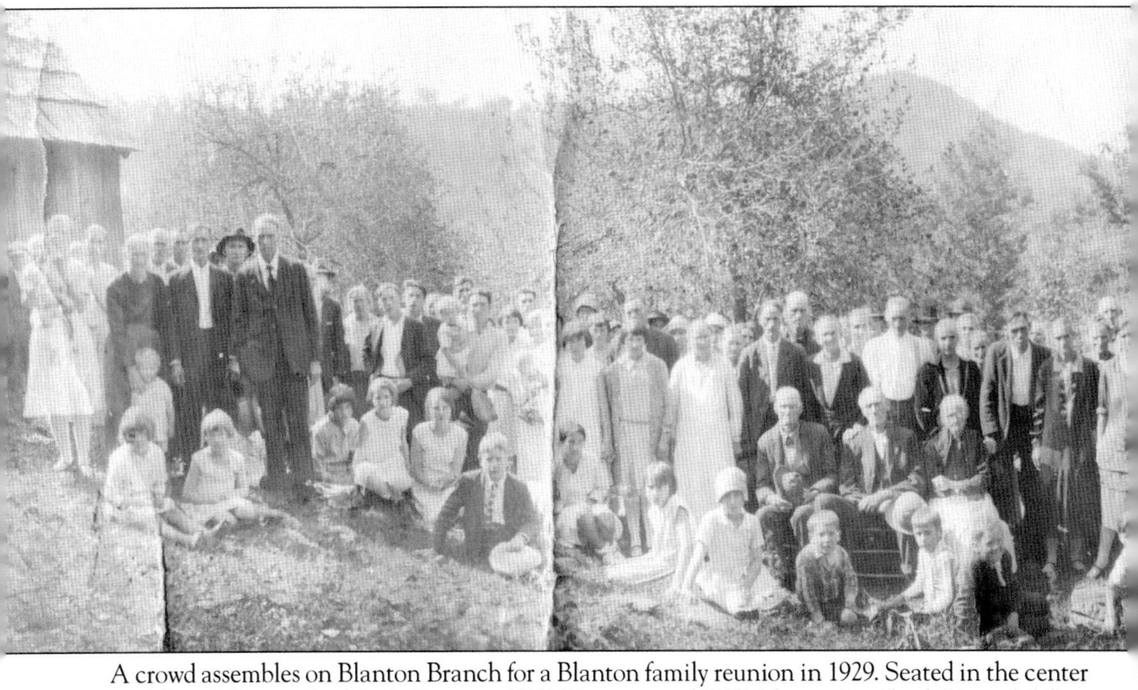

A crowd assembles on Blanton Branch for a Blanton family reunion in 1929. Seated in the center are, from left to right, Mark Blanton, Will Blanton, and Will Blanton's wife, dePiney Adeline Ensley Blanton. Children include Carrie Blanton Wagner, Gladys Shuler Henson, Willard Norman, Brodee Shuler Wiley, Edith Parris Jones, Audrey Shuler Springer (wearing hat), Lucas

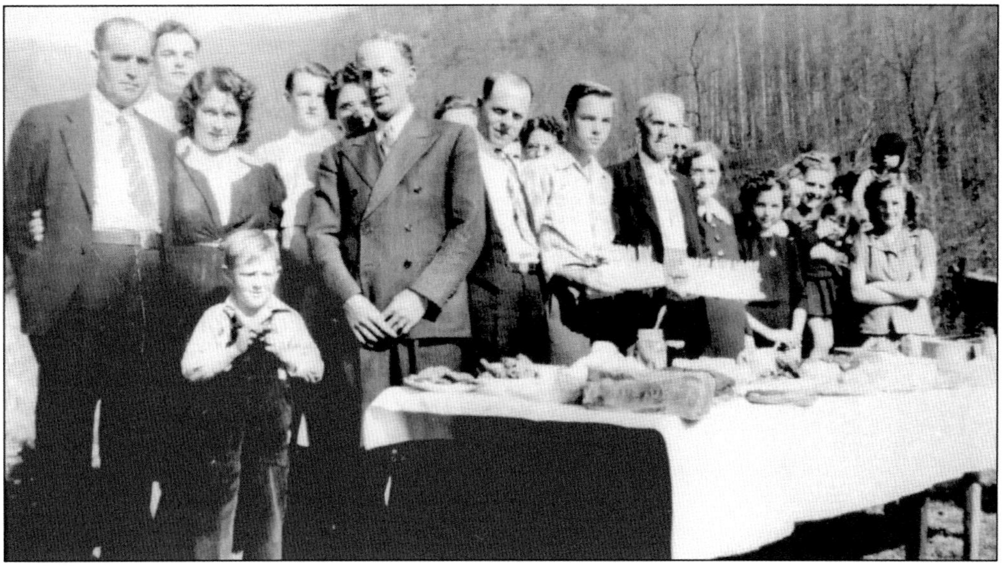

The family of Estes Bryson gathered at his Buff Creek home in November 1943 to celebrate his 74th birthday and the 15th birthday of one of his grandsons, *Asheville Citizen-Times* columnist Bob Terrell. Pictured from left to right are Claude Bryson, Kenneth Terrell, Martha Bryson, Joe McClure (boy in front), Roy McClure, Emma Bryson, Clyde Bryson, Lou Bryson, Cicero Bryson, Birdell Terrell, Bob Terrell, Estes Bryson, Raymond McClure, Tennie Bryson, Eddie Lou Terrell, Nettie McClure, Irene Bryson, Nancy Bryson, Bobby O'Kelly (boy in back), and Betty McClure. (Courtesy of Gene McClure.)

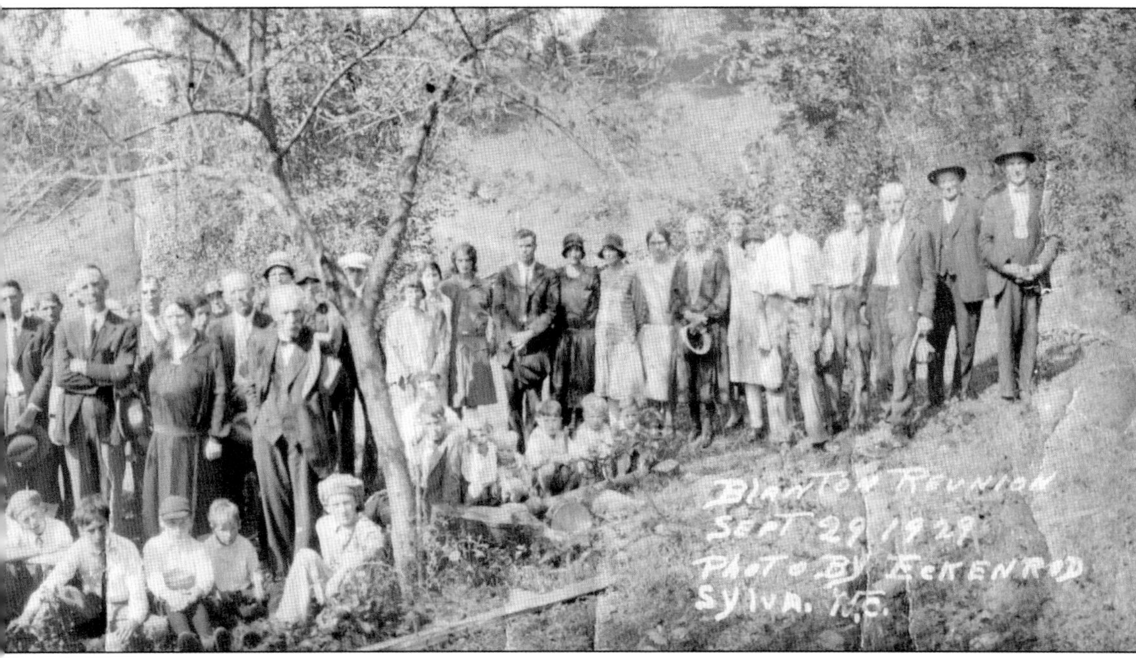

Shuler, Beryl Shuler, Wade Hoyle, Cecil Blanton, and Charles Blanton. Others present were Gold Hoyle, Roy Blanton, Julie Crawford, Beulah Cogdill Ensley, Bonnie Shuler, Annie Cogdill Blanton, Julie Crawford Parris, Berie Green Pannell, Lloyd Shuler, and Julius Carson. (Courtesy of Ginger Fullbright.)

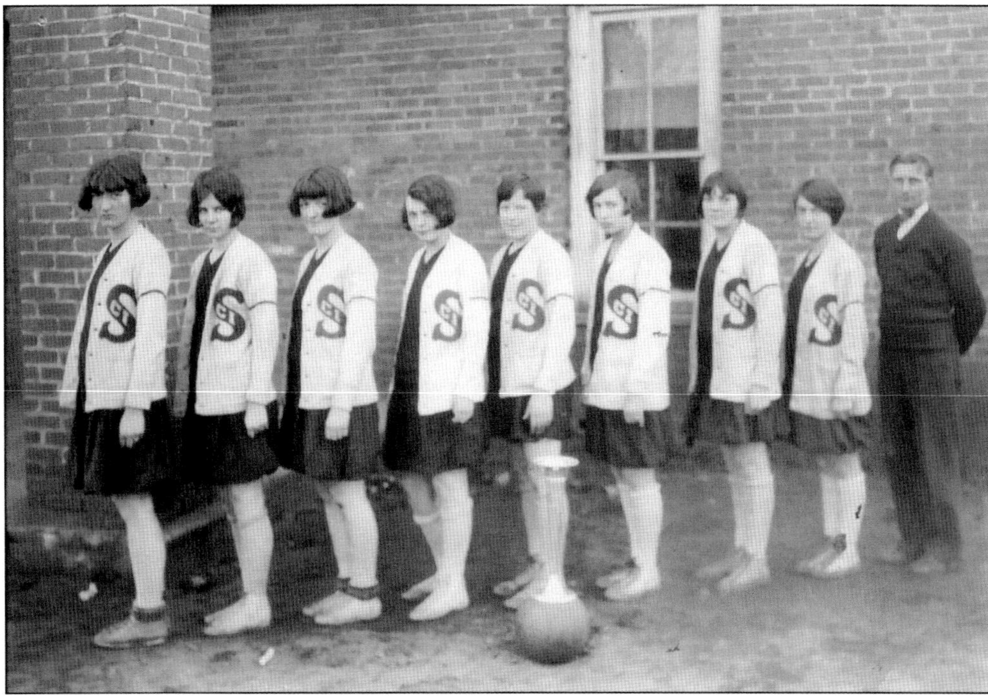

Sylva Collegiate Institute was a Baptist-affiliated, coeducational school that operated in Sylva from 1898 to 1932. Members of the school's 1928 girls' basketball team (above) included, from left to right, Jometa Higdon, Lou Hooper, Will Nell Higdon, Rebecca Ray, Hazel Higdon, Jessie Higdon, Pauline Calhoun, and Peggy Burford, with coach Manor G. Roberts. The institute's original dining and society hall is shown below. (Courtesy of Rachel Phillips.)

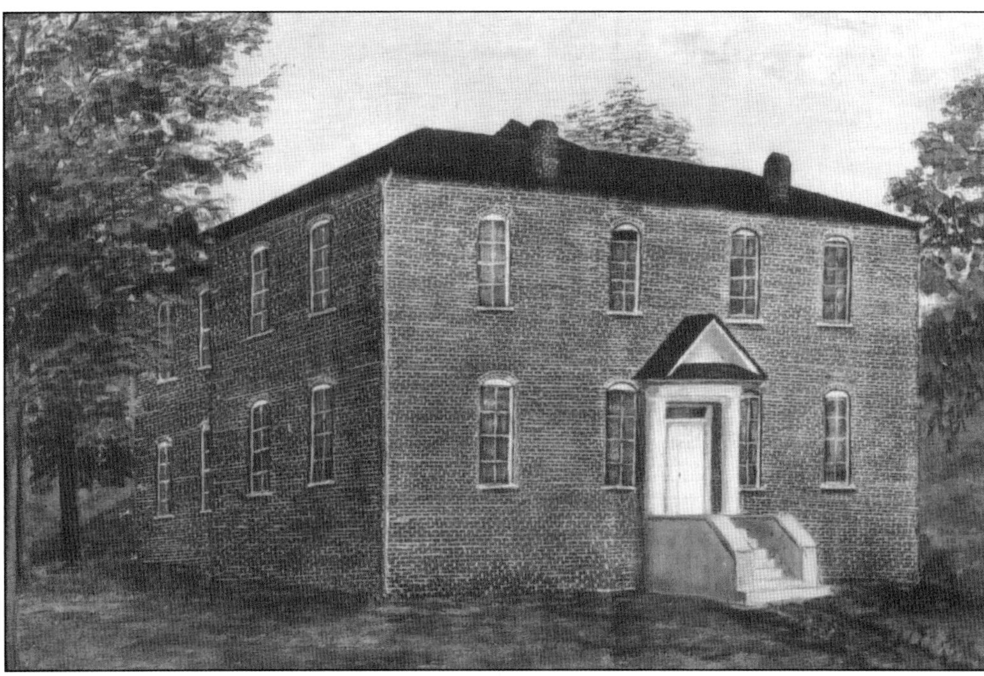

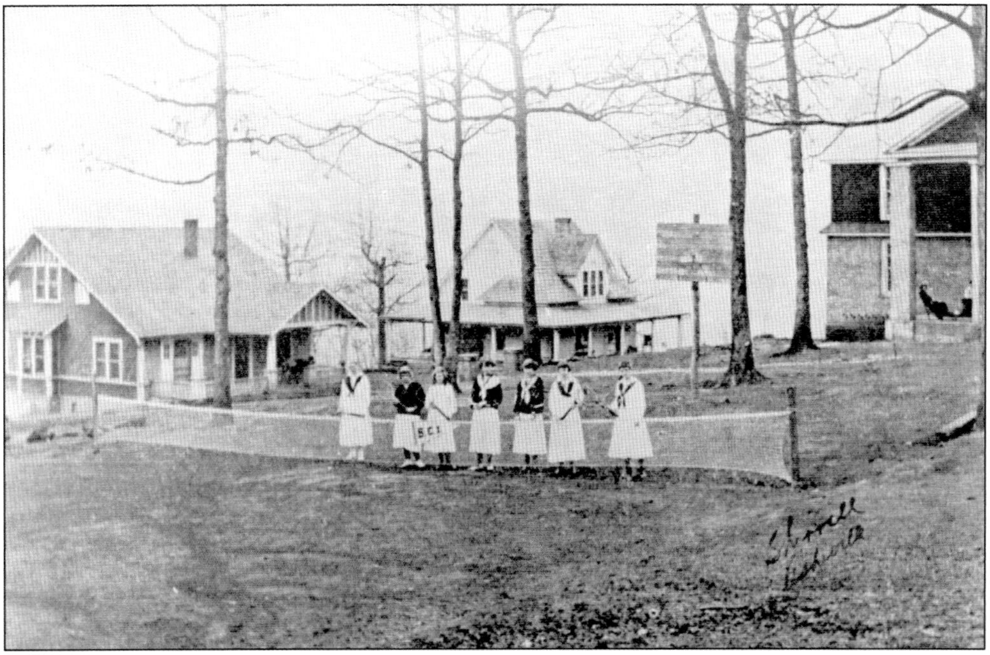

Sylva Collegiate Institute's tennis club is pictured on campus in this undated photograph. The school's administration building was located on the corner of Allen and Hampton Streets; the area behind it is still known as College Hill. (Courtesy of Dorris Beck.)

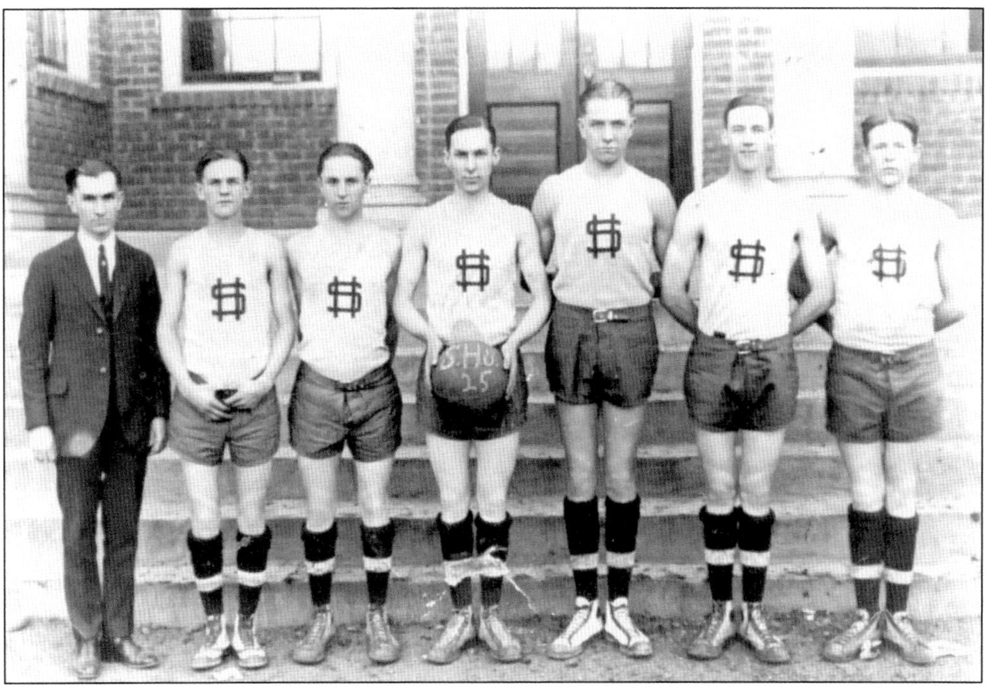

In 1925, Sylva Central High School sponsored its first men's basketball team. Pictured from left to right are coach V. B. Cooper, Harrison Cathey, Felix Potts, Dick Potts, Arthur Fincannon, Sayre Moore, and Ralph Sutton. (Courtesy of Rachel Phillips.)

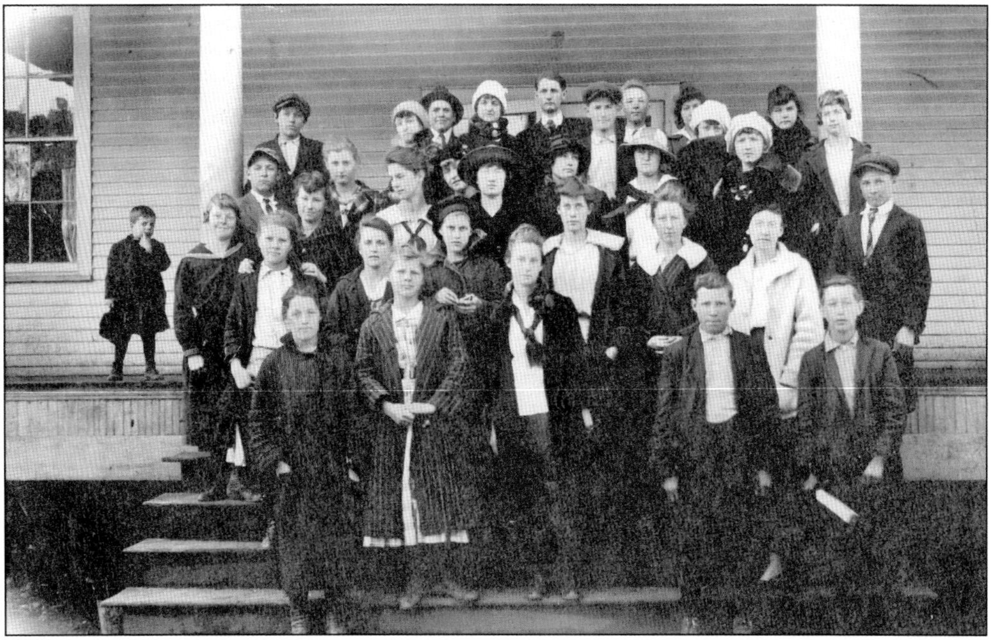

Sylva High students gathered on the school's steps in 1917 include Bessie Higdon, Ruth Hensley, Elizabeth Candler, Lavinia Picklesimer, Bessie Mae Moss, Christine Cathey, Myrtle Henson, Nettie Franklin, teacher Laura Sullivan, Zada Ashe, Jim Ashe, Nita Garrett, Margaret Candler, Dorothy McKee, Julian Cathey, Rebecca Cathey, Clyde Buchanan, Bob Garrett, Everett Harris, Christine Nichols, and Grace Cogdill. The small boy on the left is John Lambert Hooper. The school building was located where the town swimming pool has been since the 1930s. In the landscape below, which was taken around 1920 from Sylvan Heights, the school is the large building on the left, and the Jackson County Courthouse is on the right. (Above courtesy of Audrey Jones Tritt; below photograph by George Sherrill, courtesy of Ann Melton.)

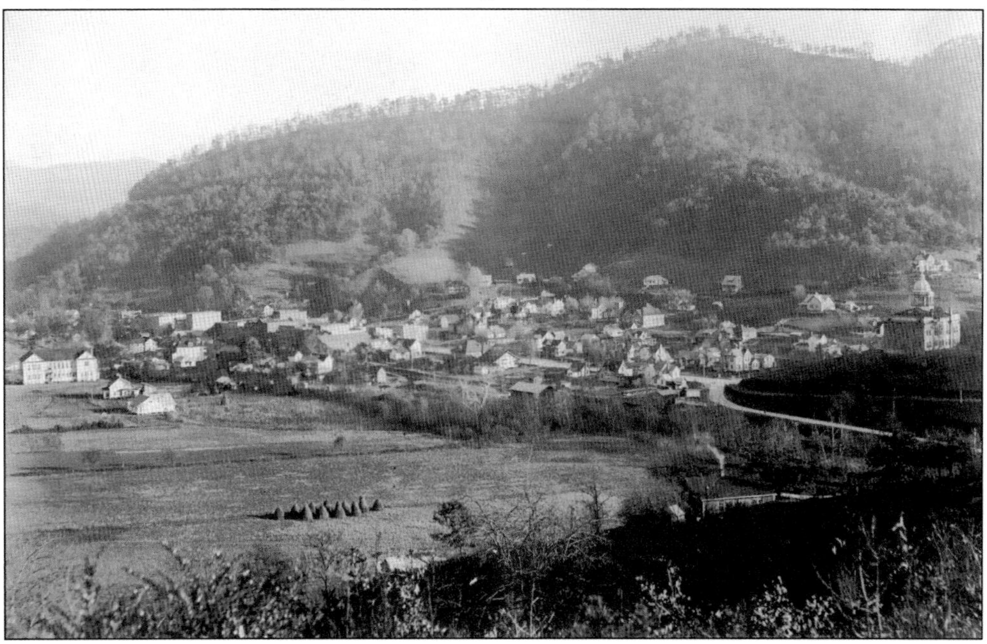

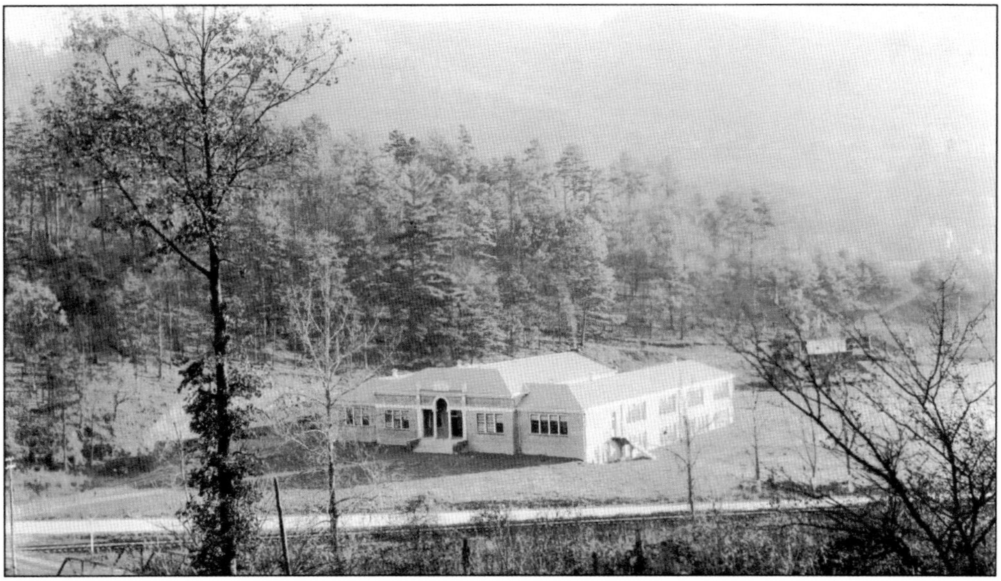

Sylva High School (above) was built in 1924 in what is now Mark Watson Park. An elementary school was added to the right of the high school five years later. The members of Sylva Elementary's seventh-grade class pose below in 1936. Seen from left to right are (first row) Jimmy McLain, Elsie Hyatt, Dorothy Queen, mascot Frank Crawford Jr., Grace Lloyd, Virginia Clark, Dorothy Warren, Irene Paxton, Willa Mae Clemmons, and Homer Franklin; (second row) Kathleen McGiness, Mildred Sumner, Geraldine Price, Jeanette Queen, Nancy Young, Polly Wilson, Maggie Allison, Daisy Frady, and Melita Fox; (third row) R. L. Glenn, Winnie Beasley, Ethel Wiseman, Nell Fox, Ilean Dillard, Thelma Monteith, Pearl Henson, Alma Plemmons, Mae Conner, and principal Frank Crawford Sr.; (fourth row) Joe Deitz, J. C. Dillard, Bobby Hall, Ruth Deitz, Bonnie Estes, Hadley Kilpatrick, Harry Crowell, and Ernest Jamison. (Above photograph by George Sherrill, courtesy of Ann Melton; below courtesy of Frank Crawford Jr.)

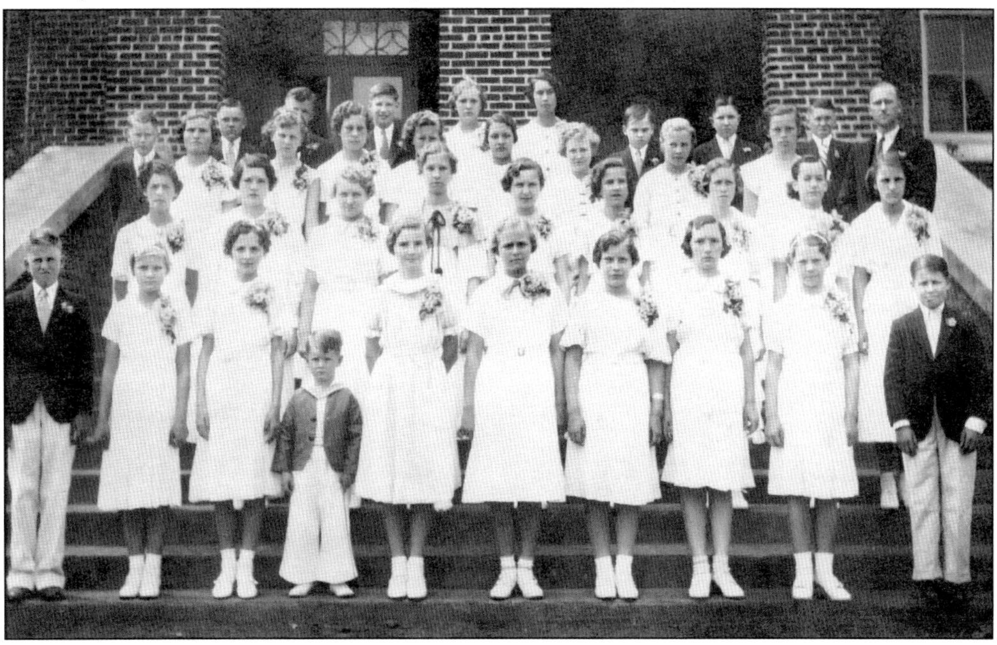

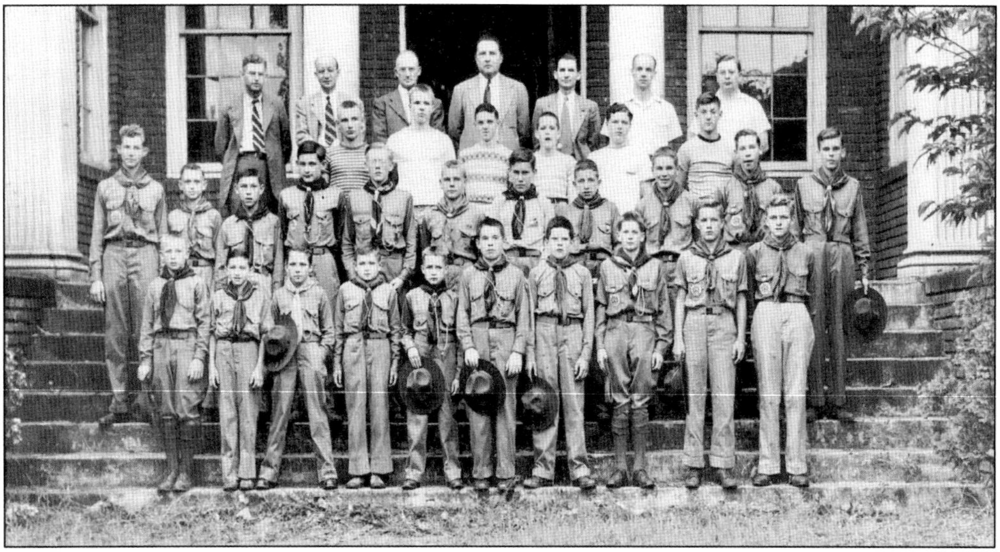

Members of a 1945 Sylva Boy Scout troop are, from left to right, (first row) Chig Cagle, Frank Holden, T. C. Shepard, John Robinson, Louis Monteith, Thornton Cabe, Charles Cope, Frank Crawford, R. L. Madison, and Jack Greene; (second row) Carroll Ashe, Ray Davis, Tommy Queen, Harold Morgan, Charles Stillwell, Boyd Sutton, Derel Monteith, William Holden, Jack Hennessee, Phillip Jones, and Bennie Reese; (third row) Joe Wild, Jim Madison, John Gibson, Dan Allison, Randall Goldman, and Walter Jones; (fourth row) Scoutmasters W. C. Hennessee, Hugh Monteith, Herbert Gibson, O. E. Brookhyser, Alliney Bryson, Dennis Barkley, and Claude Campbell. (Courtesy of Jim Madison.)

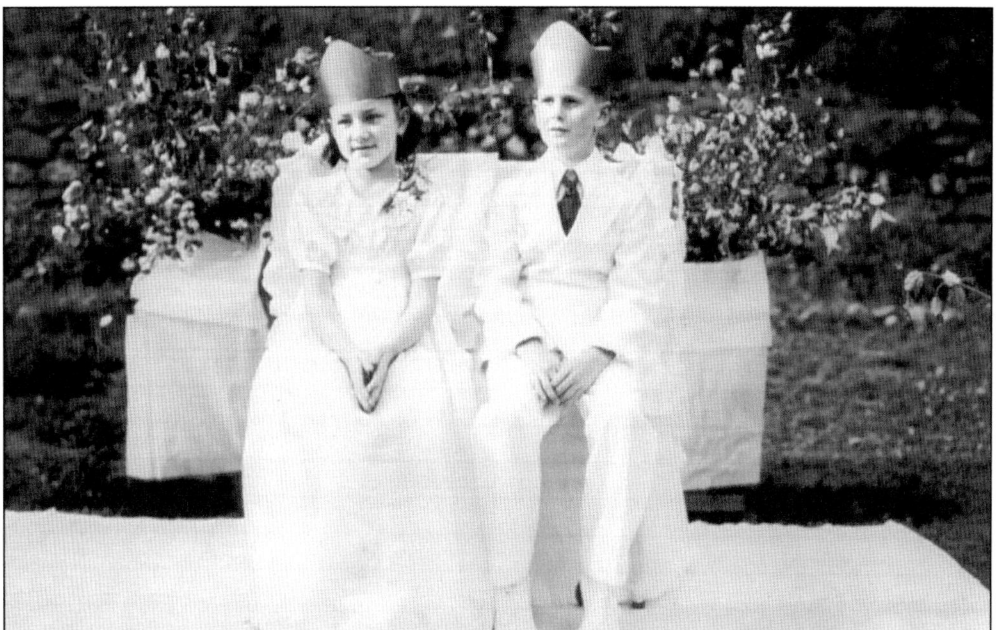

Frank Crawford Jr. and Joanne Moody, both seven years old, were chosen May Day king and queen in 1937. Sylva's annual May Day event was held in front of the clubhouse by the swimming pool. That building now serves as the Golden Age Center. (Courtesy of Frank Crawford Jr.)

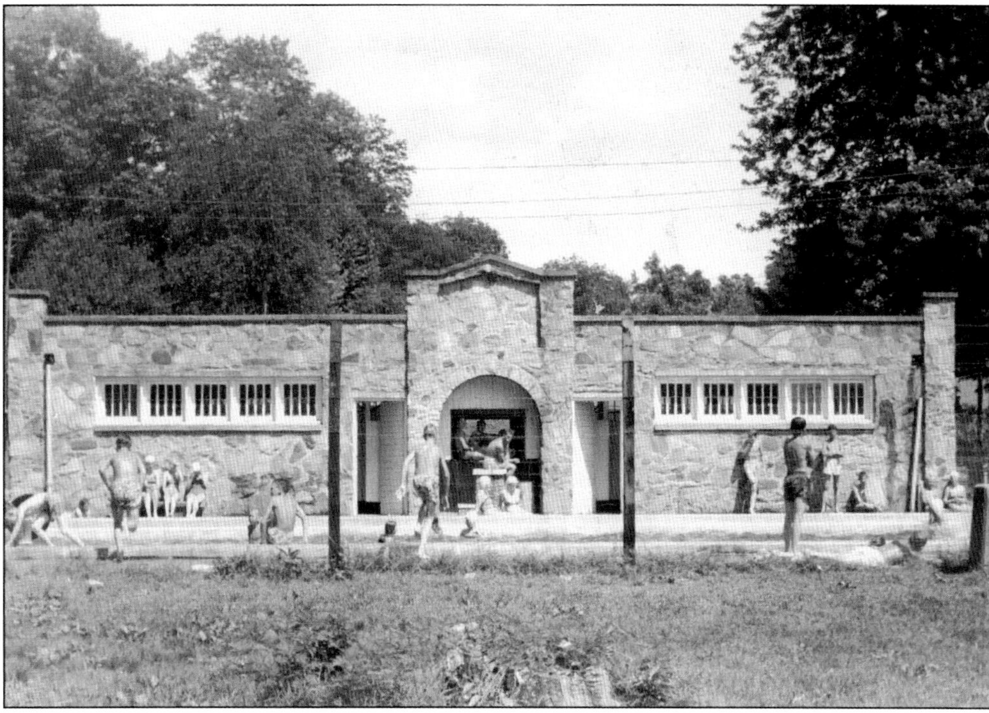

When the Sylva Swimming Pool (above) opened on June 1, 1937, it was the only municipally owned pool west of Asheville, and bathing suits rented for 10¢. Built by the Works Progress Administration, the old pool was torn down in 1969 to make way for the Roscoe Poteet Pool, which remains in use after extensive renovations were completed in 2001. Below, local residents enjoy the pool during the year it opened. The six at right are, from left to right, Frank Davis, Sam Roane, Margret "Cotton" Sherrill Roane, Elizabeth "Curl" Sherrill Davis, Frank Crawford Jr., and Edith Sherrill Crawford (lying down). The others are unidentified. (Above courtesy of the *Sylva Herald*; below courtesy of Frank Crawford Jr.)

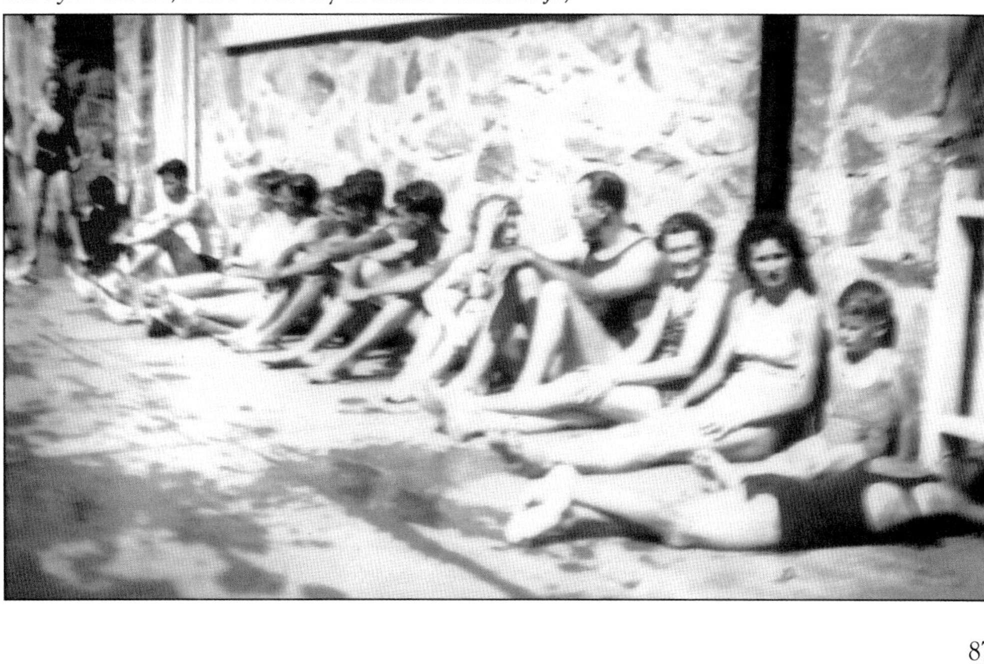

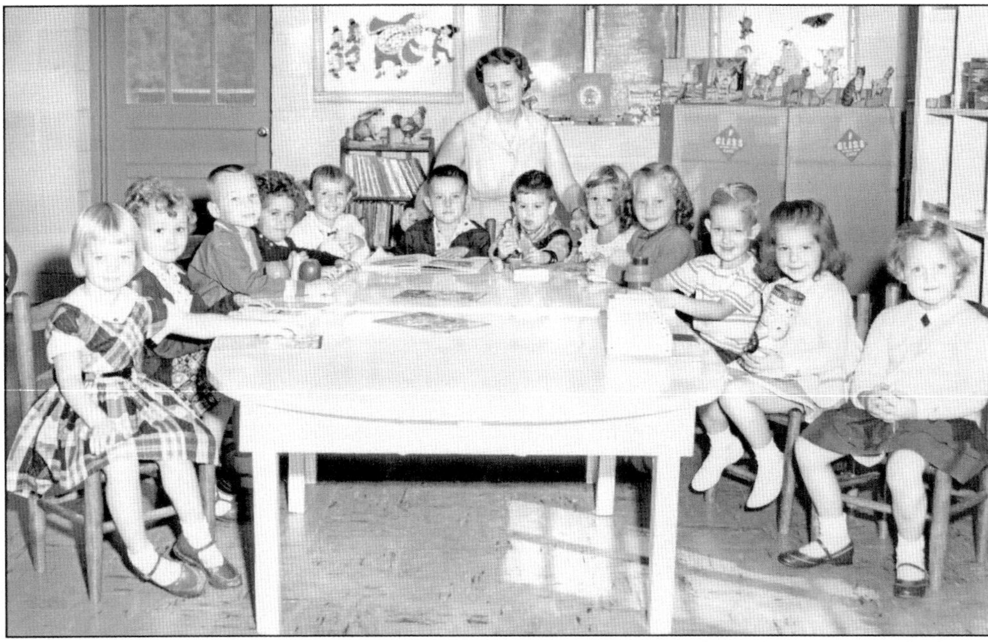

Docia Garrett's 1956–1957 kindergarten class met in the basement of St. John's Episcopal Church in Sylva. Shown from left to right are Becky Dewees, Janet Gibson, Hugh Raxter, Carolyn Wilson, Janis Stovall, Boyd Greer, Patrick McGuire, Katherine Dillard, Debbie Crawford, Keith Ramsey, Beverly Tucker, and Teresa Dillard. Garrett is standing behind the children. Jackson County Public Schools did not include kindergarten until around 1975. (Courtesy of the *Sylva Herald*.)

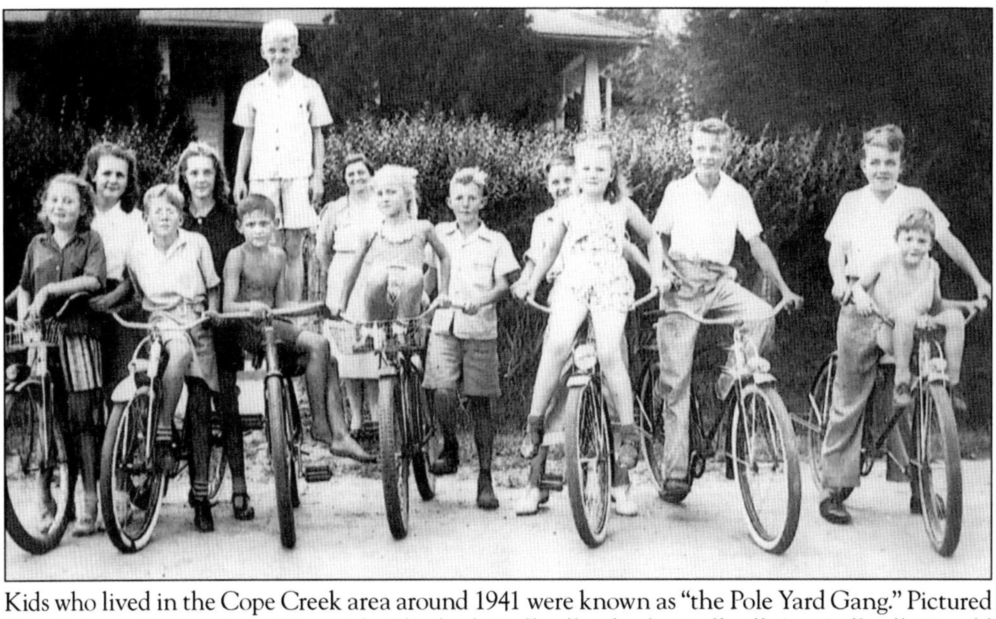

Kids who lived in the Cope Creek area around 1941 were known as "the Pole Yard Gang." Pictured from left to right are Jean Monteith, Elizabeth Stillwell, Charles Stillwell, Joy Stillwell, Harold Morgan Jr., Charles "Sonny Boy" Yonally Jr., Lula Brown, Dorothy Ashe, Carroll Ashe, Fred Conner, Mary Cole Stillwell, Ray Ashe, J. C. Brown, and E. P. "Chub" Stillwell. By the time this photograph was taken, the pole yard, which once treated tall trees with creosote for telephone and power poles, had become a log yard. (Courtesy of Ray Ashe.)

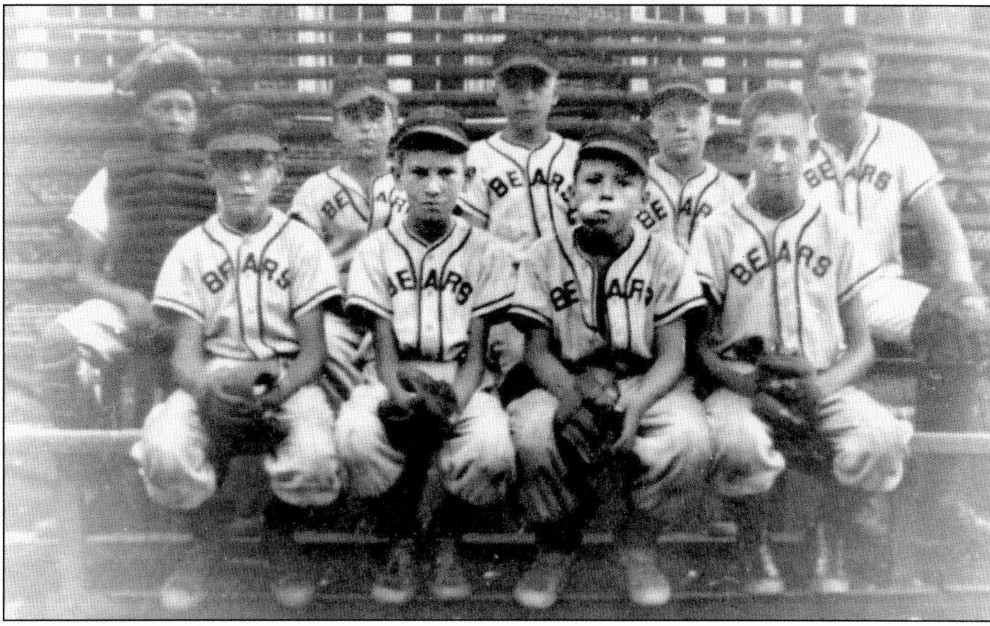

The 1954 Bears, a local little league team for boys ages 9 through 12, included, from left to right, (first row) Tom Jones, Bill Fox, Scotty Cooper, and Richard Williams; (second row) Alan Allman, Tom Kelly, Forrest Bryson, Tommy Allen, and Tom Fox. (Courtesy of Bill Fox.)

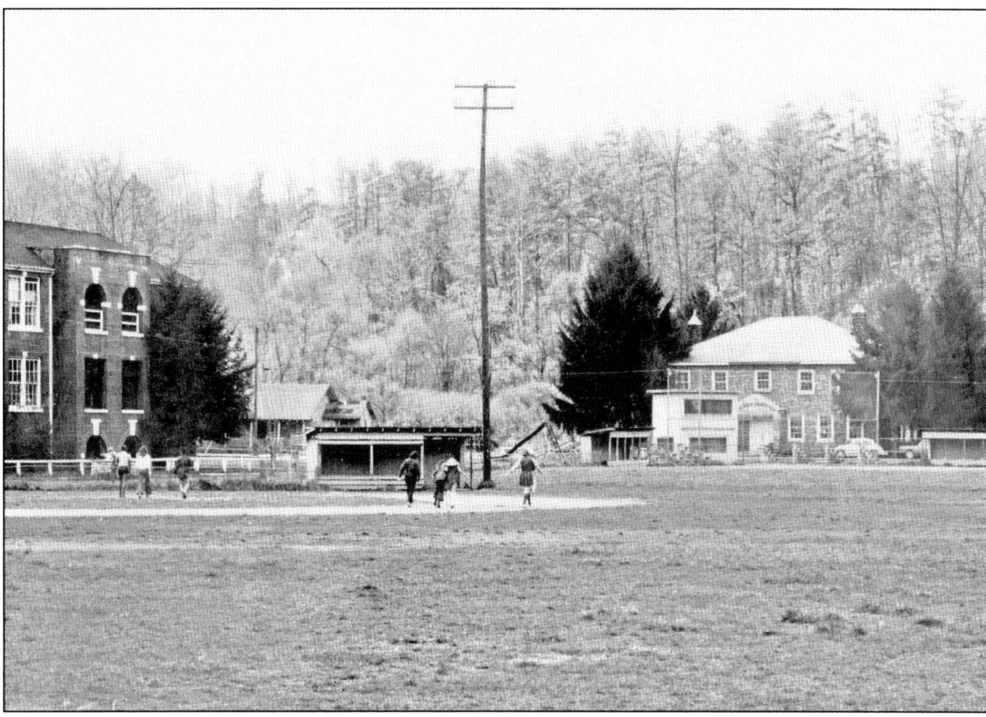

Sylva Elementary School (left) opened in 1929 at what is now Mark Watson Park. The rock building to the right is the old high school agricultural building, which housed the Jackson County Recreation and Parks Department until 1999. The elementary school, in use until Fairview Elementary opened in 1973, was razed in 1974. (Courtesy of Jackson County Schools.)

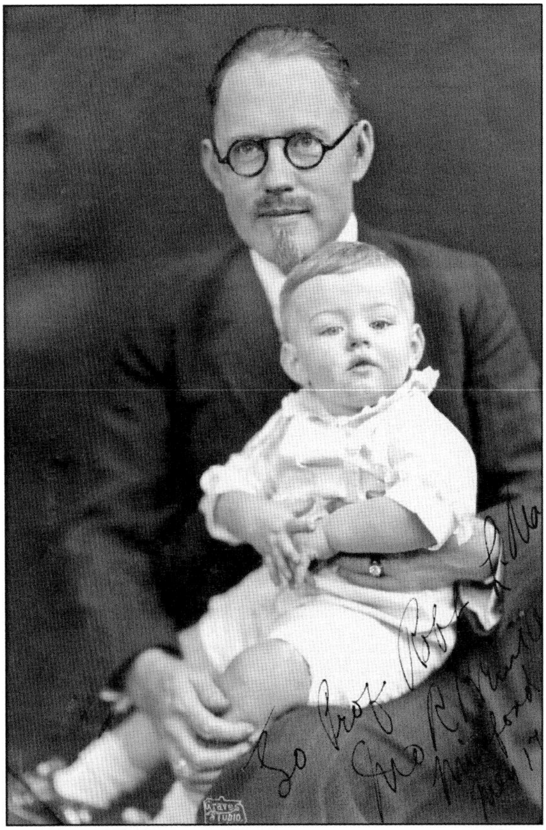

Jackson County's most notorious native son is Dr. John R. Brinkley (left, with his son "Johnnie-Boy"), who was born east of Sylva and orphaned at age 10. After attending medical school, he began treating male impotence by transplanting goat glands into aging men and performed hundreds of surgeries at hospitals he founded in Milford, Kansas; Del Rio, Texas; and Little Rock, Arkansas. When Kansas authorities stripped him of both his radio and medical licenses, he moved to Del Rio and constructed his radio transmitter in Mexico. Brinkley, who once owned the most powerful radio station in the world, ended his career in bankruptcy court. He died a broken man in 1942. Brinkley's radio show introduced country music luminaries like the Carter Family as well as Sylva talent like Samantha Bumgarner (below). In 1924, the Lovesfield resident was probably the first Appalachian banjo player to cut a commercial record. (Left courtesy of Western Carolina University Special Collections; below courtesy of the *Sylva Herald*.)

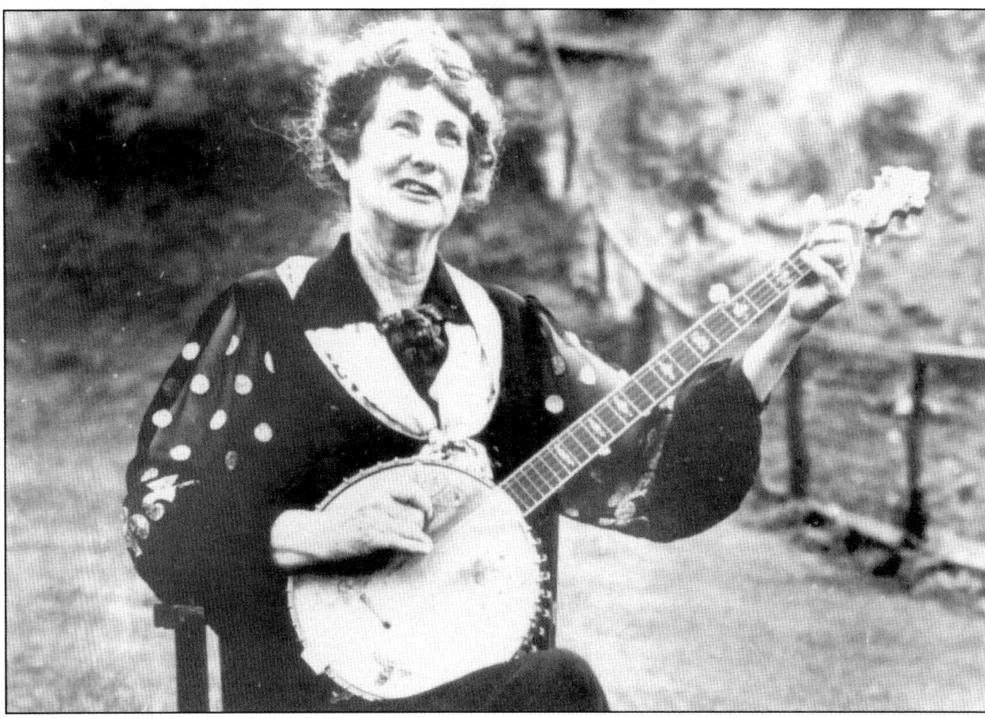

Fiddler Harry Cagle, who operated several downtown service stations through the years, performed with his band, the Country Cousins, at the 1982 World's Fair in Knoxville, Tennessee. Cagle, who died in 1998 at age 80, learned to play from Samantha Bumgarner. During a 1989 interview, he said that Bumgarner had taught him to play the banjo because she preferred the fiddle and needed a banjo player. He wanted to learn the fiddle, too, but had to teach himself. "I played the banjo, but I watched that fiddle," he said in 1989. As a teenager, Cagle went to Texas with Bumgarner to play on Dr. John Brinkley's radio show. (Courtesy of Carroll Cagle.)

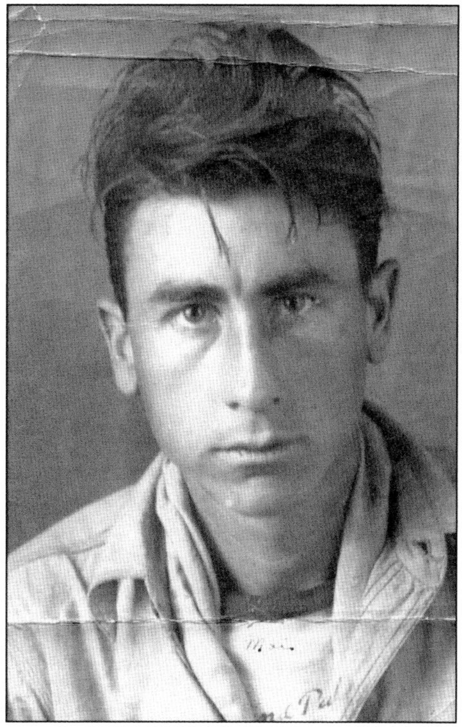

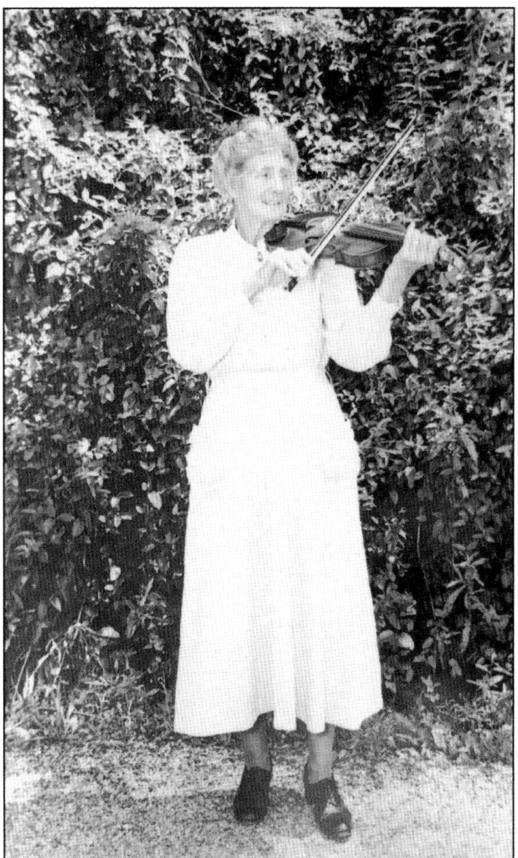

Legendary local musician Samantha Bumgarner plays her fiddle at her Lovesfield home. According to a flyer she used to advertise performances, each event promised "musical entertainment composed of string music and singing" at a cost of 75¢ for adults and 50¢ for children. The flyer also claimed the performance would be "a strictly clean and high-class rendition of old-time music." The manager was listed as "Aunt" Samantha Bumgarner. (Courtesy of Wanda Cagle.)

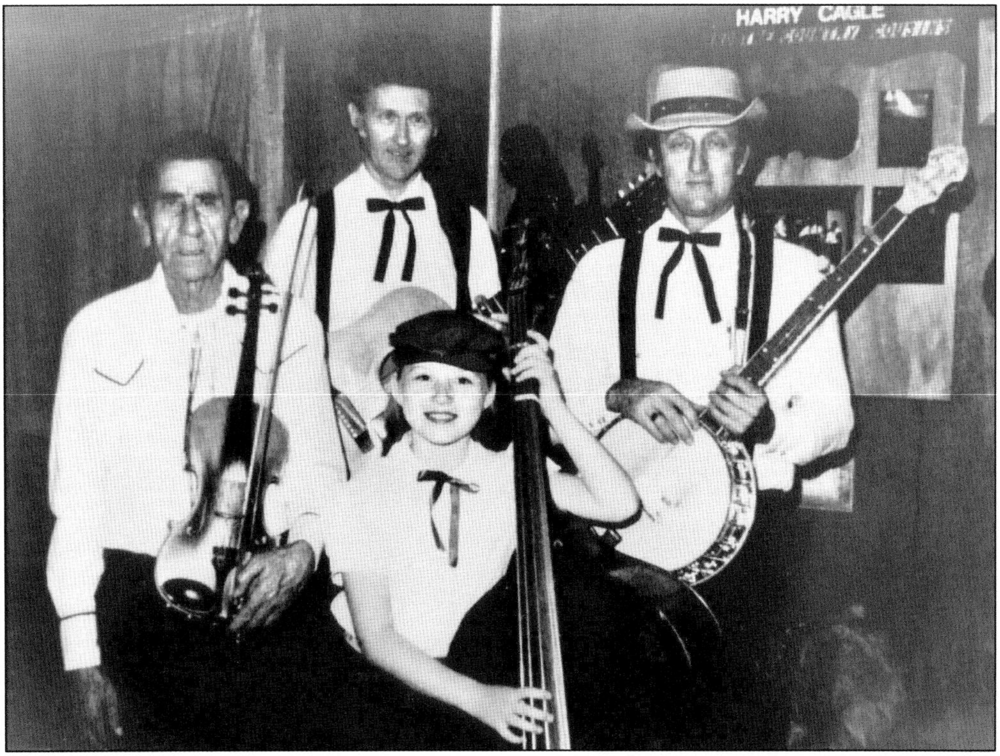

Fiddler Harry Cagle (far left) is pictured with the Country Cousins in 1982. At that time, band members were Joe Deitz (left), Chrystal Deitz (center), and Bill Deitz. Other Country Cousin lineups included Hayes Nicholson, Claude Buchanan, and Phil Stovall. (Courtesy of Joe Deitz.)

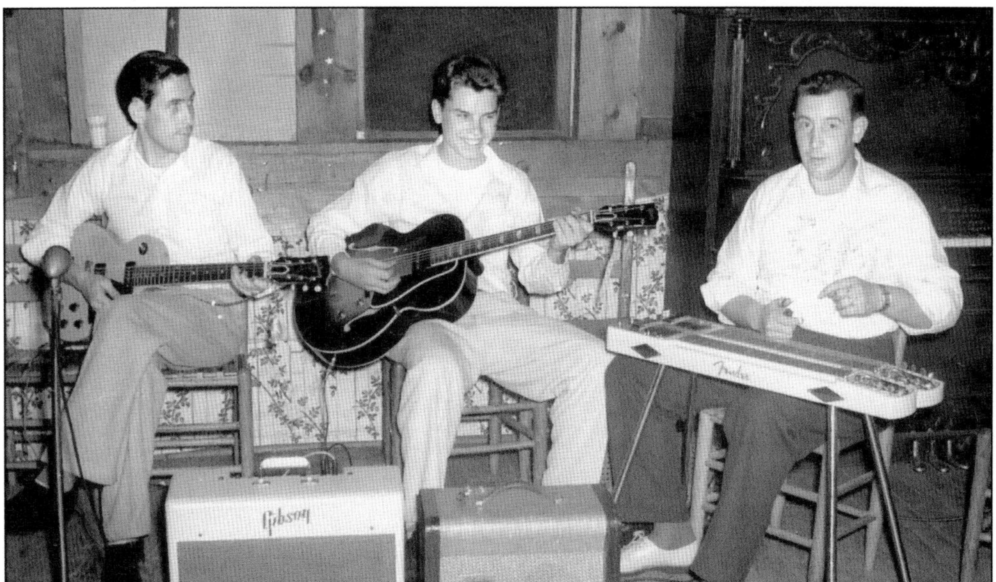

Perry Rhodes (left), Scroop Lewis (center), and Wallace Swann formed a local band that played around Sylva and across the region in 1949. Harry Cagle sometimes performed with the group. (Courtesy of Nancy Browning.)

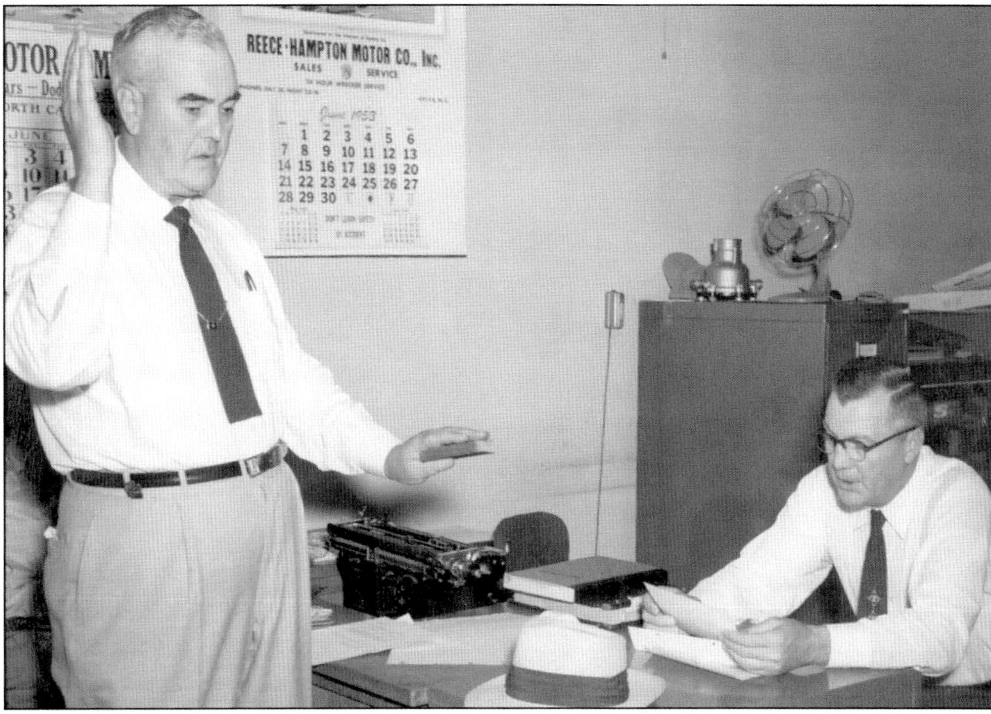

Mayor Roscoe Poteet (left) receives the oath of office from superior court judge Dan Moore in the above photograph, taken in June 1953. Poteet served as Sylva's mayor for more than 20 years, from 1953 to 1976. Moore held the office of North Carolina governor from 1965 to 1969 and later served on the state supreme court. Below, a younger Moore (right) stands on Main Street with pharmacist Gilbert Bess, who operated Sylva Pharmacy. (Above courtesy of the *Sylva Herald*; below courtesy of June Bess Anderson.)

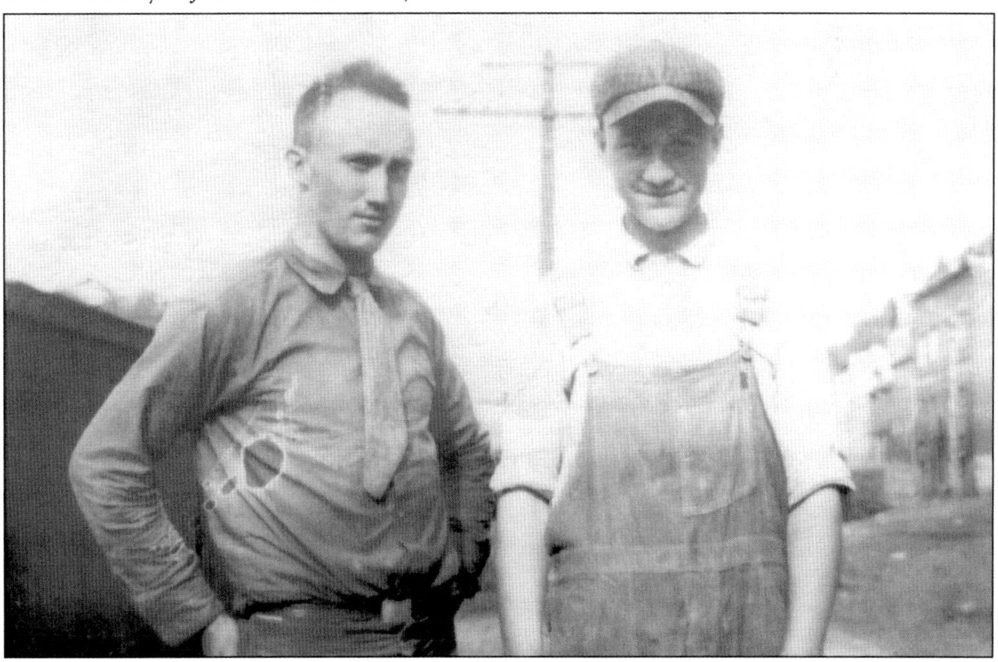

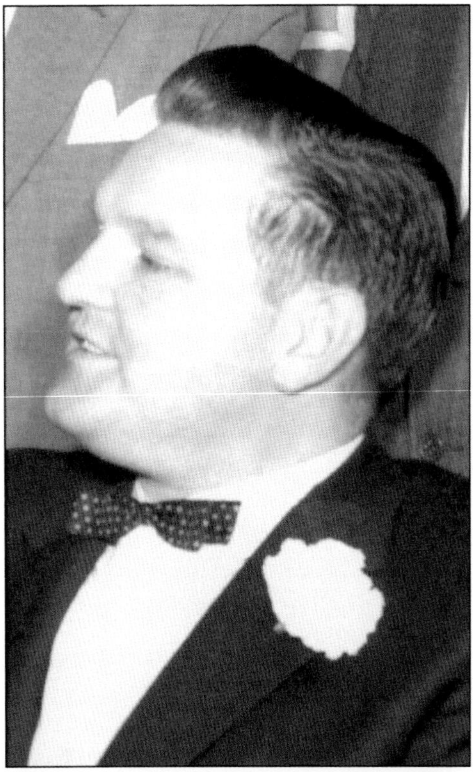

In addition to Gov. Dan Moore and Sen. Gertrude Dills McKee, elected officials who have made local history include Congressman David Hall (above), the only Jackson County resident ever elected to the U.S. House of Representatives; U.S. District Court judge Lacy Thornburg (below left), who served as North Carolina's attorney general; and Sylva Town Board member Danny Allen (below right), the first African American to be elected to public office in Jackson County. Hall was elected to Congress in 1958 but died in 1960 before completing his term. Thornburg held the office of attorney general from 1985 to 1993 and was appointed to the federal bench in 1995. Allen served on the town board from 2001 to 2007 and mounted an unsuccessful bid for mayor in 2005. (Courtesy of the *Sylva Herald*.)

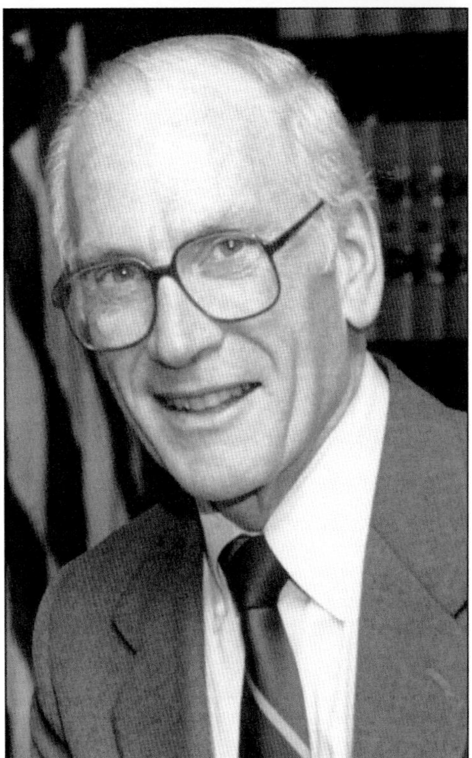

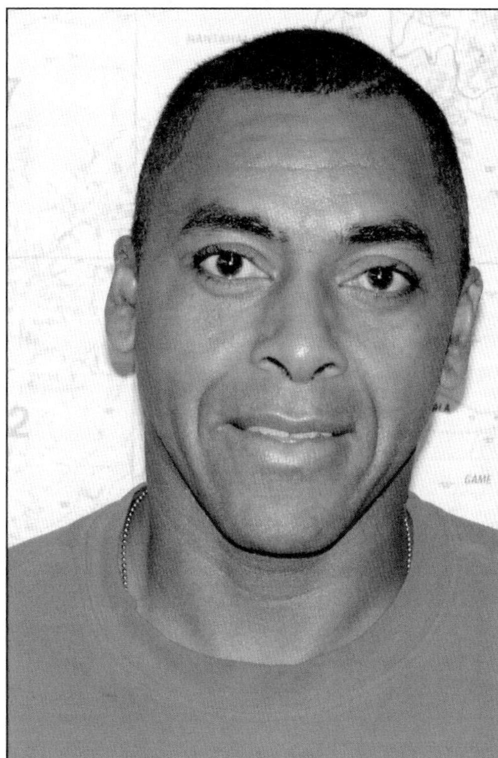

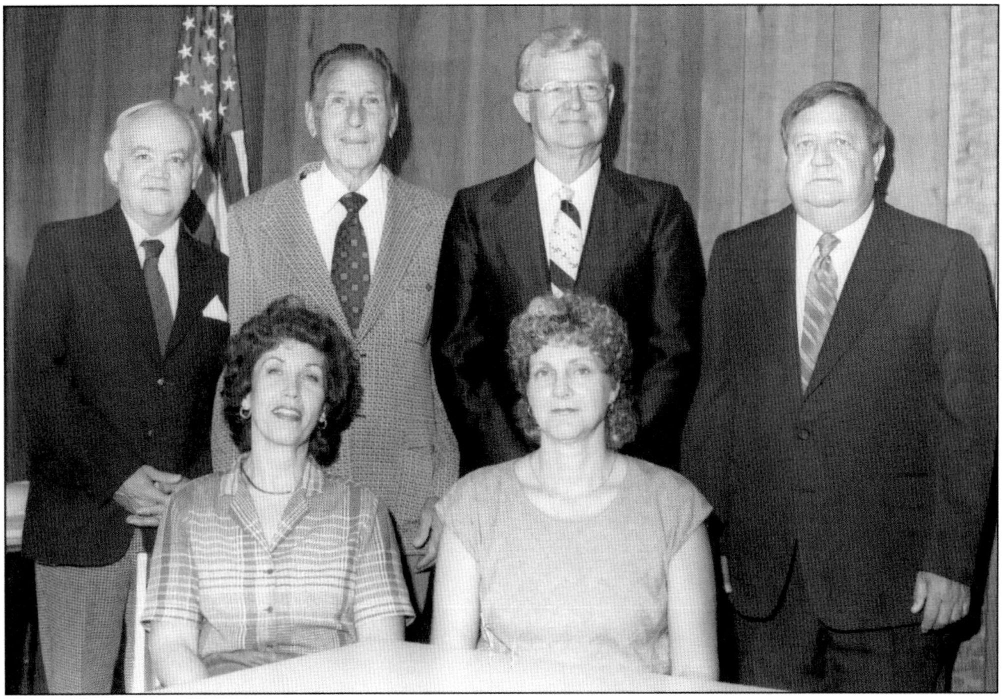

Mayor Brenda Oliver (front left) is both the first woman elected to the Sylva Town Board and the town's first female mayor. She won her town board seat in 1981 and became mayor after John Bunn resigned in 1992. Oliver was elected to the post in 1993 and won reelection bids in 1997, 2001, and 2005. The members of the town board elected in 1985 are, from left to right, (first row) Brenda Oliver and Audrey Tritt; (second row) Johnny Ahlin, Frank Buchanan, Mayor T. C. Lewis, and Harry "Straw" Stephens. (Courtesy of Audrey Jones Tritt.)

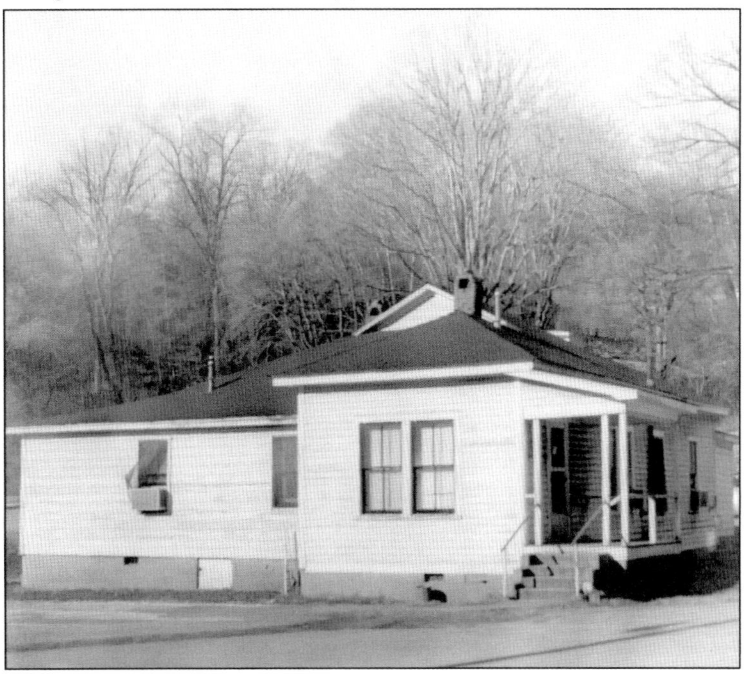

This building, which traditionally housed Sylva High School principals and later the welfare department, once stood just behind the present Sylva City Hall in the vicinity of the current swimming pool. (Courtesy of the *Sylva Herald*.)

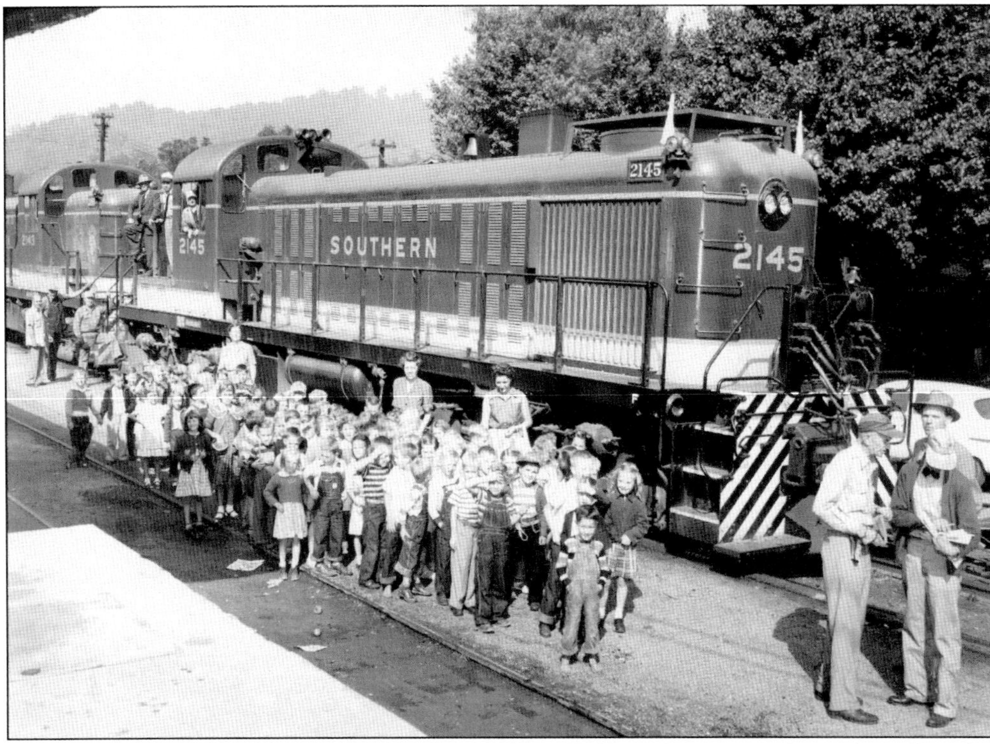

Sylva Elementary School teachers Emily Tompkins (left), Arline Evans (center), and Evelyn McMahan took their first-grade classes to see the train at the old Sylva Depot, which was torn down in the 1970s. The above photograph is thought to date from the late 1950s. The old Sylva School (below), which opened as Sylva Central High in 1924, became part of Sylva Elementary when Sylva-Webster High School was established in 1960. The building ceased to be used as a school during the 1973–1974 year, when Fairview Elementary opened. A grassroots effort by the community failed to convince commissioners to spare the building, which had seen use by the Kudzu Players as a community theater. It was razed in 1990. (Above courtesy of Arline Evans; below courtesy of the *Sylva Herald*.)

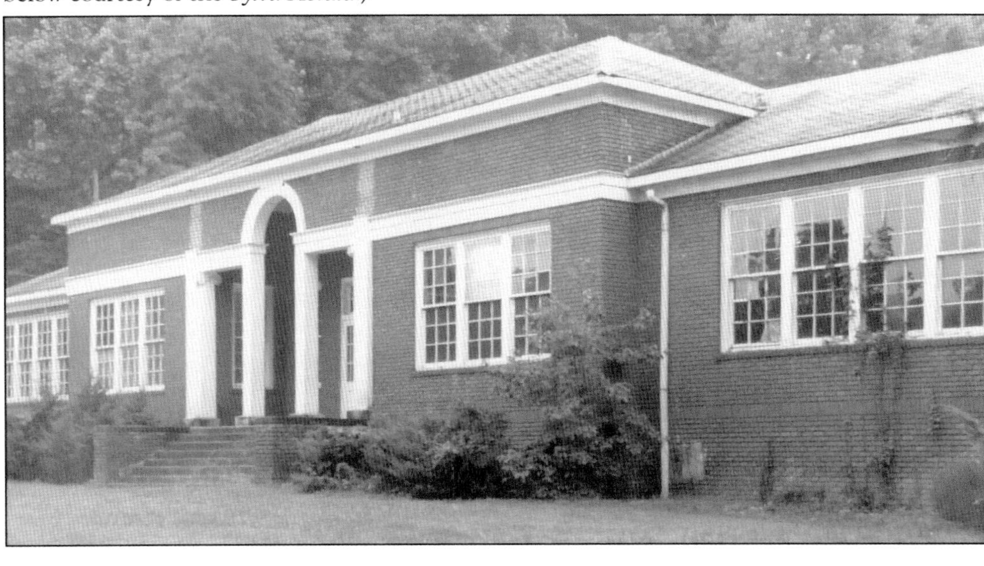

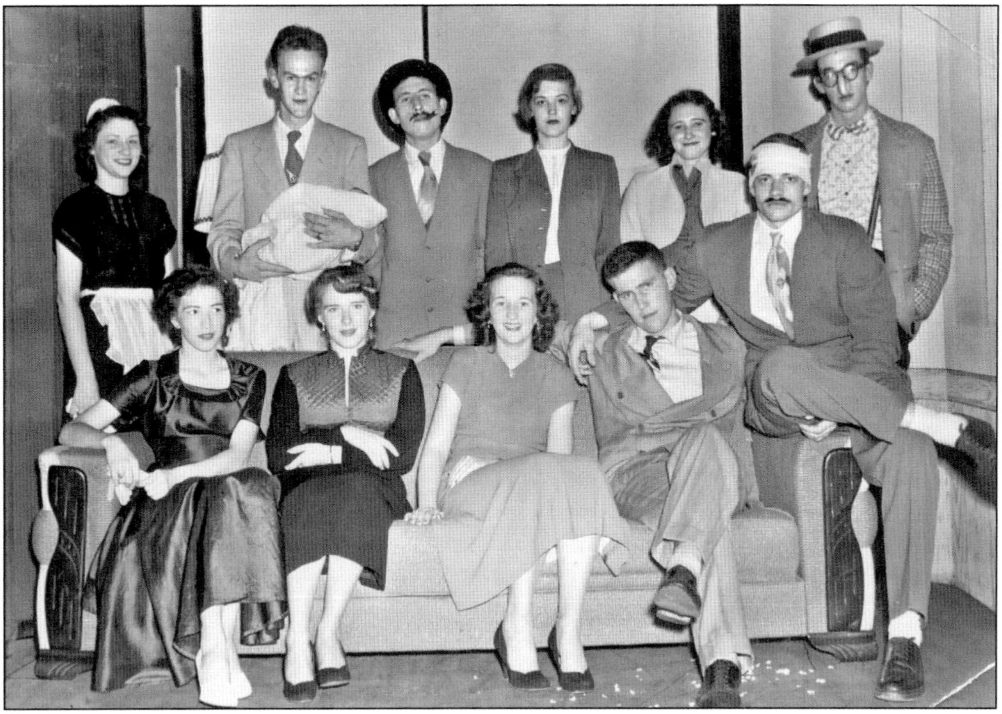

Cast members of a Sylva High School senior class play (above) from the late 1940s or early 1950s include, from left to right, (first row) Loqueta Holden, Libby Dillard, Doris Middleton, unidentified, and Zollie Fincannon; (second row) Joann Moody, ? Parks (holding baby), Perry Rhodes, unidentified, Dottie Fincannon, and Jack Morris. Sylva High's 1953 senior class, the largest the school had seen at that time, gathers on the school steps in the photograph below. (Courtesy of Nancy Browning.)

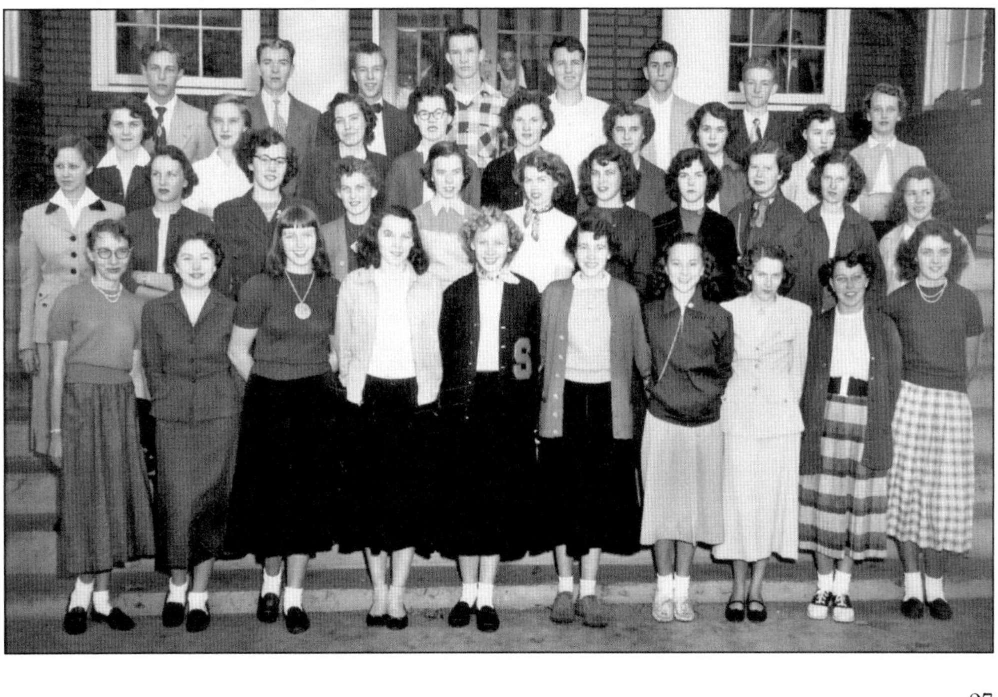

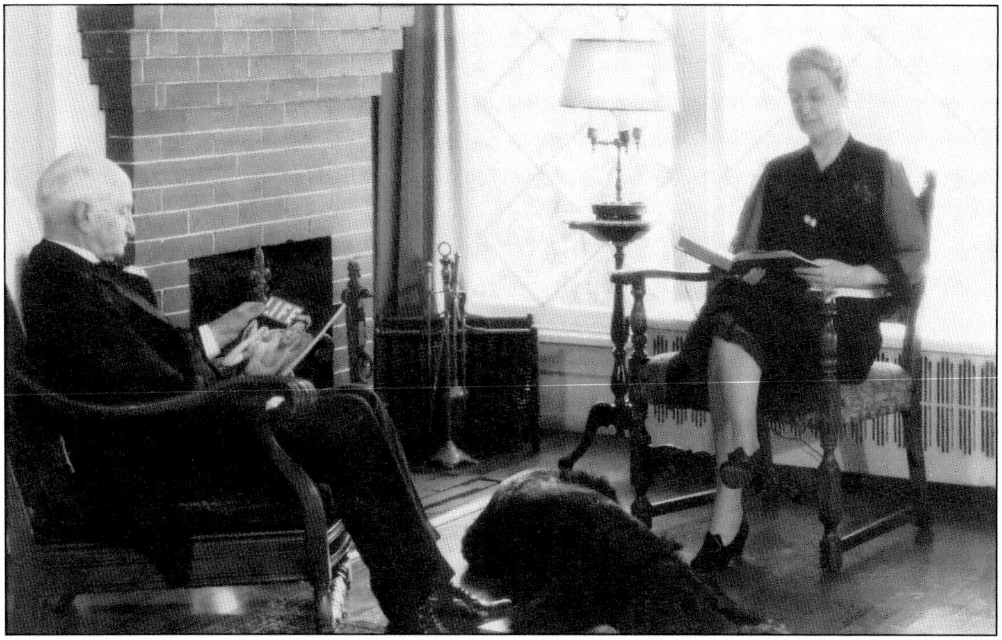

Gertrude Dills McKee (right), North Carolina's first woman senator, and her husband, leading Sylva businessman E. L. McKee, are in the living room of their Main Street home, which was torn down around 1964 to make way for the First Baptist Church sanctuary. Gertrude McKee was the daughter of Dillsboro founder William Allen Dills. (Courtesy of Ann McKee Austin.)

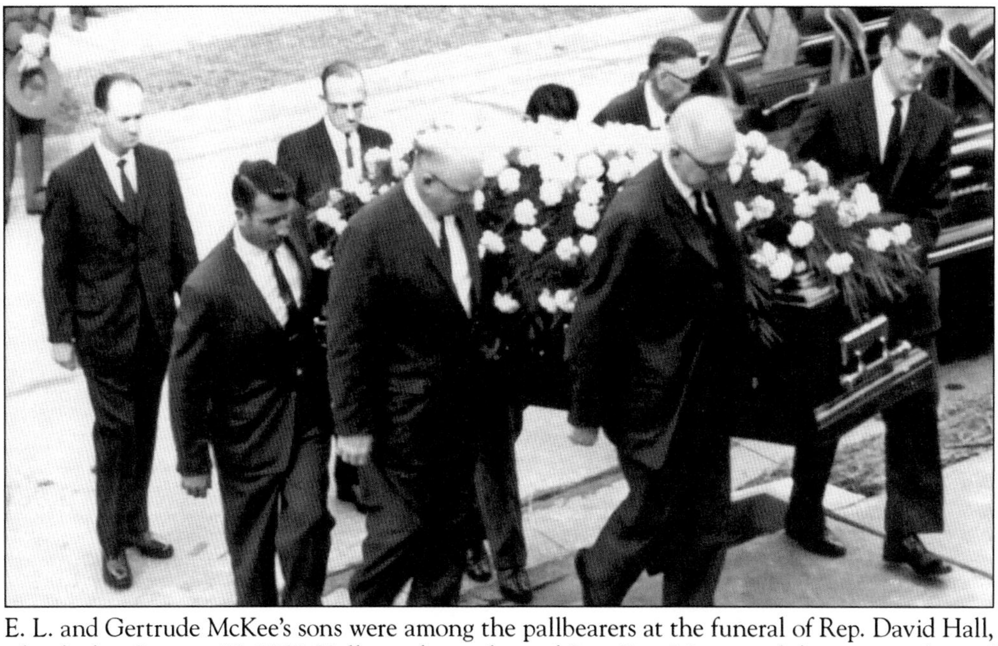

E. L. and Gertrude McKee's sons were among the pallbearers at the funeral of Rep. David Hall, who died on January 29, 1960. Hall was the nephew of Gov. Dan Moore and the great-nephew of the McKees. Pallbearers included, clockwise from far right, Judge Lacy Thornburg, who served two terms as North Carolina's attorney general; William McKee; Lyndon McKee; Ernest Burch; unidentified, Joe Ted Wilson; Andrew Wilson; Fred "Snuffy" Hooper; and Malcolm Brown. (Courtesy of the *Sylva Herald*.)

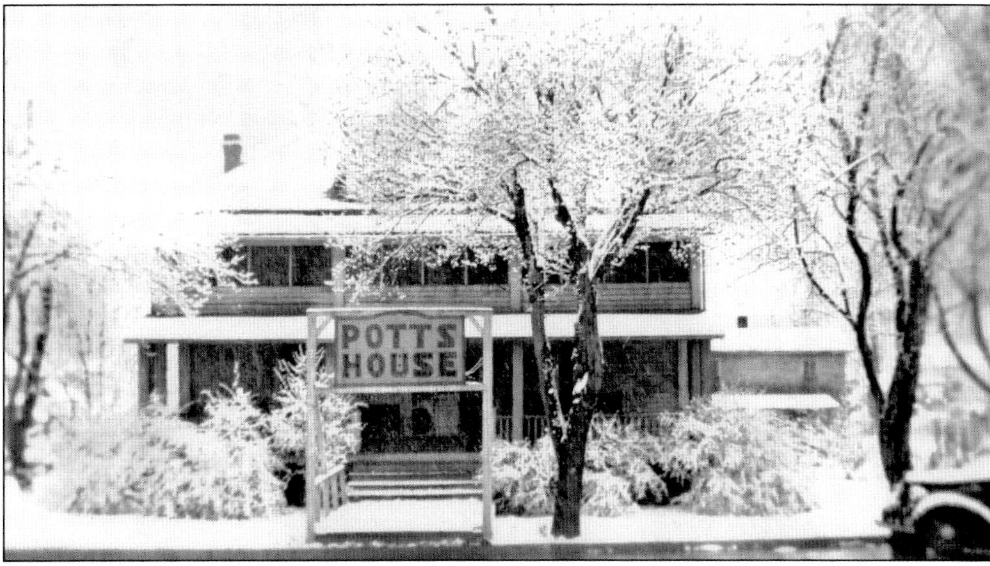

The Sylva Hotel, known as the Potts House when the above photograph was taken in the 1940s, was located across Railroad Avenue from the former train depot. The former Allison House on Cowan Street, below, was built by Cornelius Buchanan and his wife, Katie Keen Buchanan, in 1894, around the time of this photograph. J. W. McKee bought the house from Buchanan in 1909, and McKee's wife, Carrie, and daughter Dorothy sold the residence to Charlie Allison in 1923. Hattie Hilda Allison moved into the home in 1957, when she married Charlie Allison's son Edwin, and the couple lived there for 20 years before building a new house directly across the street. The Allison House changed hands three times before it was purchased in June 1984 by Dr. Clay Smallwood and his wife, Katherine, who restored and renovated the structure and continue to reside there. (Above courtesy of Elise Terrell; below courtesy of the Town of Sylva.)

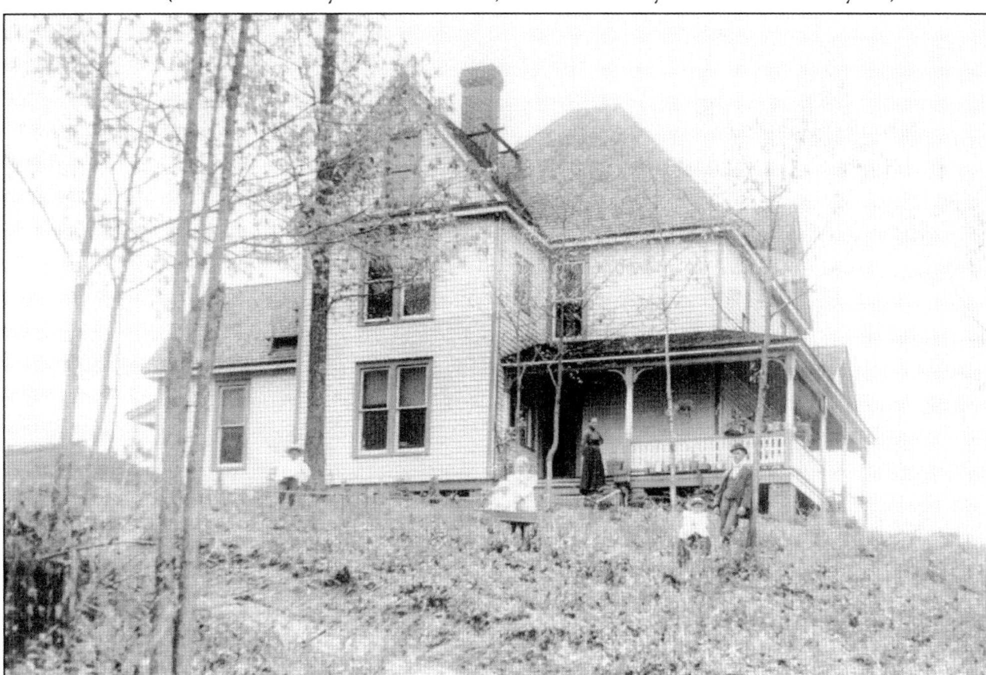

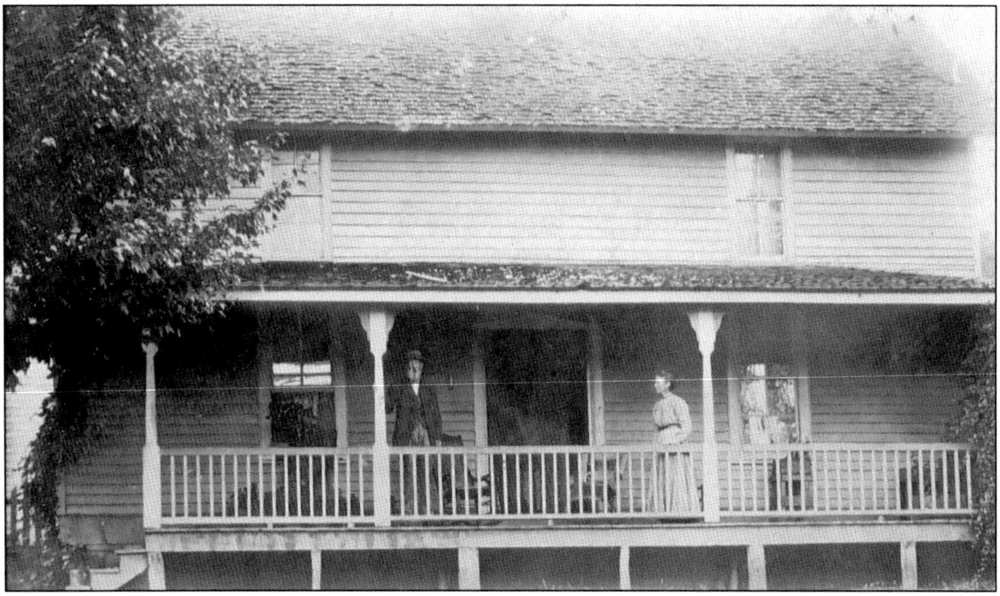

The above Allen Branch home served as the residence of Jasper and Helen Allen, for whom Allen Branch was named. It was torn down in the 1930s to make way for the home of Kenyon and Edith Moody. Jasper Allen's son Judd owned the house below, which was built in the 1890s. It was later sold to Charlie Allison, whose daughter Mary was known to drive her buggy down Allen Branch to school. Charles Rector and Elizabeth Liner Moody bought the house in 1921 and enlarged it to establish one of Jackson County's early tourist homes. Also operating Moody's Dairy, Charles delivered milk to Sylva by horse-drawn wagon. His grandson Maurice Moody and Maurice's wife, Mary Ellen Beck Moody, restored the home in 1995 and continue to live there. (Courtesy of Maurice Moody.)

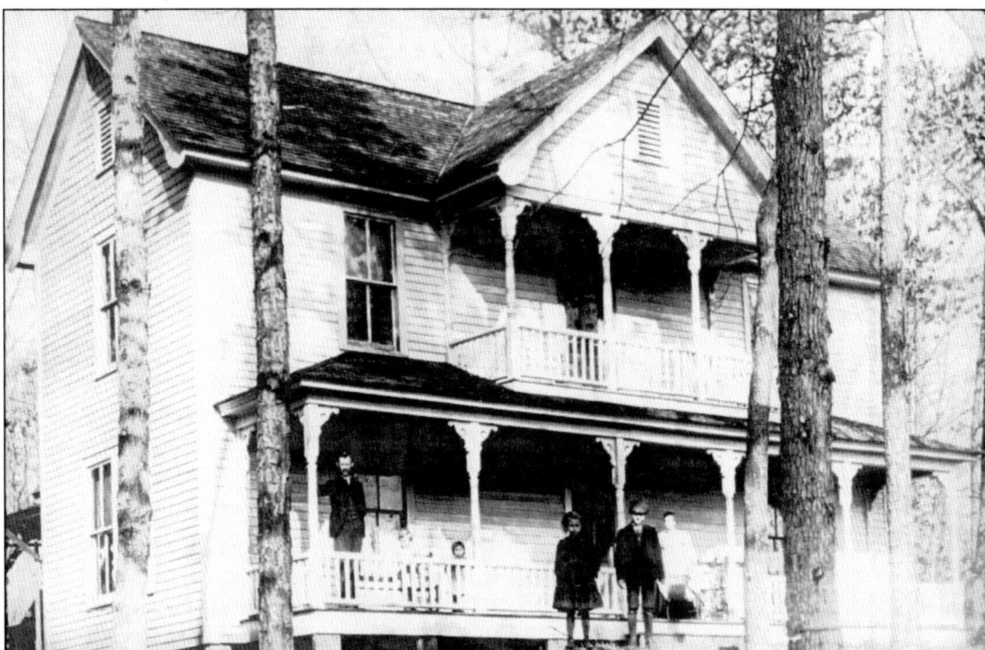

John and Eileen Dillard and their son Paul posed for the photograph at right in February 1946, when Eileen and Paul arrived in the United States. The couple met in England during World War II, when John was in the U.S. Army and Eileen was in the Royal Air Force. They fell in love and married before John was sent to France with the Allied Forces. When John drove Eileen and their son to his home in Dillardtown, everyone came running out to welcome Eileen, who the newspapers said was the first "war bride" to arrive. Dillardtown, which is just outside Silva's city limits, still had a frontier look in 1919, when the below image of Robert L. Bryson and his mother, Sarah W. Bryson, was captured beside a log cabin. (Right courtesy of Eileen Dillard; below courtesy of Robert L. Bryson.)

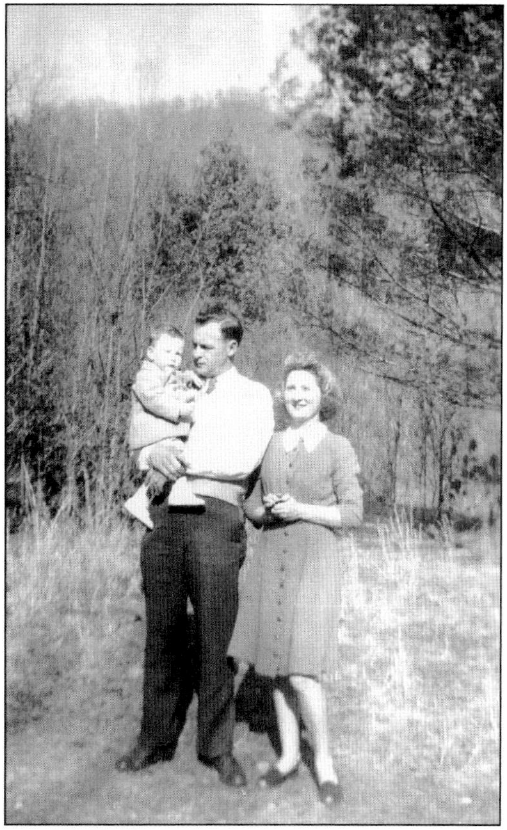

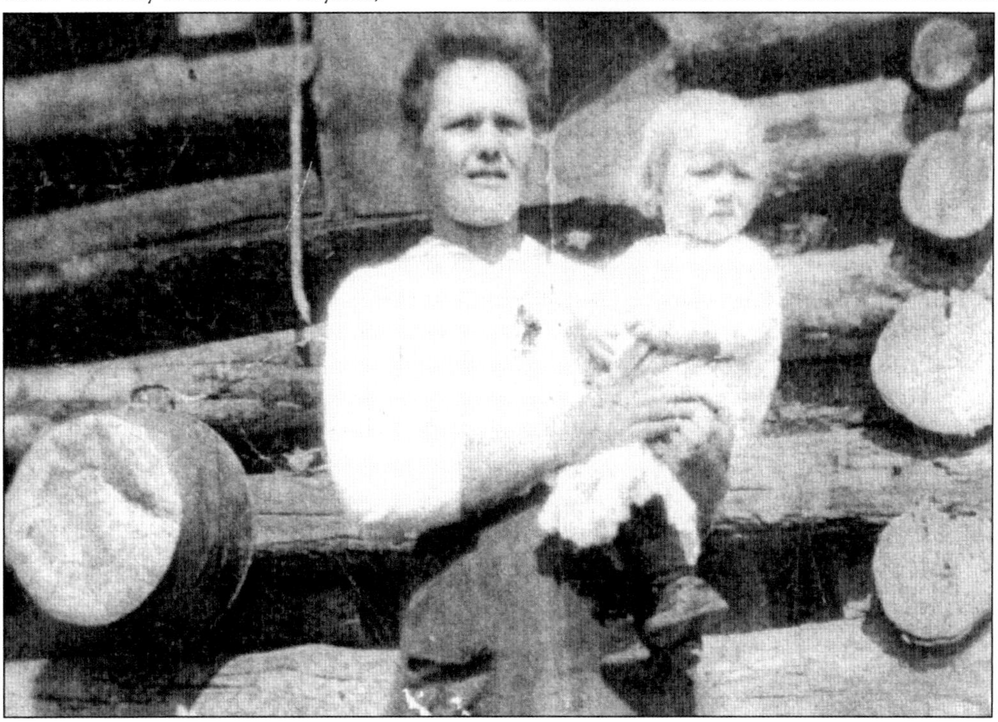

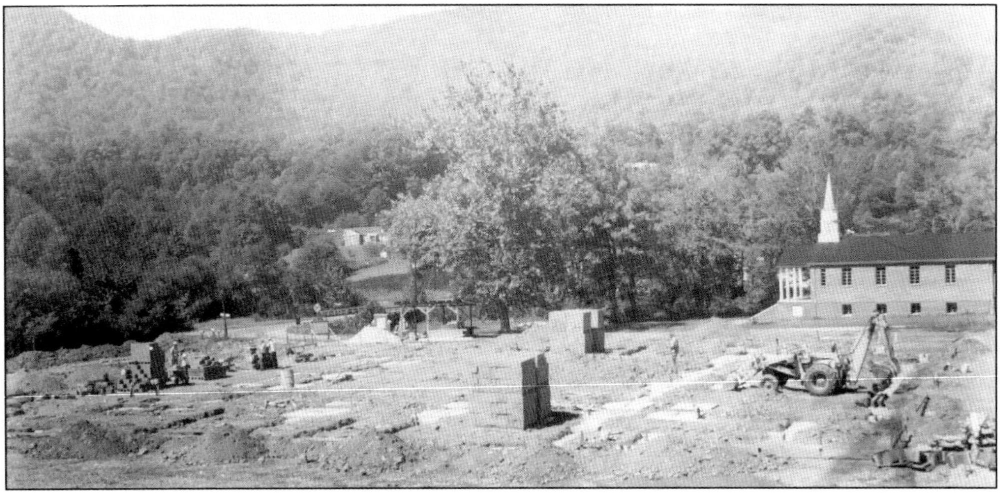

Liberty Baptist Church—pictured around 1970, when construction was beginning for the Jackson County Community Service Center—was established in 1871 as Scotts Creek Liberty Baptist Church and was first located in a log cabin on Daniel Bryson's farm. The congregation purchased the church's current site in 1899 for use as the county's first African American school. A one-room school was built in 1900, and the church began holding its services there. In 1906, an adjacent church building was constructed. That structure was replaced in 1942 by a stone church, which was destroyed by fire in 1958. The current brick church was built after the blaze. (Courtesy of the *Sylva Herald.*)

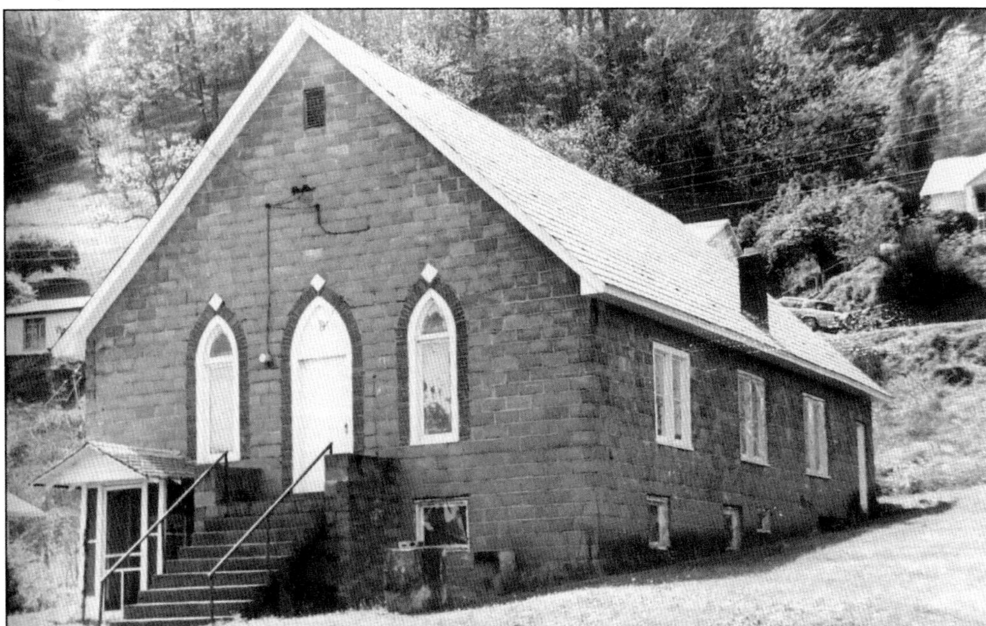

Now God's Holy Tabernacle, this building was constructed during the 1940s to house Maize Chapel African Methodist Episcopal Church. Organized near the Hog Rock mines in 1895 as Black Branch Methodist, Maize Chapel purchased property in Tannery Flats about 1910 because many of its members had moved there to work at the Harris-Reese Tannery. A plank building was constructed in 1914; the present block building was erected around the original church. (Courtesy of the *Sylva Herald.*)

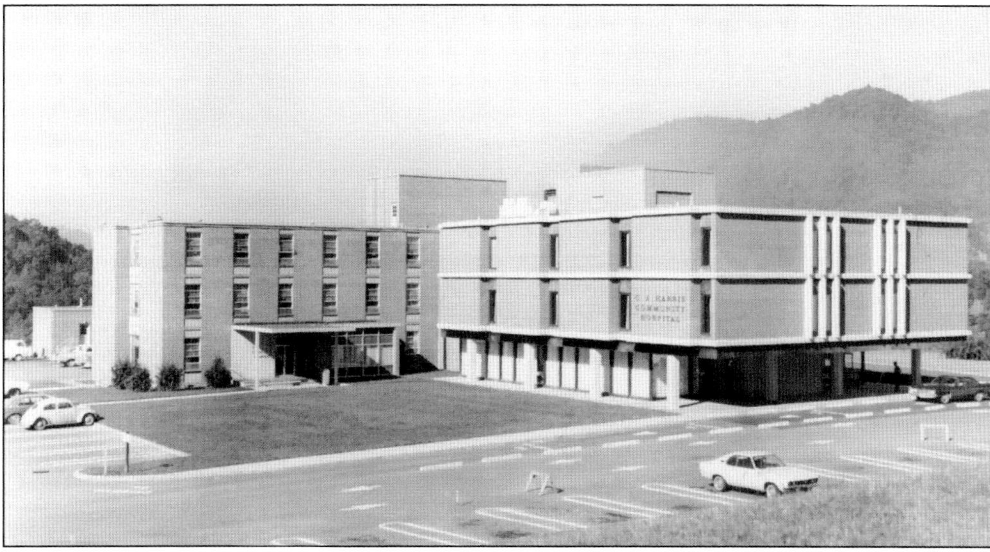

C. J. Harris Community Hospital underwent a major expansion that was completed in 1971. The project included a three-story addition and two separate one-story additions, bringing the total number of beds to 80. Another expansion in 1994 brought the number of beds to 86. As the hospital expanded, so did its service area, with more than half of its patients from outside Jackson County. The facility changed its name from C. J. Harris Community Hospital to Harris Regional Hospital in 1994. (Courtesy of the *Sylva Herald*.)

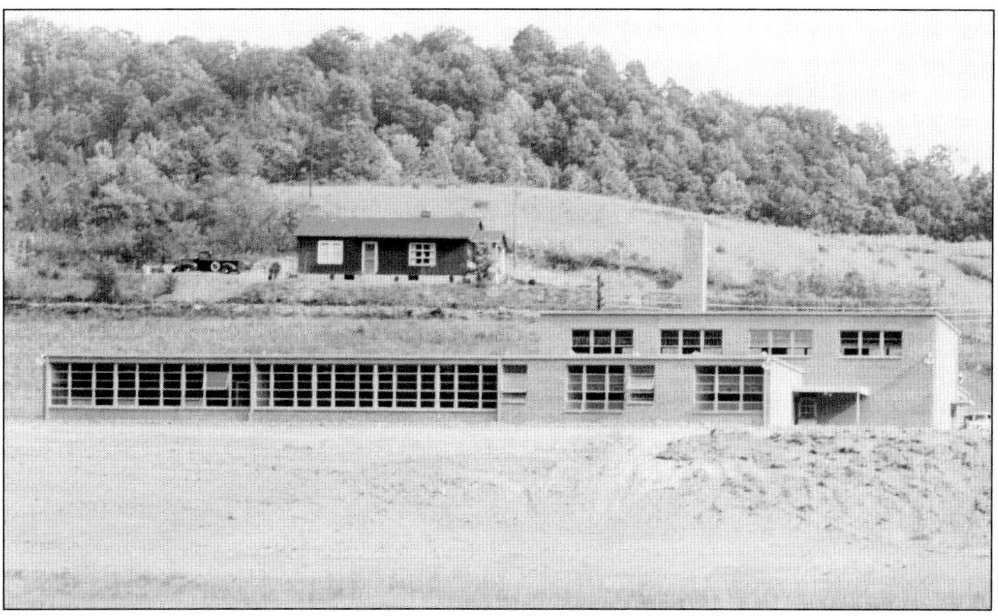

The Jackson County Schools Central Office, located between the present Harris Regional Hospital and Jackson County Community Service Center, was constructed around 1960 as the Colored Consolidated School. According to *The History of Jackson County*, it was used for only a few years before closing in 1965 in compliance with the 1964 Civil Rights Act. African American students then enrolled in the county's other schools. (Courtesy of the *Sylva Herald*.)

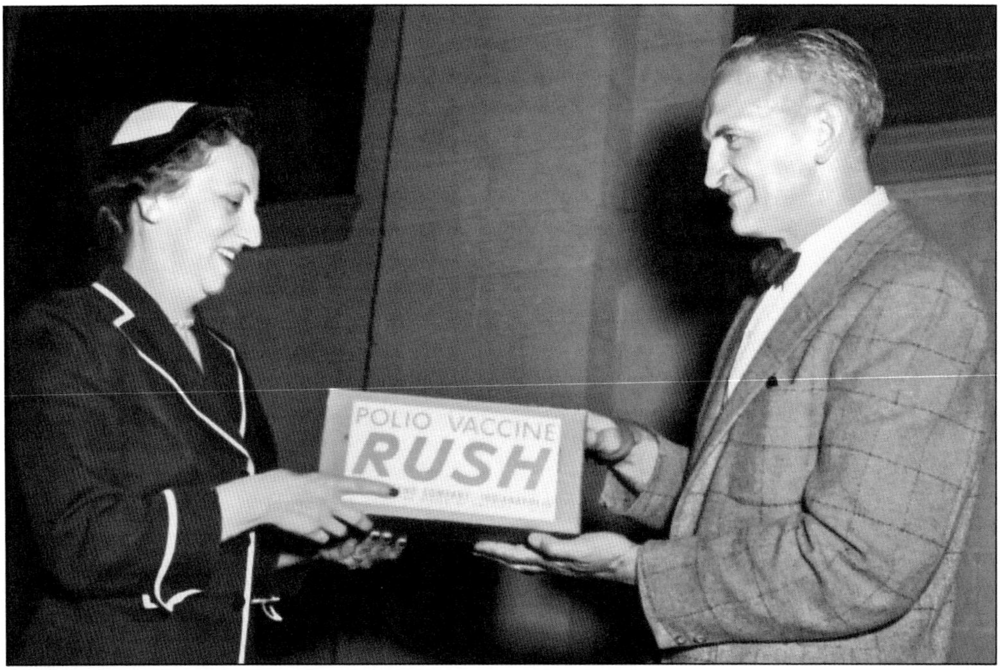

Jeannelle Moore (left), chairman of the local chapter of the National Foundation for Polio Prevention, hands the first shipment of Salk anti-polio vaccine to Dr. Dick Slagle, acting health officer for the district health office, in April 1955. (Courtesy of the *Sylva Herald.*)

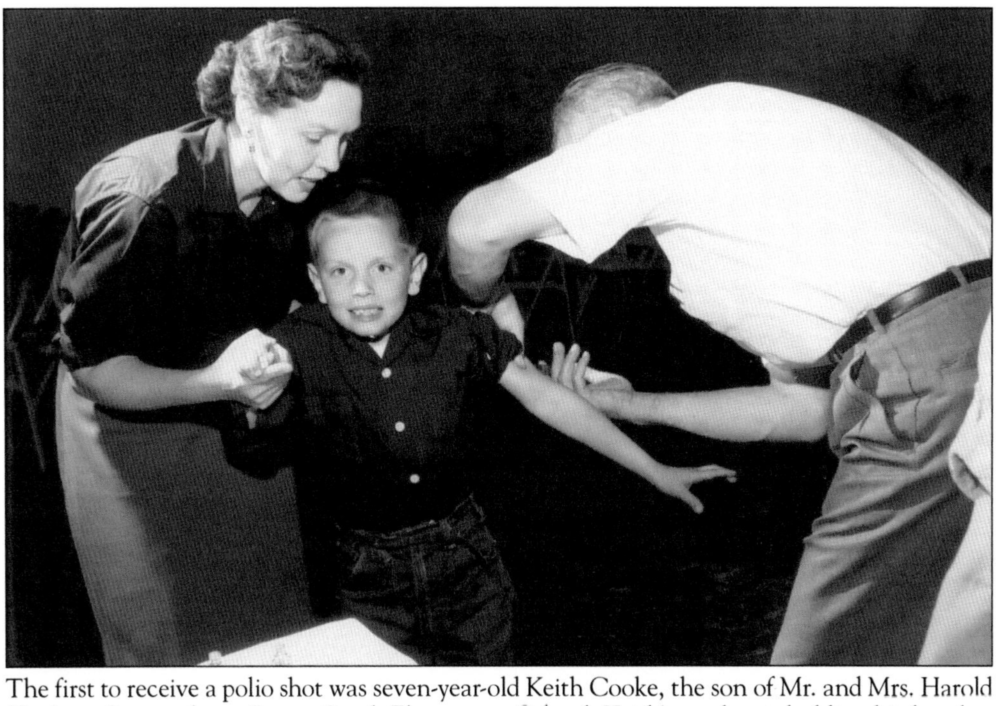

The first to receive a polio shot was seven-year-old Keith Cooke, the son of Mr. and Mrs. Harold Cooke, a first-grader at Scotts Creek Elementary School. Keith's mother is holding his hand as Dr. Dick Slagle administers the injection. More than 200 children in the first and second grades at Scotts Creek School were vaccinated on this day. (Courtesy of the *Sylva Herald.*)

Three

TRADE AND COMMERCE

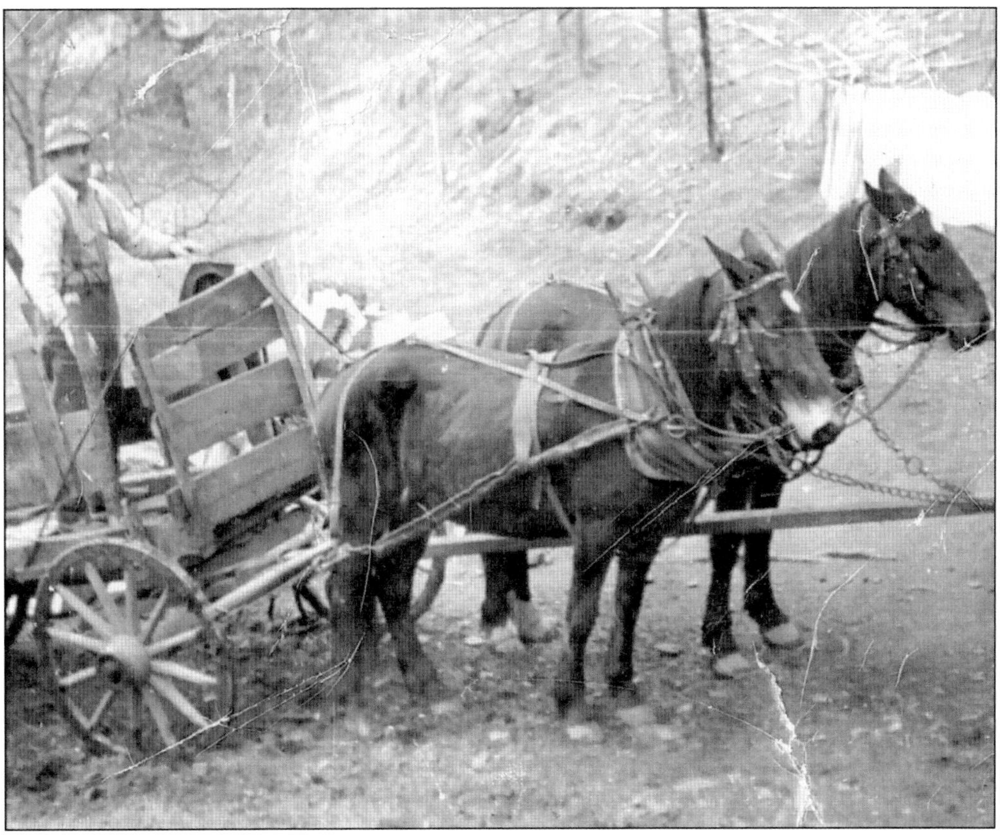

Allen Fisher delivers a load of firewood to Cal Clayton on Buff Creek in 1940. Fisher used the mares, Daisy (left) and Gyp, for logging as well as to pull his wagon, according to his son Lawrence. In addition to firewood, Fisher hauled logs to the pole yard, which was located near the present-day N.C. 107 and Cope Creek Road intersection. (Courtesy of Lawrence Fisher.)

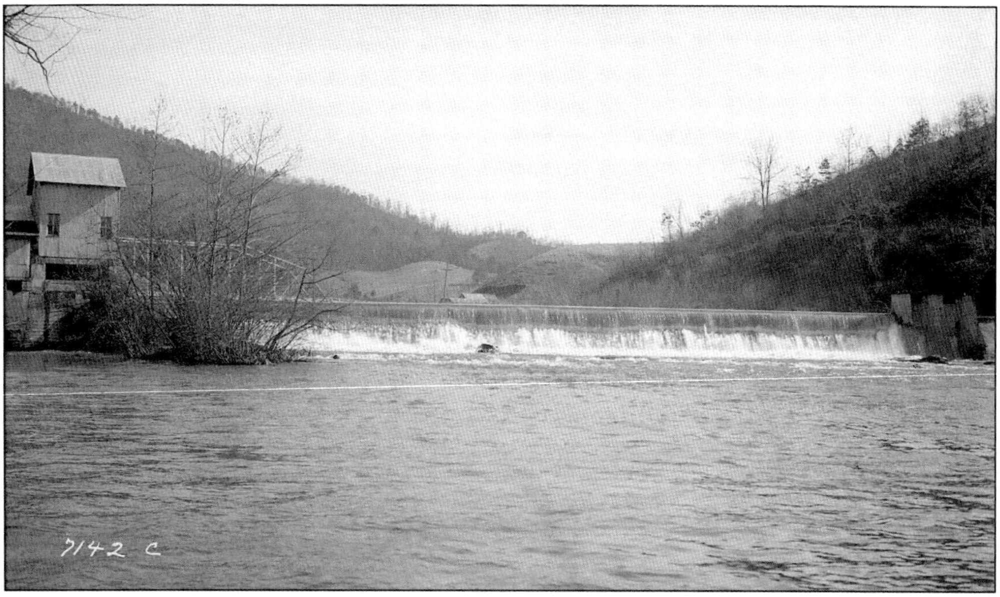

Built in 1914 by early Jackson County entrepreneur C. J. Harris to provide power for his Harris-Reese Tannery and to light the streets of Sylva and Dillsboro, the Dillsboro Dam was acquired by Nantahala Power and Light in 1957, when Nantahala purchased the Dillsboro and Sylva Electric Company. The dam is now owned by Duke Energy, which bought Nantahala in 1988. (Courtesy of the National Archives.)

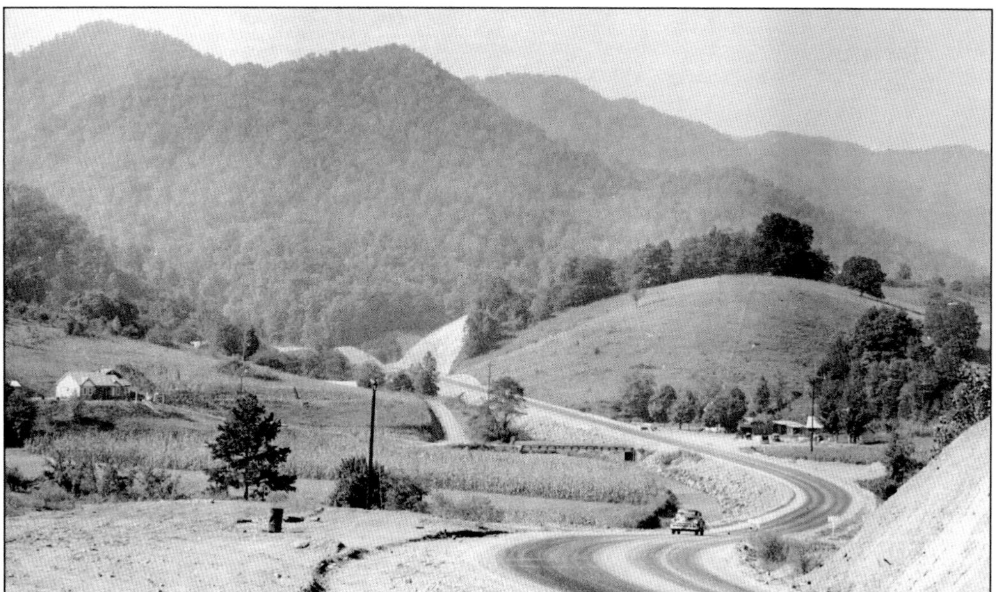

A new section of U.S. 23/441 between Dillsboro and Franklin was opened to traffic in mid-September 1955. This photograph, which ran in the *Sylva Herald* on September 22, shows the roadway near the mouth of Old Savannah Creek (Sutton Branch), with the Enley Cope house at far left and the Lela Hall home at right. According to the newspaper, the new highway has "gradual, well-balanced curves where once hairpin turns prevailed," and the old road was "narrow and winding at this point." (Courtesy of the *Sylva Herald*.)

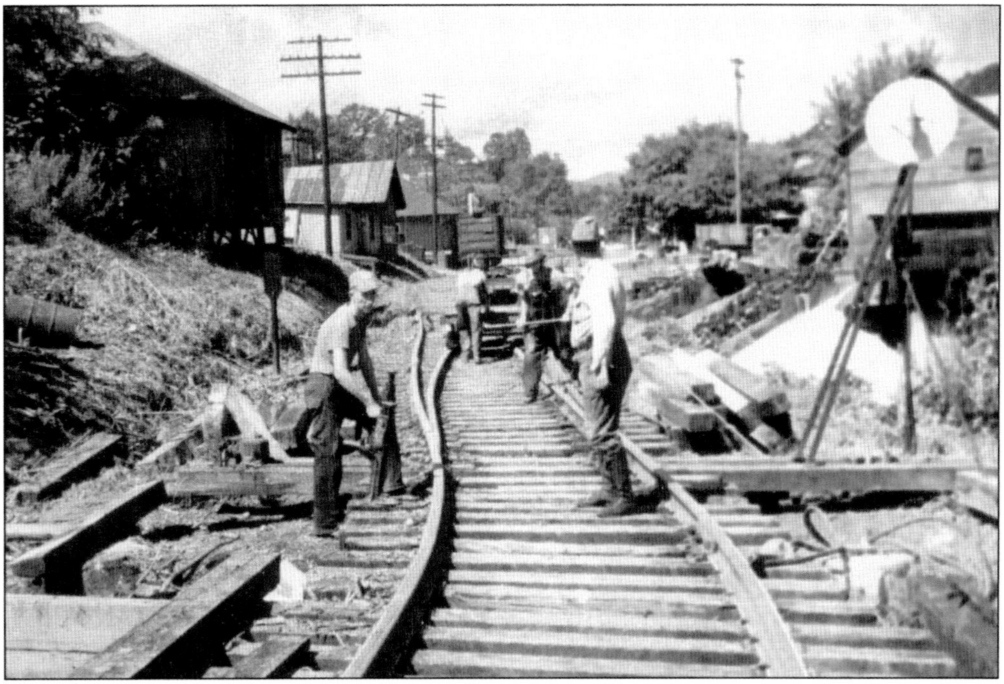

Railroad laborers (above) repair damage to a downtown section of track caused by Jackson County's greatest natural disaster: the flood that occurred on August 29–30, 1940. Visible buildings include the Asheville Mica Company (second from the left), the old Sylva Depot (just past the mica shed), and in the distance, the Jackson County Courthouse. The flood also damaged a trestle over Scotts Creek (below) near the mouth of Cope Creek, causing it to collapse under the weight of a Tuckaseigee and Southeastern train. (Above courtesy of the *Sylva Herald*; below courtesy of the National Archives.)

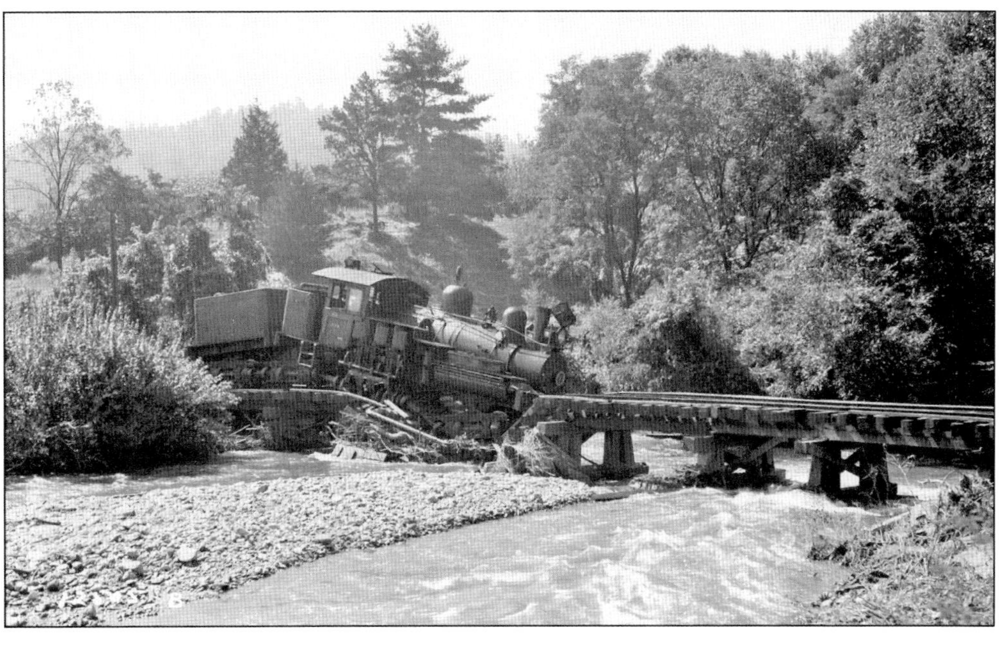

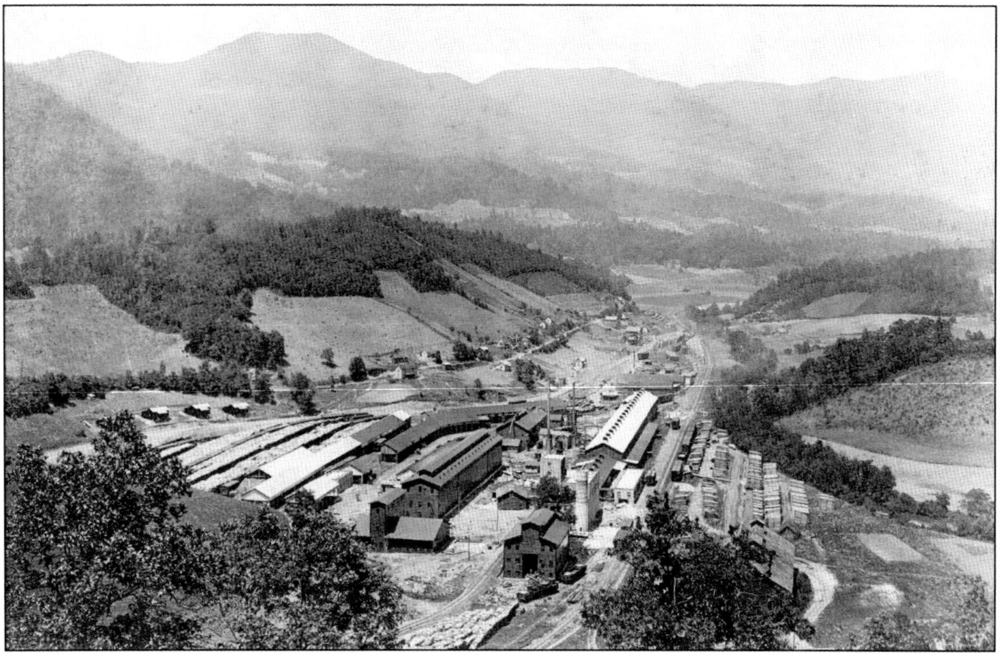

The buildings along Main Street and Chipper Curve Road that now comprise Jackson Paper have been a source of employment for local residents since C. J. Harris founded a tannery on the banks of Scotts Creek in 1901. According to *The History of Jackson County*, that tannery went by several names—Harris-Reese, Harris, Sylva, and Parsons—before it was bought by the Armour Leather Company in 1915. The plant boiled tannic acid from chipped chestnut wood and used it to cure, or tan, industrial-grade hides for machine belts and shoe sole leather. Armour purchased the company in order to expand extract production and supply tannin to its 14 other tanneries. By 1922, the tannery was curing 300 hides a day and employing around 150 people; the extract plant was producing about 62,000 barrels of tannin extract from 45,000 cords of chestnut wood. Armour closed in 1957 when the demand for shoe sole leather, the Sylva plant's main product, dropped sharply due to the increased use of man-made materials. (Courtesy of Hattie Hilda Allison.)

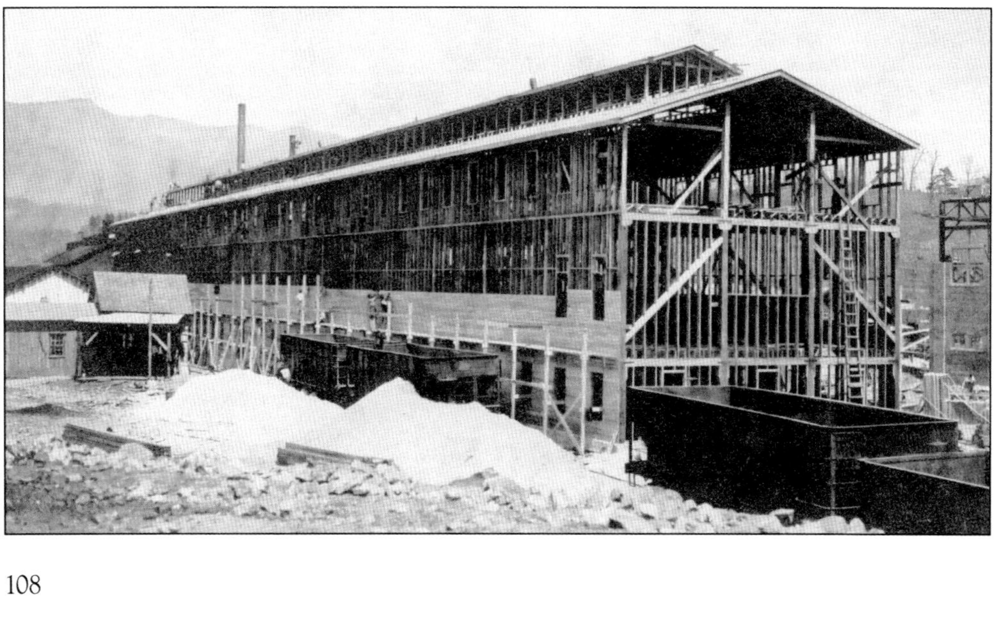

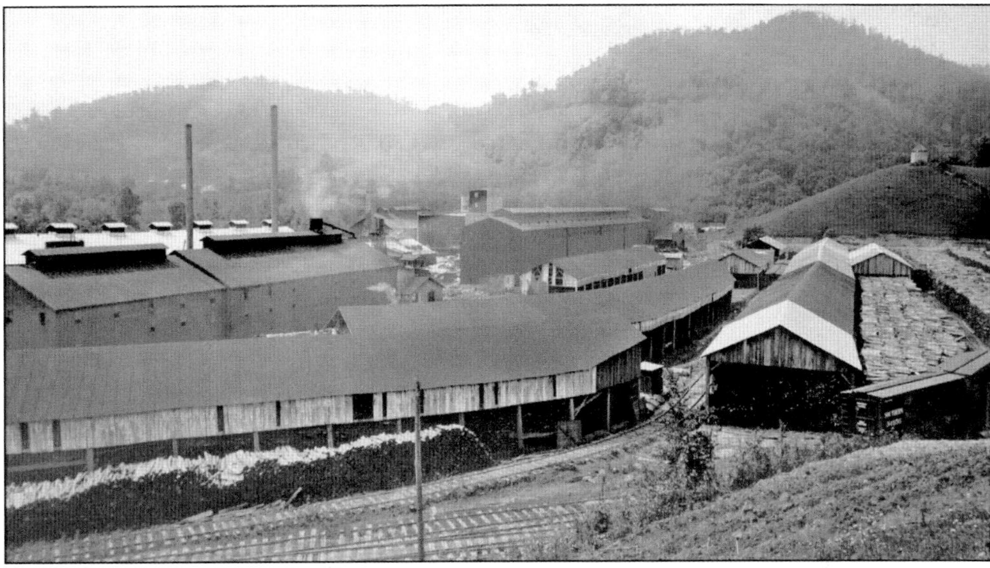

Papermaking became a part of the local economy during the tannery's heyday. E. L. McKee, who was managing the tannery for Armour, realized a new paper production method could make use of the plant's byproduct of chestnut chips. McKee persuaded George Mead, who had developed a process to make cardboard from boiled wood chips, to open a paper plant next door, and the Sylva Paperboard Company began creating both tannin extract and cardboard. By 1955, the company, then known as Mead, was the largest manufacturer in Jackson County, employing more than 300 and operating its own 10,000-acre forest. Despite Mead's success, the corporation experienced financial trouble due to environmental problems and closed its Sylva plant in 1974. The facility was sold to the Dixie Container Corporation, which reopened the plant as Jackson Paper around 1982. The aerial photograph below shows the Mead plant after a portion of Scotts Creek was relocated to facilitate the firm's expansion and operation. (Above courtesy of Hattie Hilda Allison; below courtesy of the *Sylva Herald.*)

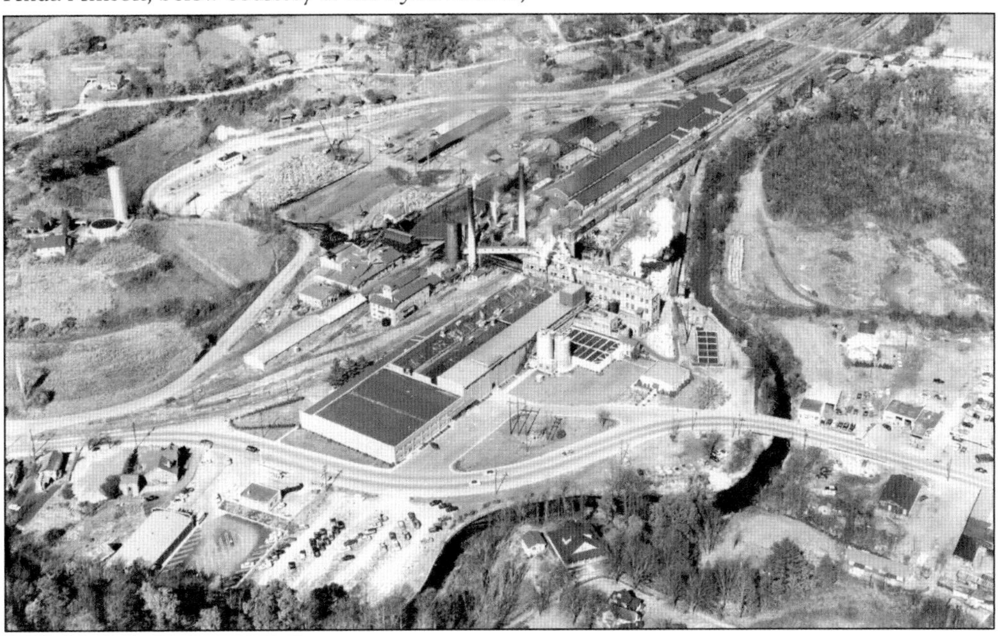

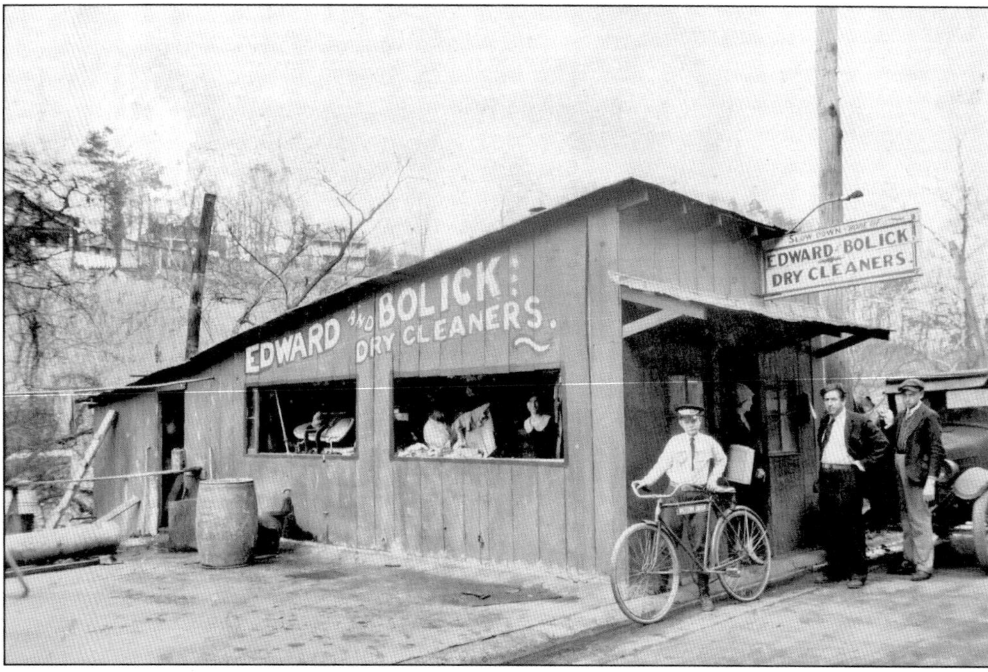

Edwards and Bolick Dry Cleaners, pictured during the 1920s, once stood on Mill Street near its east intersection with Main. Mack Golwyn and Lulu Garland Edwards owned the business along with the Bolicks and operated a Western Union telegraph office in the same location. The woman inside the front window is Ella Bolick. The Western Union delivery boy, Charlie Woodard, carried telegrams all over town and later opened Charlie's Restaurant in Waynesville. Lula Edwards stands in the shadows behind Woodard. The two men are Mack Edwards (left) and Willie Monteith, who delivered the dry cleaning and later owned a downtown laundry. (Courtesy of Sandy Owens.)

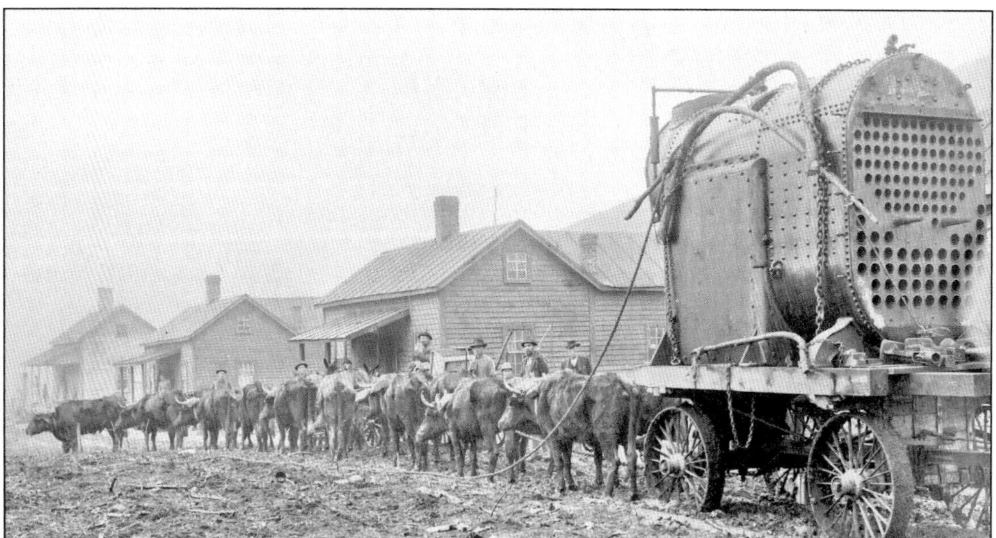

A boiler bound for the Cullowhee Normal School (now Western Carolina University) makes its way through Sylva on March 4, 1910. (Courtesy of Western Carolina University Special Collections.)

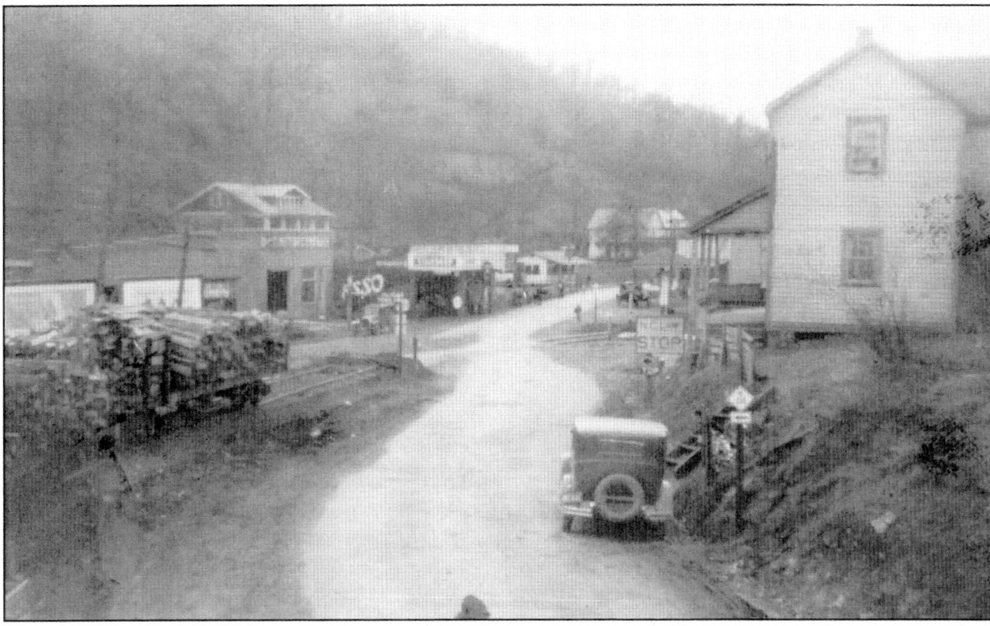

These photographs of the intersection of East Main Street and Chipper Curve Road were taken in 1930. In the picture above, the house above the Coffee Shop (center left) served as the Frank and Mayme Bailey residence at that time. The original Coffee Shop (center), operated by the Baileys and located just west of the current restaurant, is visible here. Chipper Curve Road was the main highway into Sylva from the east and was designated U.S. 19-23 and N.C. 10. A highway sign indicates traffic should turn left for N.C. 106 toward Cullowhee. Below, signs specify a left turn across the railroad tracks on U.S. 19-23 and N.C. 10 and a right turn for N.C. 106. Signs in both read "N.C. Law Stop," apparently referring to the railroad crossing, which was relocated slightly to the east in the 1960s. The building that now houses Hall's Tire Service (left) appears then to have been a Chevrolet dealership and a Standard gasoline station. The current home of the WSG Bath and Lighting Gallery (right) bears a "Motor Company" sign, possibly B&T. That building, part of which has been removed, later operated as the Hooper Motor Company until the business was purchased by Don Scott. (Courtesy of the North Carolina Department of Transportation.)

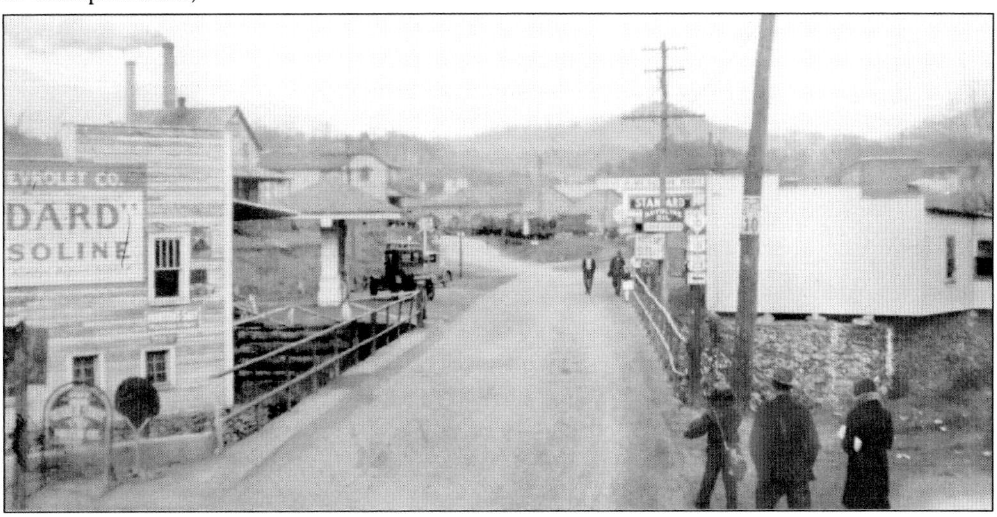

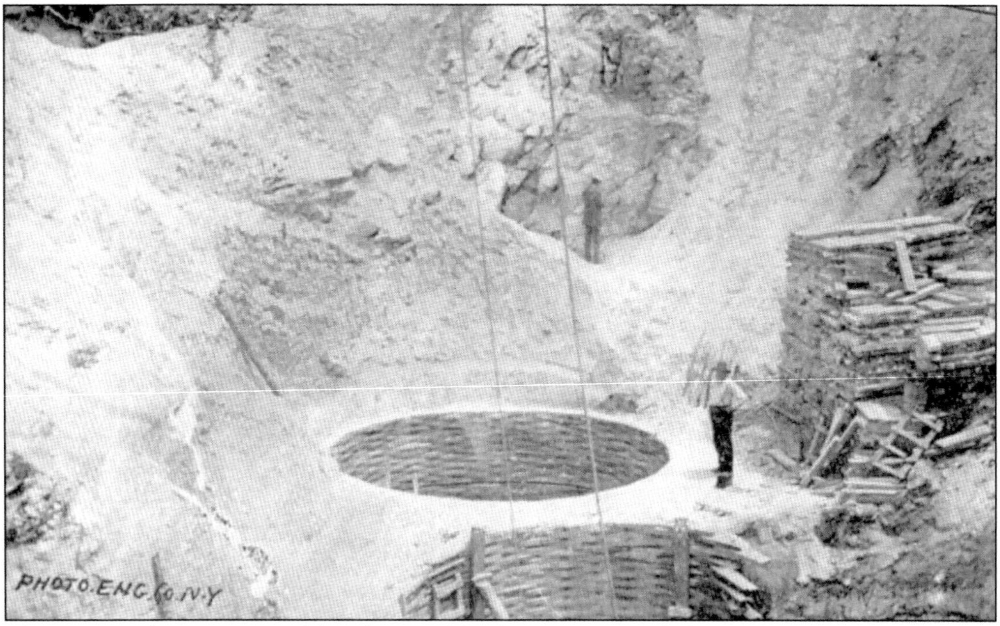

The Harris Clay Company (above) mined kaolin at Hog Rock from 1888 until around 1926. The round pits measured 15 to 20 feet across and 80 to 100 feet deep, and the clay was lifted out in buckets by mule-powered winches. The washed and dried kaolin was pressed into bricks and transported by a mule tram to Dillsboro, where it was loaded into boxcars for rail shipment. Pottery made from Harris clay was featured at the 1904 World's Fair in St. Louis. Another important mineral in Jackson County's history was mica, which was mined throughout the county. The 1884 arrival of the railroad made mica mining feasible, and the two world wars created a demand. The last trimming shed (below) in Sylva was operated by the Asheville Mica Company on Mill Street in the vicinity of the current Ward's Plumbing parking lot. That shed was torn down in 1982. (Above courtesy of Western Carolina University Special Collections; below courtesy of the *Sylva Herald*.)

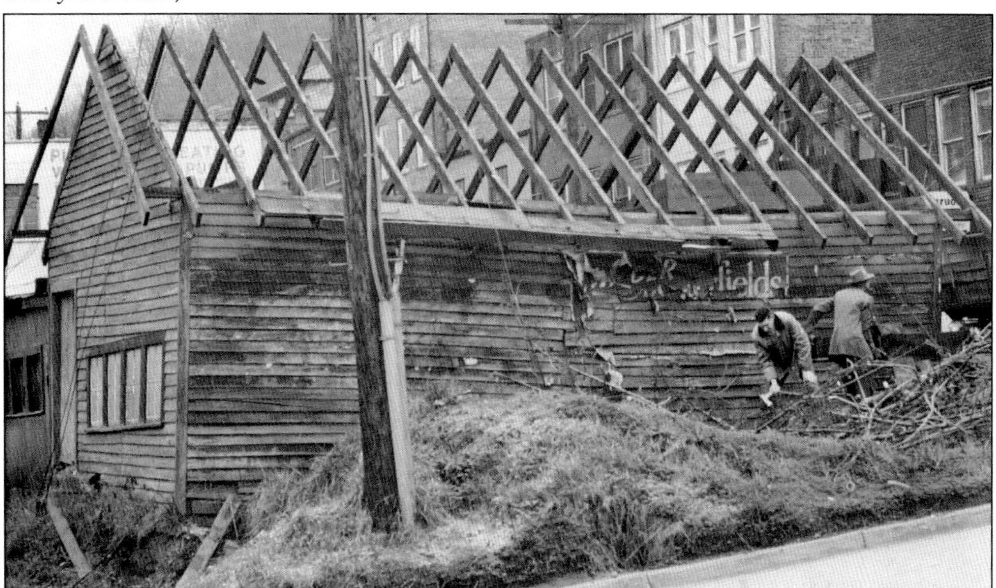

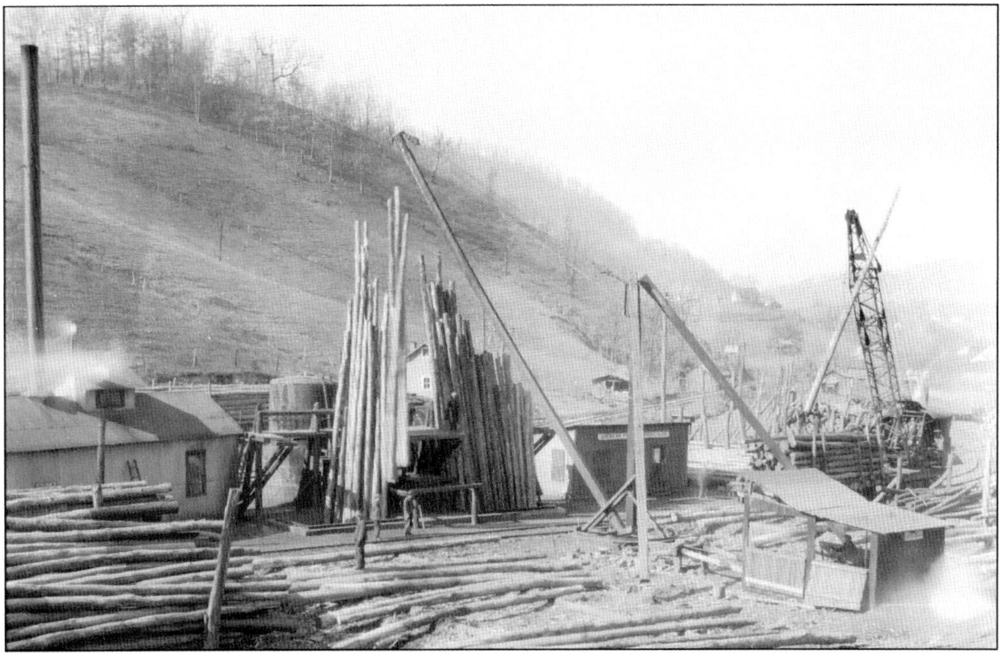

The pole yard, located near the intersection of N.C. 107, Cope Creek Road, and Walter Ashe Road, once treated tall trees for telephone and power poles. Opened by the Carolina Pole Company in 1923, it employed 60 men and treated some 30,000 poles a year in vats of creosote. By the early 1940s, it had become a log yard where loggers brought timber to be loaded onto the Tuckaseigee and Southeastern Railroad's spur line. From there, the logs were taken to East LaPorte to be sawn at the Blackwood Lumber sawmill. (Courtesy of Dorris Beck.)

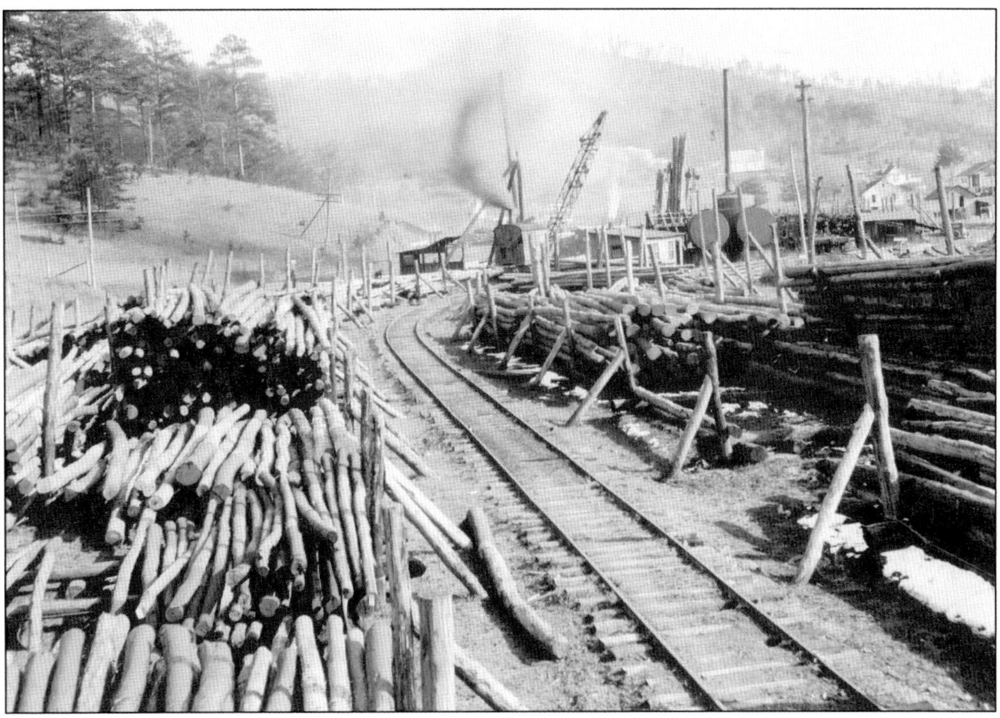

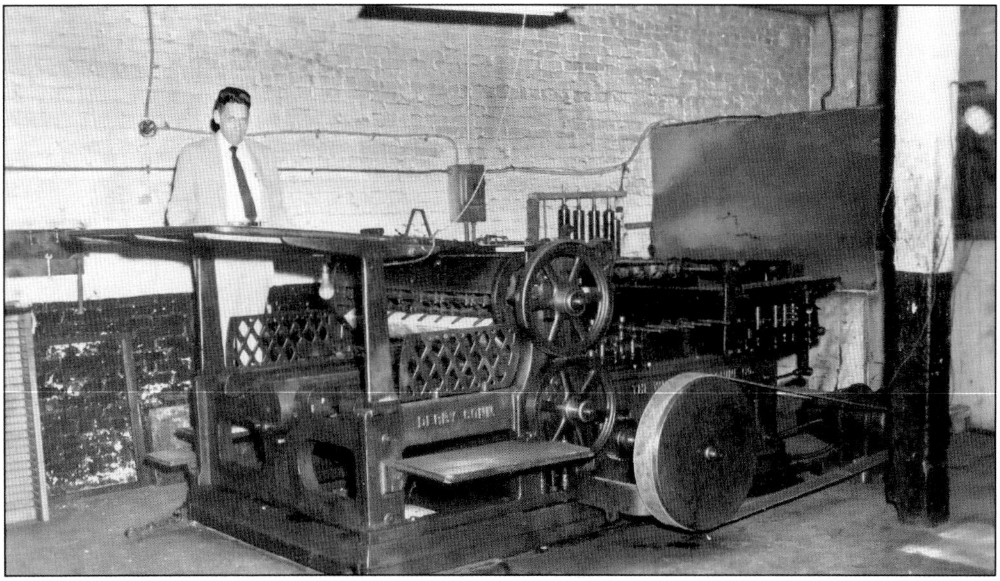

J. A. Gray, the grandfather of current *Sylva Herald* publisher Steve Gray, bought out his partner, J. M. Bird, in 1950. Gray remained publisher of the *Herald*, Jackson County's oldest newspaper, until his death in 1963. In front of Gray is the newspaper's first printing press, a four-page flatbed that was initially set up in the old Lyric Theater (more recently Merriweather's and then Micheal's on Main) before being moved to the building the *Herald* has occupied since 1950. (Courtesy of the *Sylva Herald*.)

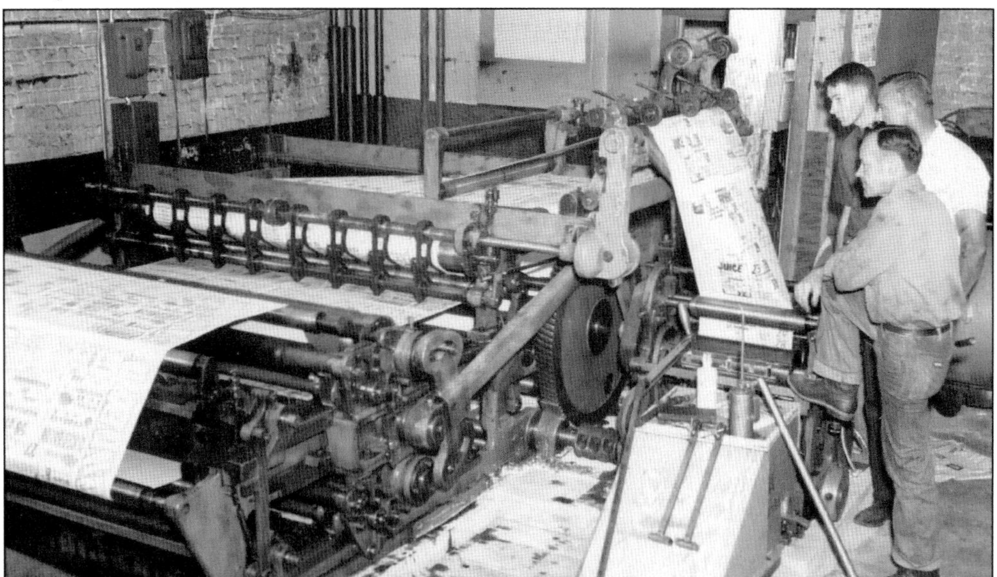

Employees Al Cunningham (front), Sam Beck (center), and Harold Norman (back) check out the *Herald*'s Cox-o-type press, purchased in May 1967. The Cox-o-type, an eight-page flatbed that printed papers from rolls of newsprint rather than single sheets, was the last press used to print the newspaper in Sylva. The *Herald* made the switch from metal type (hot type) to offset in 1974 and has been printed in Franklin since that time. The final front page printed in the newspaper's Sylva pressroom is on display in the *Herald* lobby. (Courtesy of the *Sylva Herald*.)

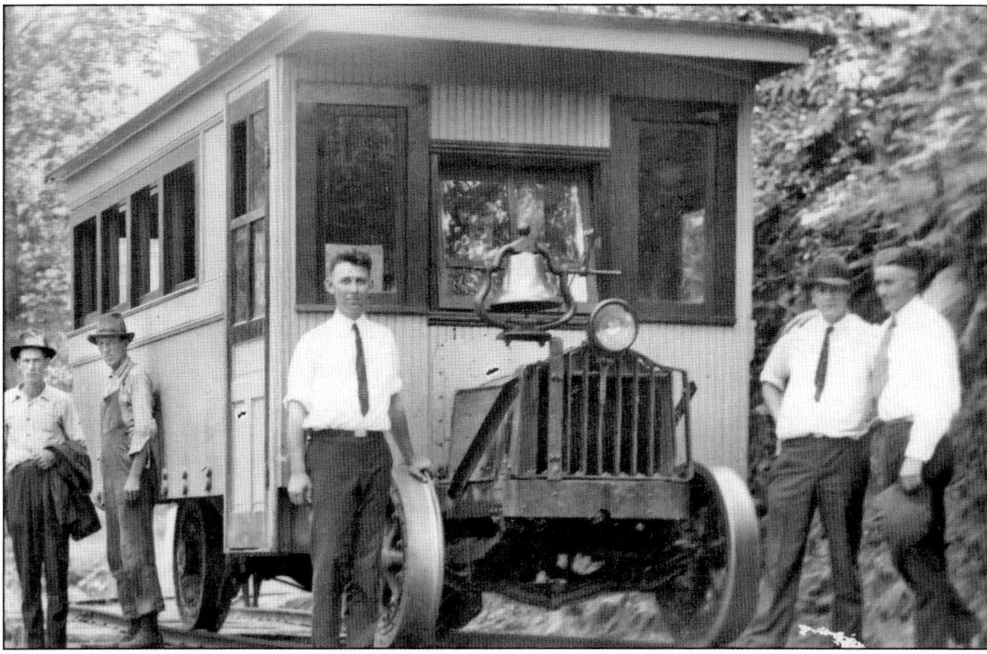

The Blackwood Lumber Company trolley, shown around 1930, transported people from East LaPorte to Cullowhee and Sylva. From left to right are two unidentified, Ed Hooper, Jim Potts, and Bethel Gunnells. (Courtesy of Sue Phillips.)

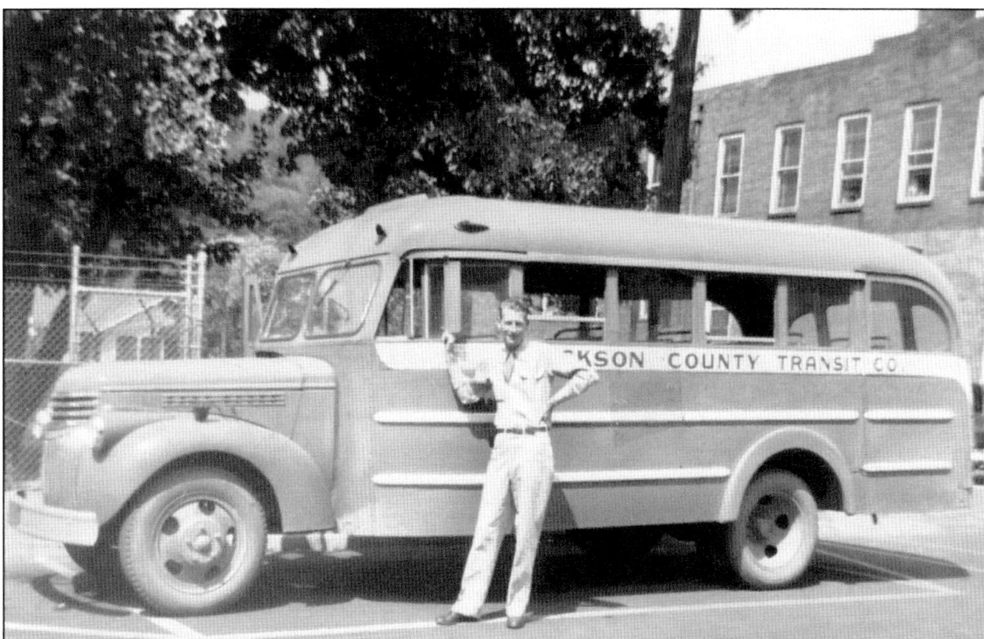

Manager and driver Venoy Reed stands with a Jackson County Transit Company bus at the west end of Main Street around 1949. The Hotel Lloyd is at right. Started by Reed's cousin Jennings Bryson, the company ceased operations in August 1952. According to a 1948 schedule, destinations from Sylva included the Beta School, the Old Mill Inn, Webster, Love's Field, and Cope Creek. (Courtesy of Western Carolina University Special Collections.)

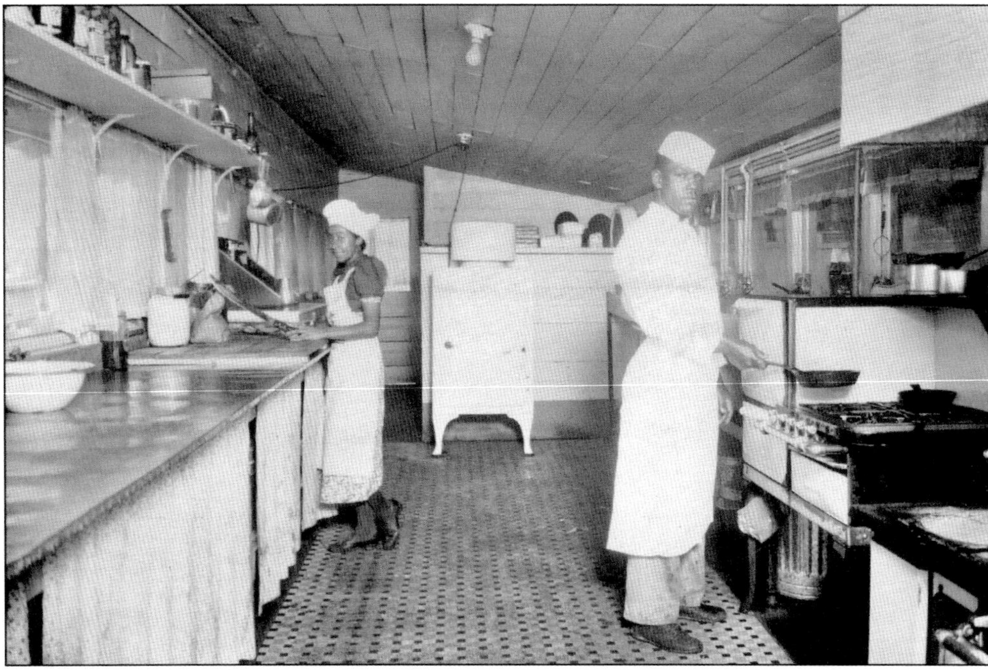

Annie (left) and Farrell Dorsey, pictured above, were among the cooks at the Coffee Shop in 1939. Established by Frank and Mayme Bailey in 1926, the popular restaurant is still located just east of the downtown business district. Emerson Phillips, on the left in the photograph below, managed the Coffee Shop, which was then in a frame building leased by Phil Stovall. Behind the counter is waitress Mae Snyder Bryson, and Phillips's wife, Rachel, is seated. Visible in the background are bottles of beer; on-premise beer sales were legal then but subsequently voted out. Sylva voters approved the sale of beer and wine again in the 1990s. (Courtesy of Rachel Phillips.)

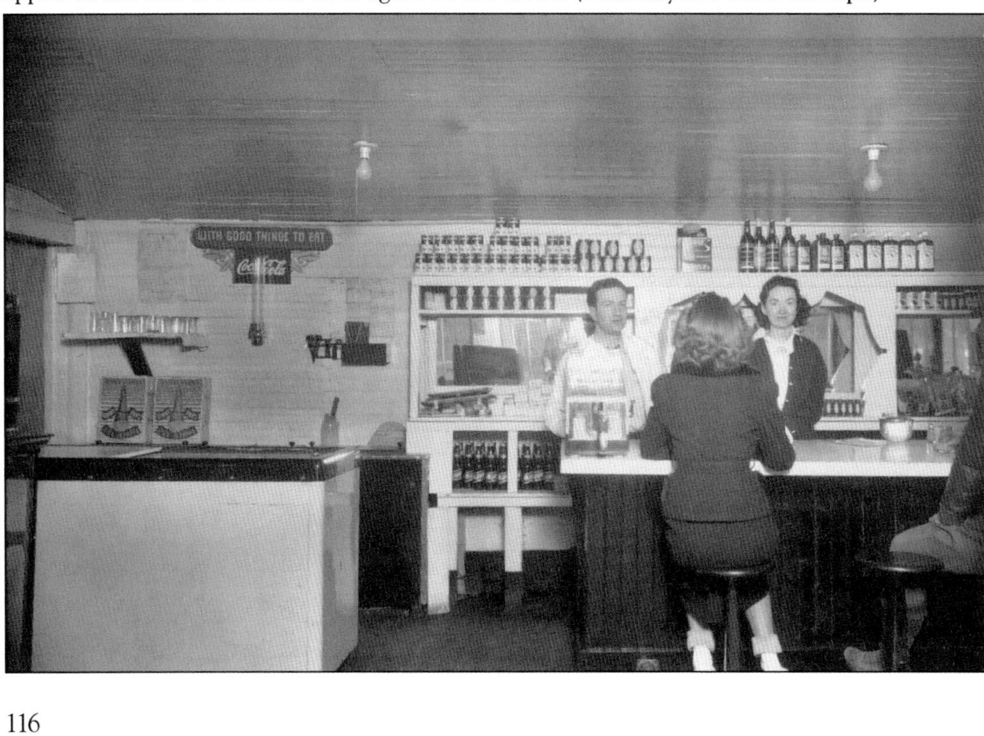

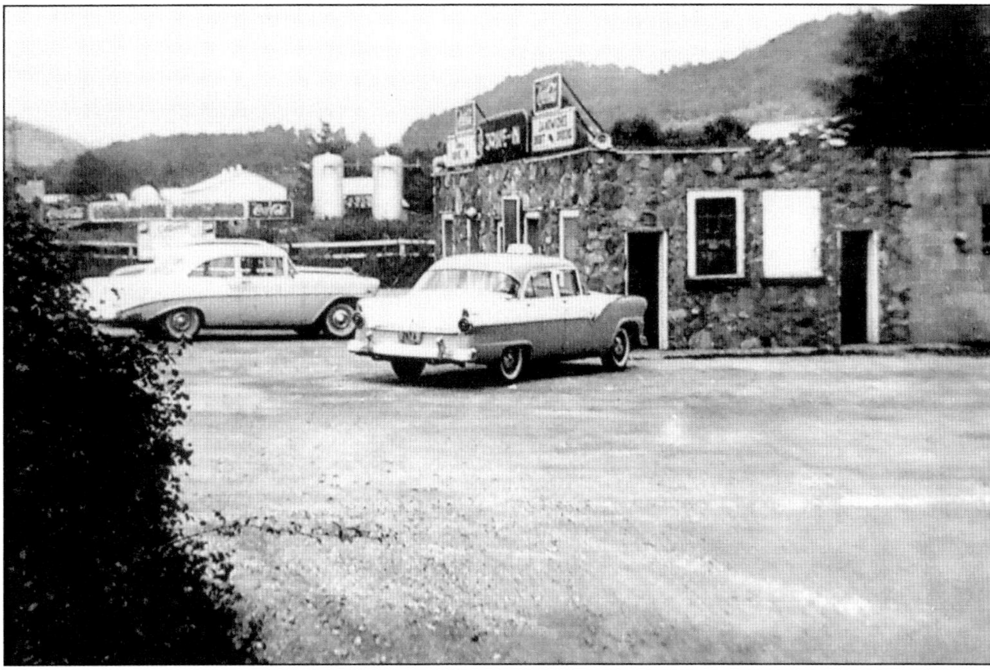

Troy's, a popular drive-in and local hangout during the 1950s, stood on Skyland Drive. Opened by Troy Robinson in the early 1950s, it was operated later in the decade by Thad and Viola Deitz. (Courtesy of Teresa Deitz.)

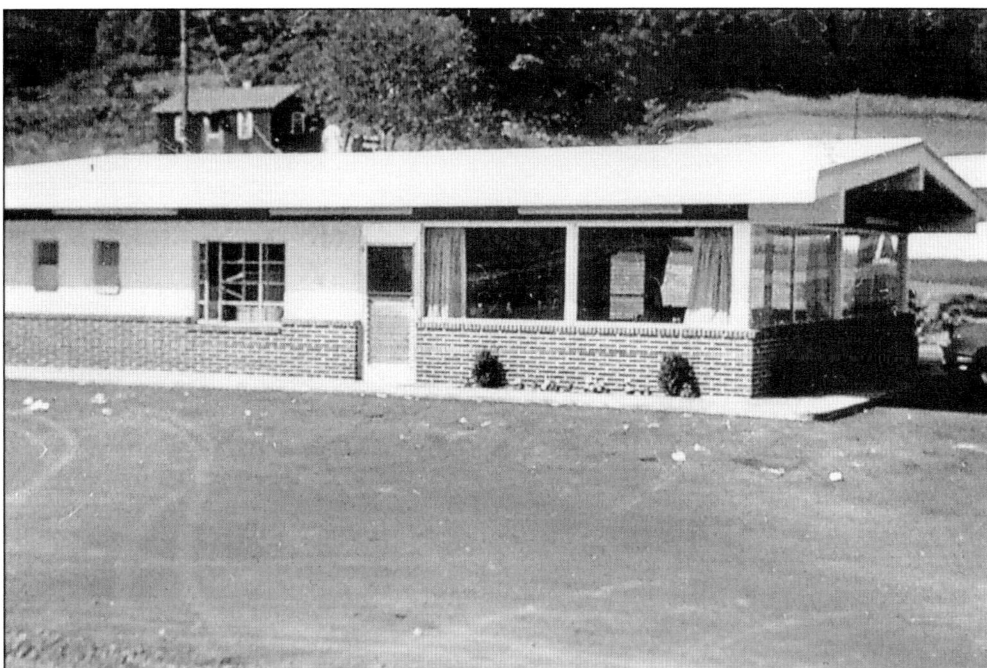

The Rebel Restaurant was Sylva's teenage hangout during the 1960s. Located in what is now Sylva Plaza, it was at one time owned and operated by Thad and Viola Deitz. (Courtesy of Teresa Deitz.)

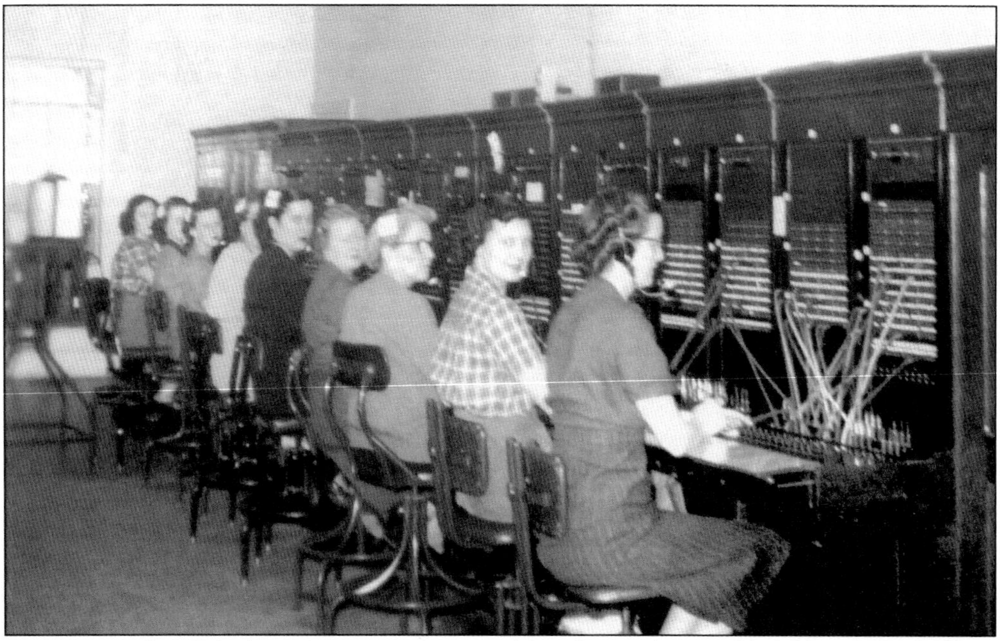

Western Carolina Telephone Company operators (above) man the switchboard in 1949, when the office was located on Main Street above Velt's Café. Pictured from left to right are Edna Mason, Merele Carter Aldridge, Evelyn Reed, Becky Wilson, Gertie Anderson, unidentified, Joan Cagle, Mildred Cable Johnson, and Joretta Monteith Moon. When the firm built a new office (below) on the corner of Allen Street and Old Dillsboro Road (now Municipal Drive), the switchboard moved there in 1950. Telephone offices remain on that corner, though the company's name is now Verizon. The building still stands but is not recognizable; expansion and renovations through the years have swallowed up the original structure. (Above courtesy of Hugh Moon; below courtesy of the *Sylva Herald*.)

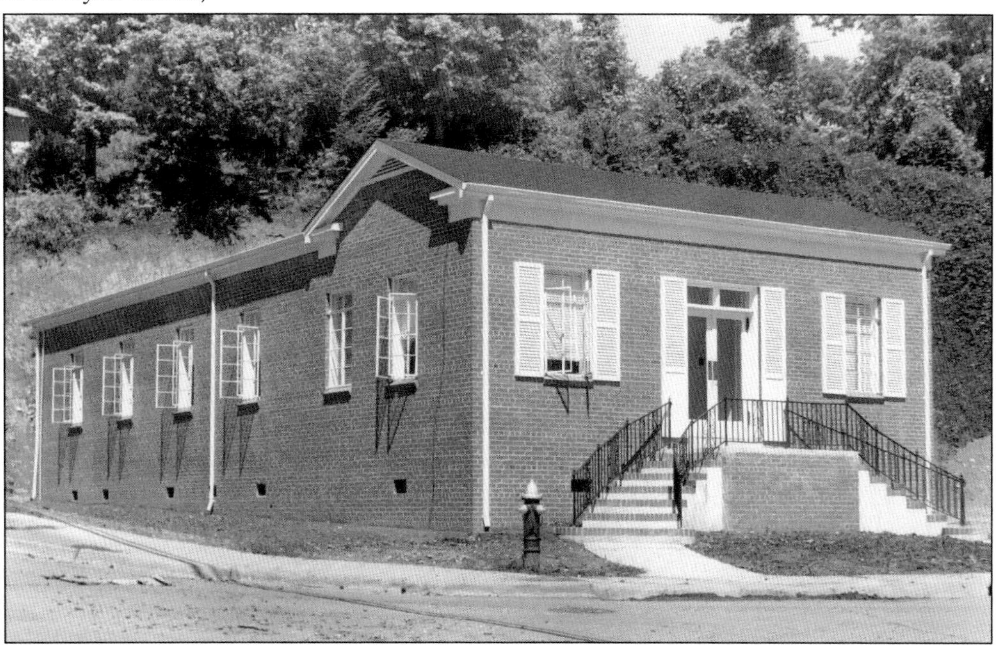

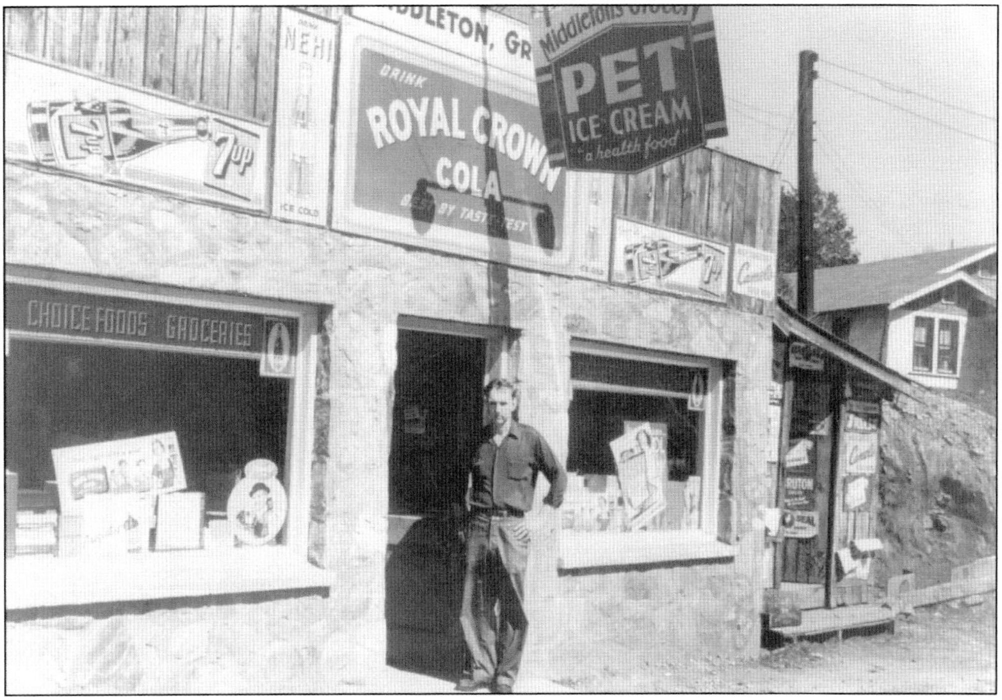

J. C. Middleton stands outside the original Middleton Grocery Store around 1950. A portion of that building remains in use as Middleton's Pawn Shop. (Courtesy of Gene Middleton.)

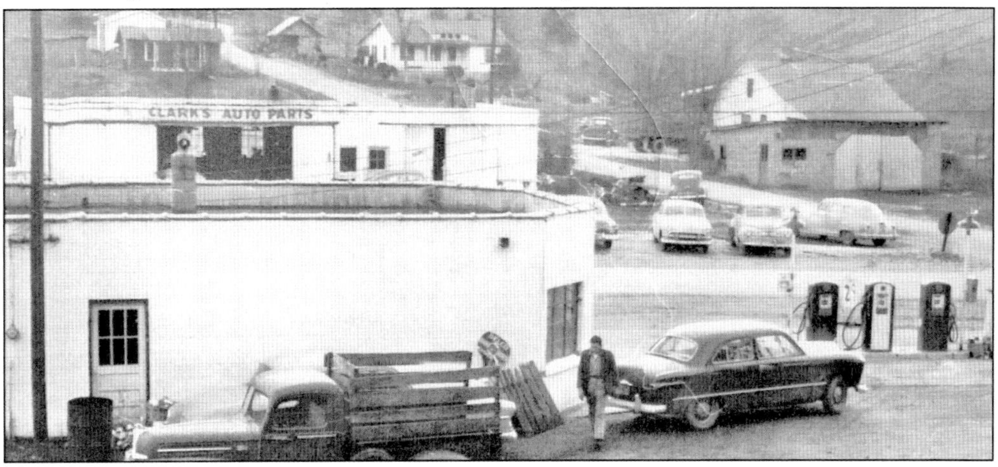

The four-way intersection of N.C. 107, Cope Creek Road, and Walter Ashe Road was less hurried in 1956, not long after Clarence Cody (pictured) opened his service station. The building in the foreground is the original station, torn down in 1967 to allow for the widening of 107. Cody's second building was razed in 1998 to make way for the present station, operated by his son Steve. Across the road is Clark's Auto Parts, which was established by Cash Clark in 1949. He was joined in that business in 1980 by his son-in-law Arthur Phillips, who continued the operation after Clark's 1988 death. John Forrest moved his Smoky Mountain Video there around 1993; when Forrest expanded a few years later, Phillips closed his automobile glass business. One house, the second on the right up Walter Ashe Road, still stands, though it has been remodeled. Macon Bank and its parking lot now occupy the other corner, replacing the old F&P Supermarket and the house and shop building that were there in 1956. (Courtesy of J. D. Patterson.)

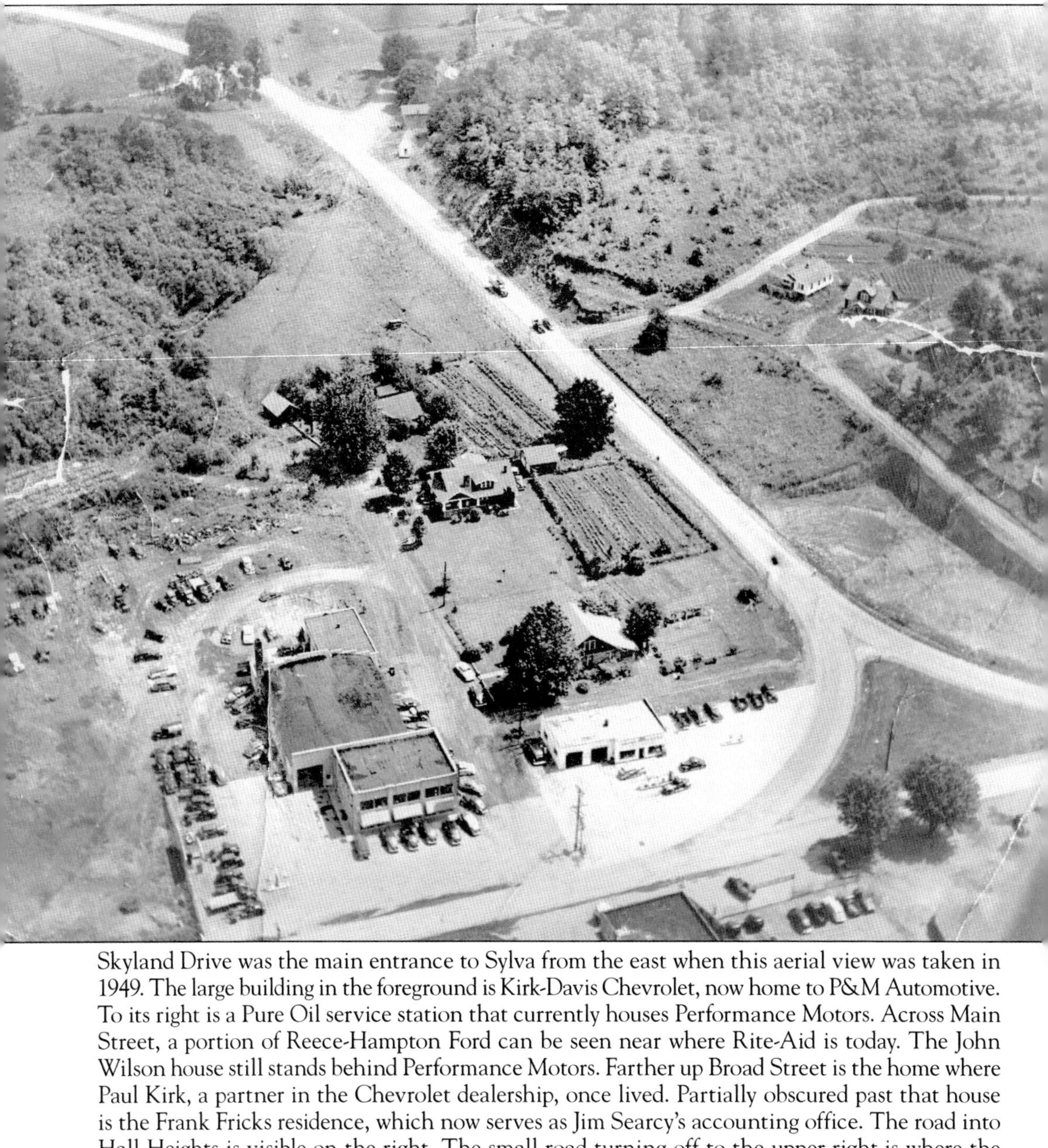

Skyland Drive was the main entrance to Sylva from the east when this aerial view was taken in 1949. The large building in the foreground is Kirk-Davis Chevrolet, now home to P&M Automotive. To its right is a Pure Oil service station that currently houses Performance Motors. Across Main Street, a portion of Reece-Hampton Ford can be seen near where Rite-Aid is today. The John Wilson house still stands behind Performance Motors. Farther up Broad Street is the home where Paul Kirk, a partner in the Chevrolet dealership, once lived. Partially obscured past that house is the Frank Fricks residence, which now serves as Jim Searcy's accounting office. The road into Hall Heights is visible on the right. The small road turning off to the upper right is where the Asheville Highway and Skyland Drive intersect today. (Courtesy of the *Sylva Herald.*)

Four

POSTCARDS FROM SYLVA

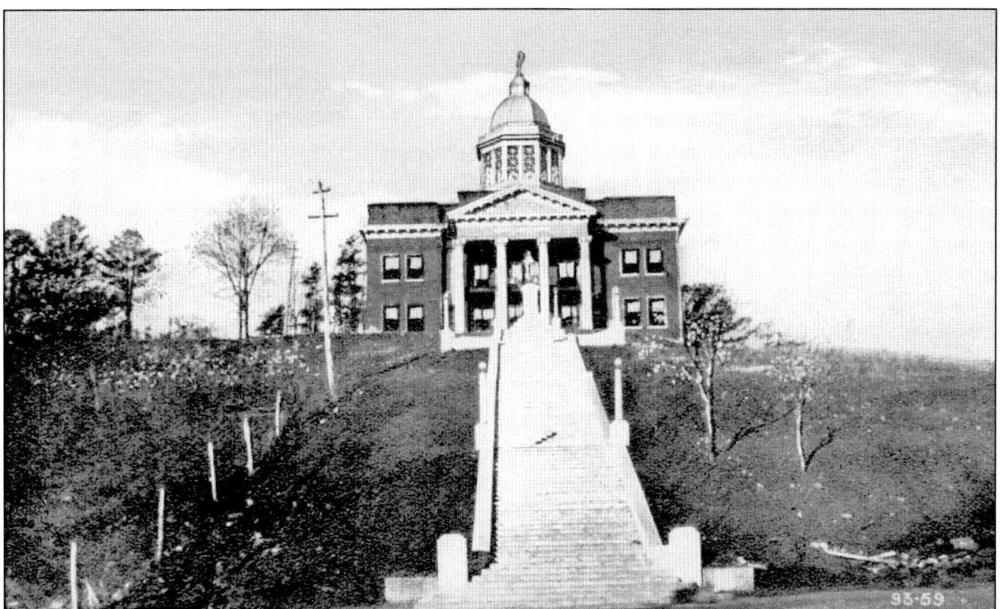

In addition to being a favorite subject for photographers, Jackson County's iconic courthouse has graced numerous postcards through the years. The card above was produced after the placement of the 1915 Confederate monument but before 1920. (Courtesy of Nick Breedlove.)

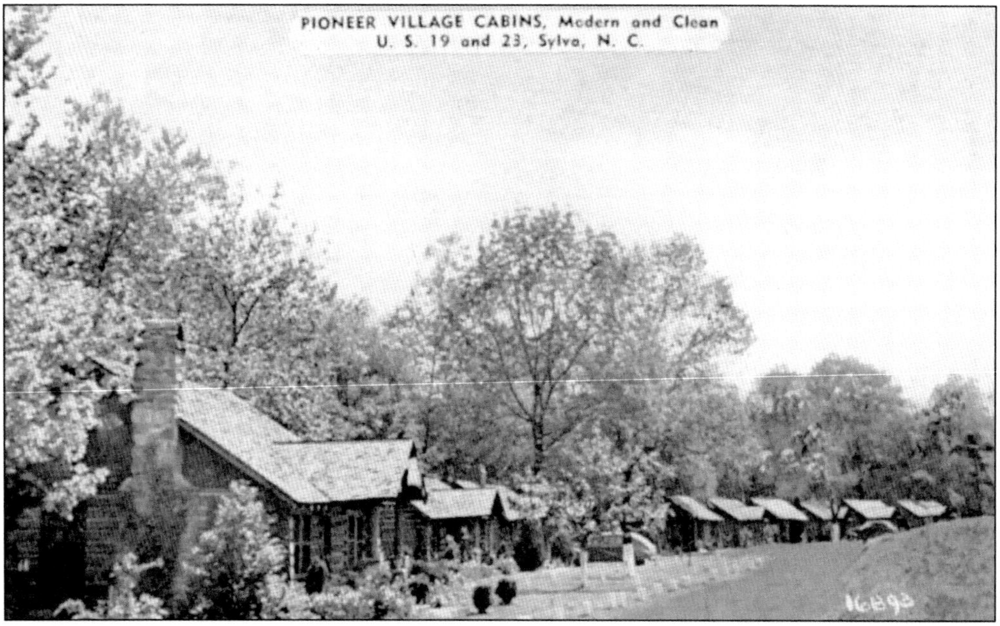

The Pioneer Cabins, described on this postcard as "modern and clean," were once located across from Mark Watson Park. The Economy Inn stands on the site now. (Courtesy of Nick Breedlove.)

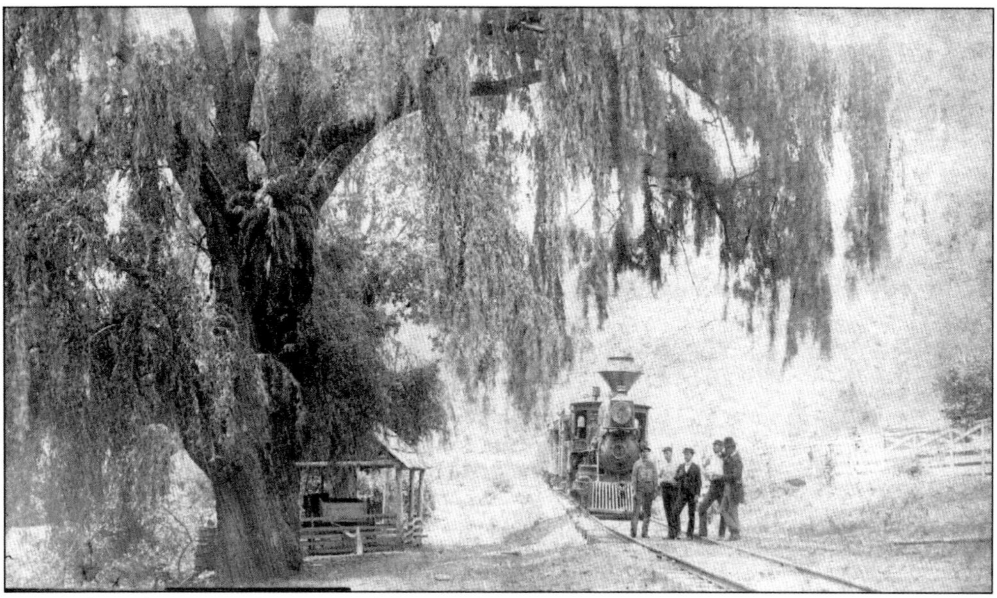

Dating from the 1880s, this postcard from Hall's Station includes area information on the back. Hall's Station, or Hall's Siding as it was known locally, was the stop Sylva-bound passenger trains made between Balsam and Addie and was a platform located in the area more commonly known as Willets. The back of the card encouraged visitors to ride the train to the mountains: "Beautiful in picturesque loveliness, grand and imposing in majesty, awe-inspiring in natural rugged beauty, and simply wonderful in all its character, the western section of this state can never be fully appreciated until it is seen. . . . Between these mountains and each mountain spur are valleys as beautiful as ever charmed the eye." (Courtesy of Western Carolina University Special Collections.)

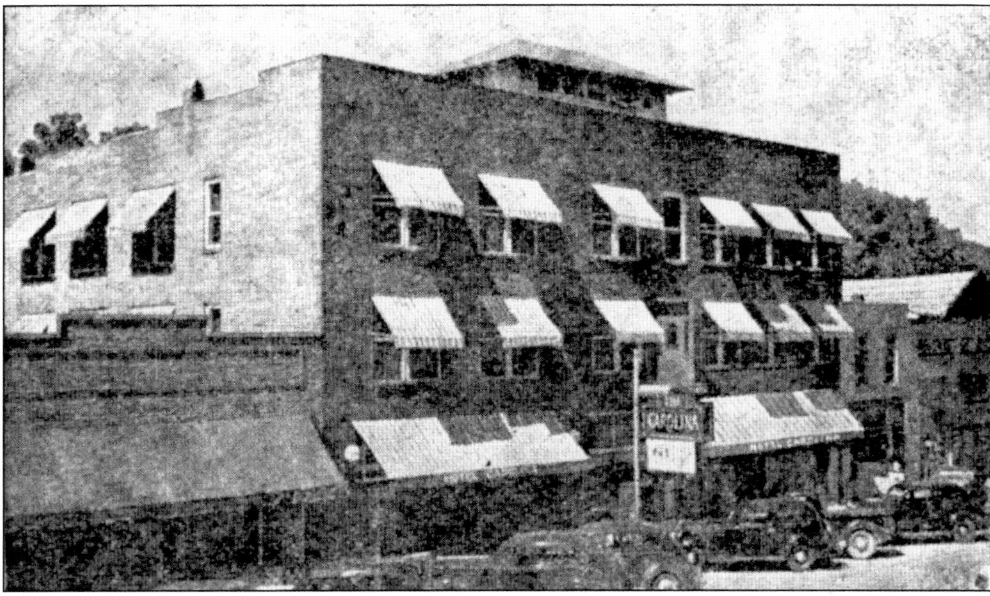

The 40-room Hotel Carolina (above), originally called the New Jackson Hotel, was built by J. S. Higdon, a mechanic who was also Sylva's first car dealer. The postcard below was mailed by a hotel guest in 1941. A variety of businesses have occupied the building's first floor in the years since the hotel closed, including the Sossamon Furniture Company for around 45 years, but the top floors are no longer in use. Businesses currently housed there are the Sylva Barber Shop, Jones Country Store, and Main Design. The card below features a hotel cook who "eats her own cooking." Longtime *Sylva Herald* publisher Jim Gray remembers the good meals served there. (Above courtesy of Nick Breedlove; below courtesy of the North Carolina Collection, University of North Carolina at Chapel Hill.)

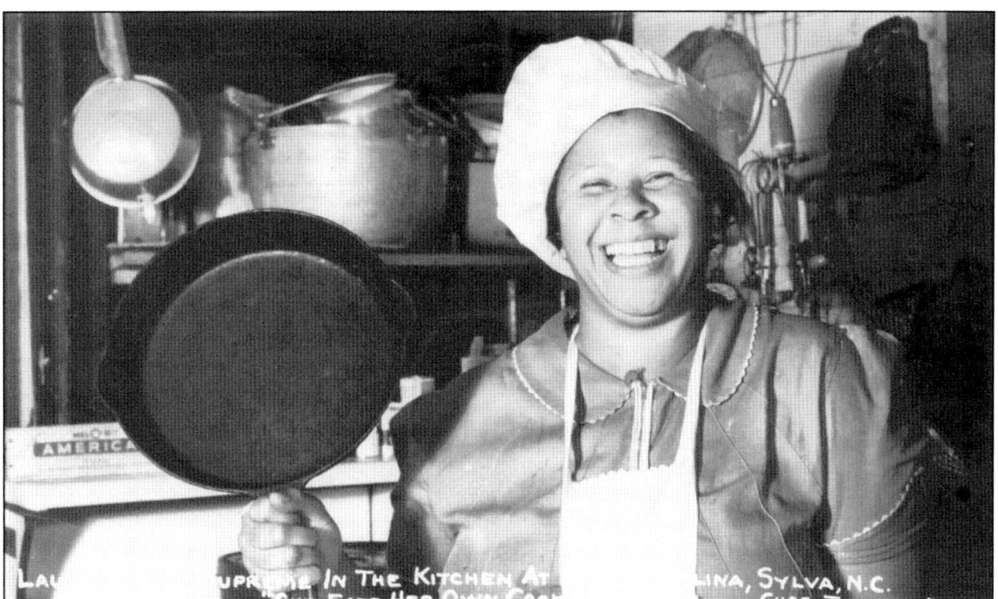

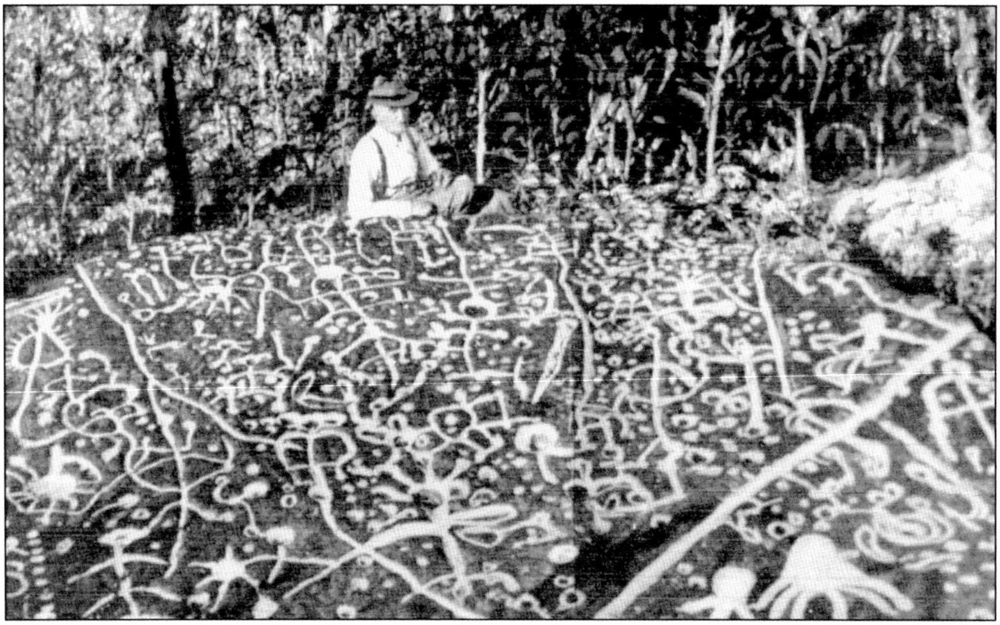

Milas Parker, who once owned the Judaculla Rock site on Caney Fork, poses with the petroglyph during the 1930s. At one time, the soapstone boulder was painted to bring out the details of the ancient Native American writing; the meaning of the symbols remains unknown. The Parker family sold the property to Jackson County some years ago, and an effort is now under way to better protect the important archaeological site. (Courtesy of Nick Breedlove.)

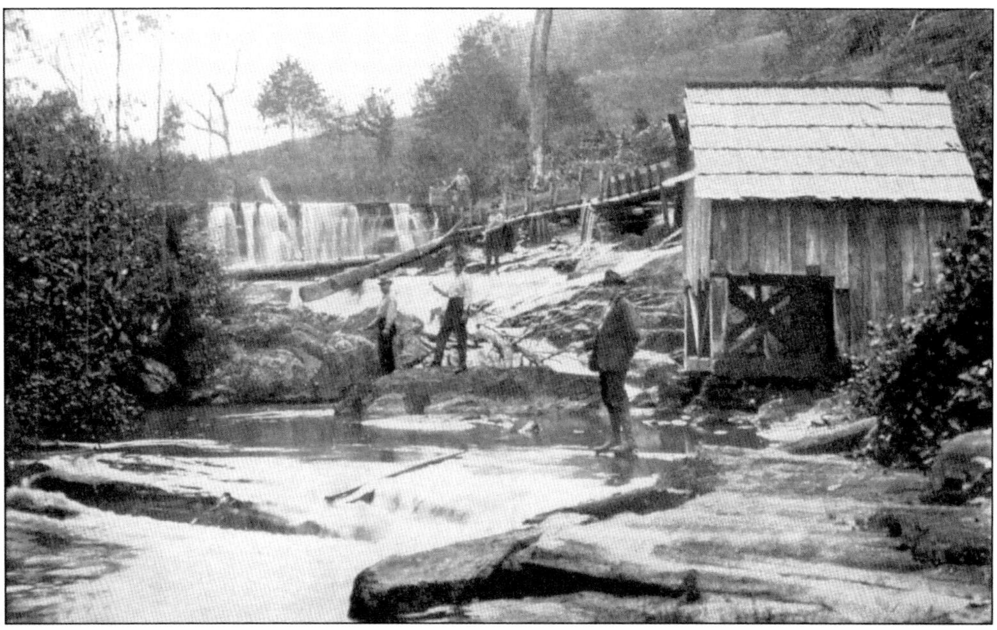

Captioned "Old Mill and Crystal Trout Water near Sylva, N.C.," this card was produced for the Sylva Rod and Gun Club. The mill once stood on Pine Creek, but the site, about a half-mile above the Glenville Dam, is now under water. Pictured are Latha Moss, Dr. Wayne McGuire, R. F. Huff, Jonah Dills, and Weaver Gray. (Courtesy of Nick Breedlove.)

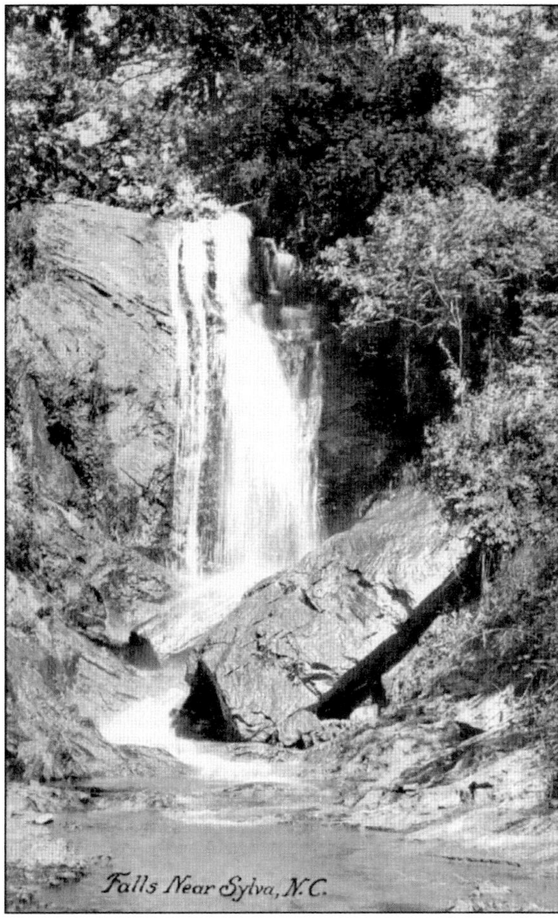

Dills Falls (right), a 249-foot-high, cascading waterfall, was located in Sylva's Dills Cove area. Sylva was reportedly the only incorporated town in the United States with a waterfall within its limits until Dills Falls was destroyed during construction of the Sylva Bypass in the early 1970s. Nestled between the Plott Balsam and Great Smoky Mountain ranges, Sylva (below) has long been a popular postcard subject, as illustrated by this 1920s card. (Right courtesy of Nick Breedlove; below courtesy of Steve Gray.)

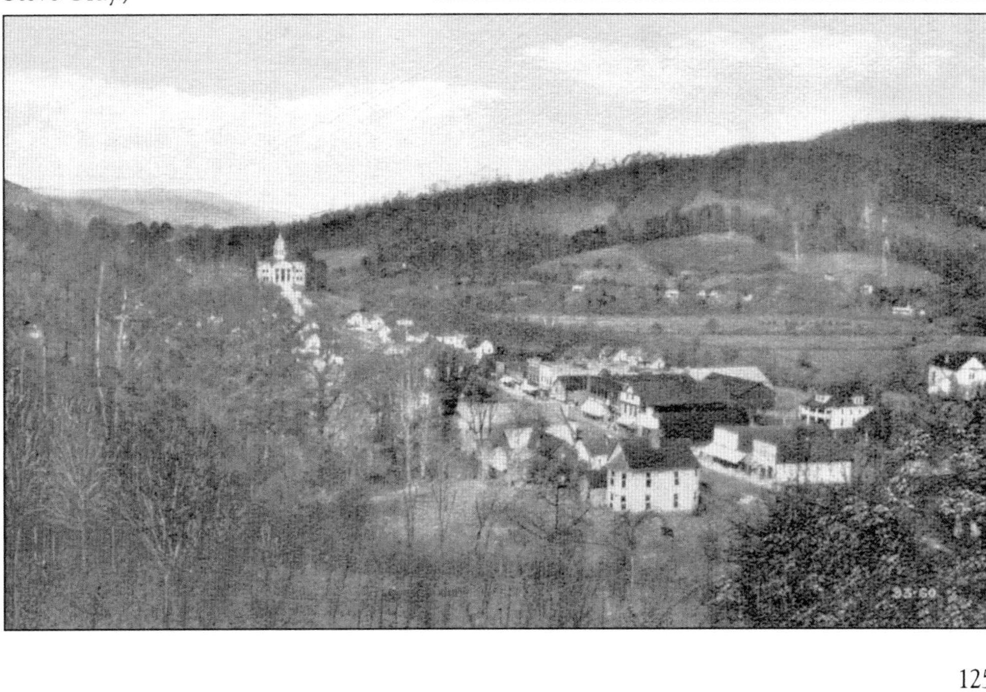

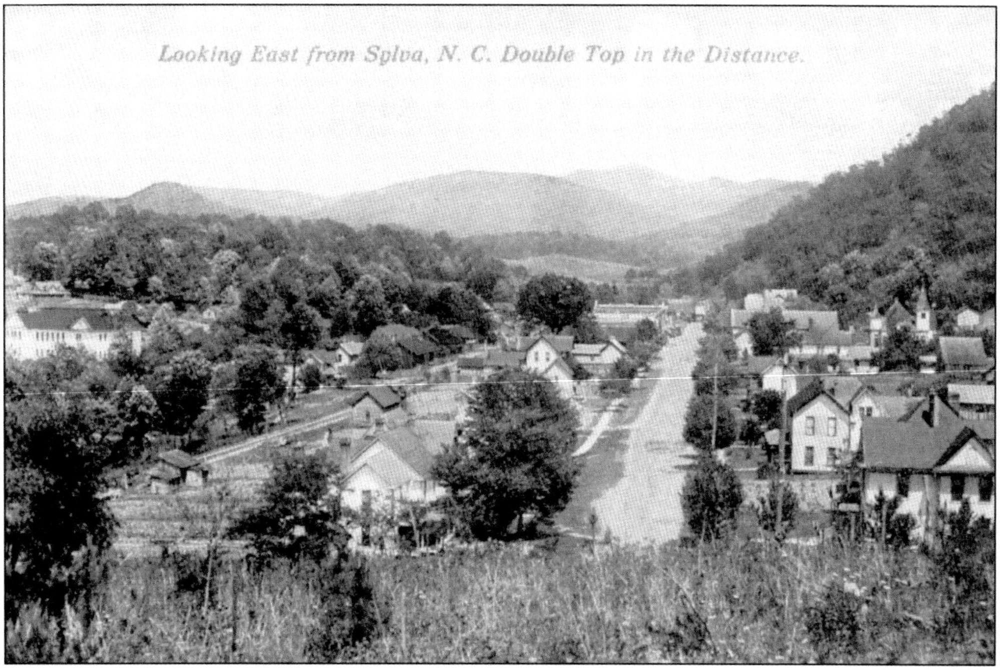

This early postcard shows a still-unpaved Main Street and predates construction of the Jackson County Courthouse. The Sylva Graded School is the prominent building at far left. The Dr. D. D. Hooper house, remodeled between 1999 and 2002 to house the Jackson County Chamber of Commerce, is on the far right. (Courtesy of Nick Breedlove.)

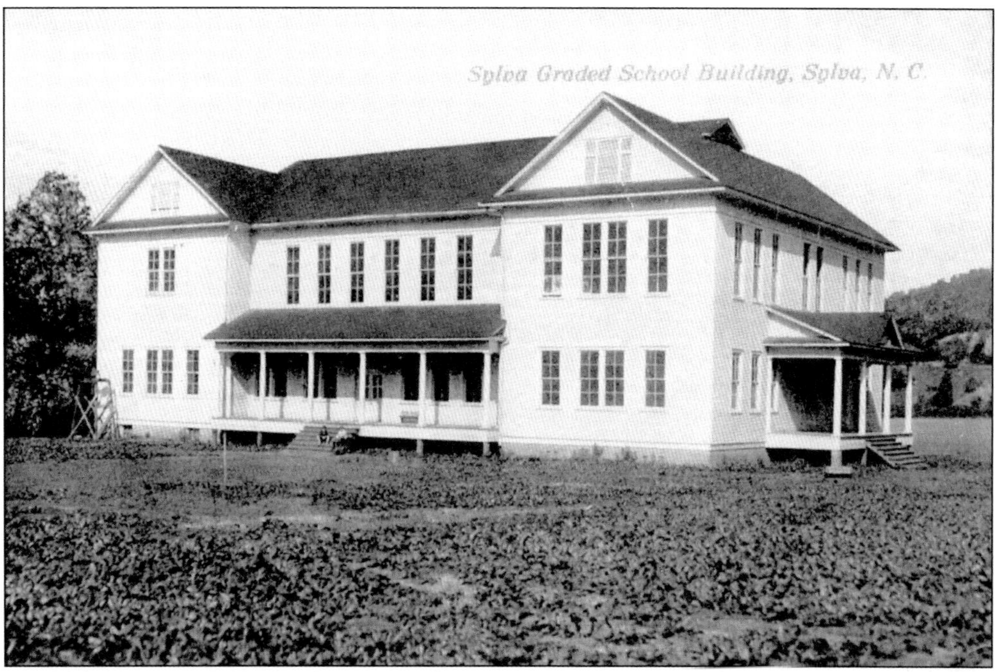

The old Sylva Graded School was once located where the town swimming pool is now. The building remained in use until 1929, when a new elementary school was built near the Sylva High School in what would become Mark Watson Park. (Courtesy of Steve Gray.)

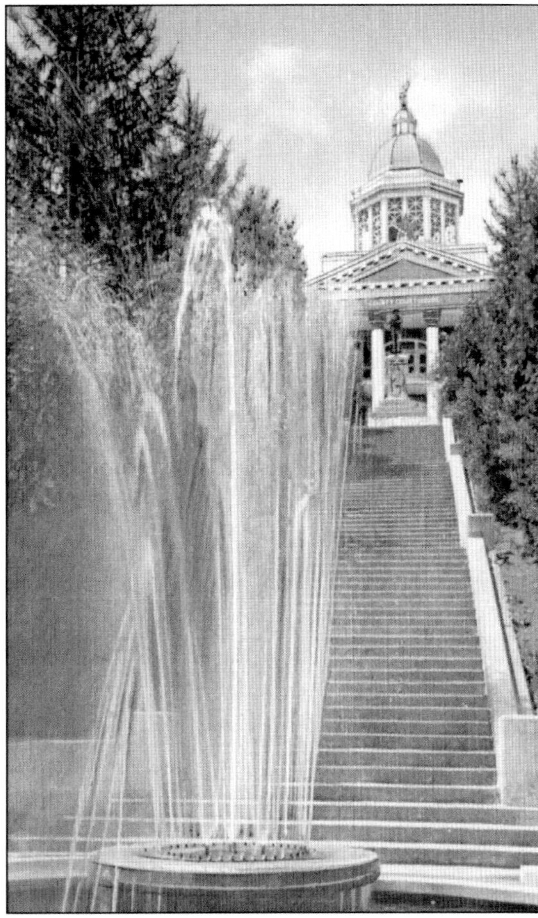

These two postcards date from the late 1940s or early 1950s, based on the size of the trees at the Jackson County Courthouse (right) and the two-way traffic on Main Street (below). The three-story building on the right, which is now part of Livingston's Photo, housed Jackson Furniture at that time. (Courtesy of Nick Breedlove.)

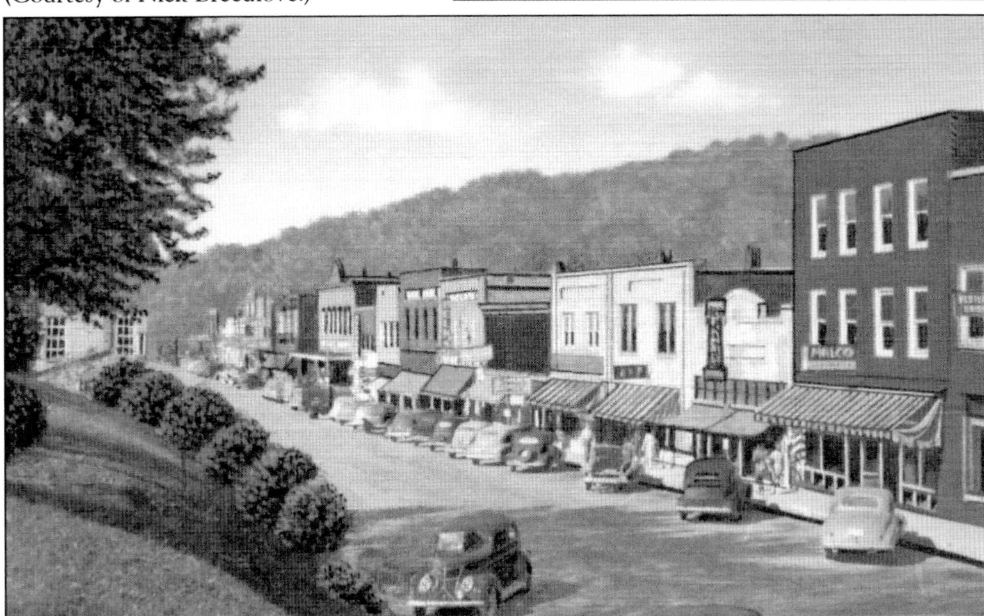